Britain, détente and changing East–West relations

While Britain's contribution to the cold war has been widely recognized there has been little work on the British role in moderating East–West tensions. In *Britain, Détente and Changing East–West Relations* Brian White presents the first comprehensive analysis of the role of successive British governments in the development of East–West détente.

The author maintains that Britain's contribution to détente from the early postwar was considerable, and constituted an important aspect of its foreign policy. He argues that Britain played a leading role as a catalyst in the 1950s and early 1960s, and thereafter enjoyed a significant if not central role in the development of détente. The key to British influence lay in skilful adaptation to the postwar structures of East–West relations coupled with a consistent view of détente. Ultimately, however, it was the failure to adapt effectively to the changing patterns of East–West relations from the mid-1960s onwards that led to the gradual decline of British influence.

This interpretative study throws new light on both the concept and history of détente and on the nature and concerns of postwar British foreign policy. It is also a central contribution to the continuing debate about Britain's role in a rapidly changing international system. As such, it will appeal to those involved in the study of British politics, contemporary British history, foreign policy analysis and international relations.

Brian White is Principal Lecturer in International Relations at Staffordshire Polytechnic, where he teaches courses on foreign policy analysis and British and American foreign policy. He is co-editor and contributor to *British Foreign Policy: Tradition, Change and Transformation* (Unwin Hyman 1988) and *Understanding Foreign Policy: The Foreign Policy Systems Approach* (Edward Elgar 1989).

Britain, détente and changing East–West relations

Brian White

London and New York

First published 1992
by Routledge
11 New Fetter Lane, London EC4P 4EE

Simultaneously published in the USA and Canada
by Routledge
a division of Routledge, Chapman and Hall, Inc.
29 West 35th Street, New York, NY 10001

Typeset in 10/12pt Bembo by
Falcon Typographic Art Ltd, Edinburgh
Printed in Great Britain by
Mackays of Chatham PLC, Chatham, Kent

*A catalogue reference for this title is available
from the British Library*

0–415–07841–5

*Library of Congress Cataloging in Publication Data
has been applied for*

0–415–07841–5

In memory of a dear friend, Elizabeth Neave

Contents

Acknowledgements

This book has its origins in a doctoral thesis which introduced many of the central ideas developed in the book, although the historical time frame and the analysis have been extended here to cover the postwar period as a whole. It is not possible, of course, to write a book or, indeed, a thesis without incurring debts to other people and institutions. I want to take this opportunity to offer particular thanks to Professors Jack Spence, Steve Smith, Peter Nailor and Roger Tooze. I have not always taken the advice of these friends and colleagues – and the responsibility for the content here is mine alone – but their encouragement and support over a number of years has been very important to me. I am also grateful to Staffordshire Polytechnic for granting me sabbatical leave and providing financial assistance for a research trip to the United States. The staffs of the Library of Congress, the John F. Kennedy Library and the Staffordshire Polytechnic Library gave helpful assistance at different times. Last but not least, without the love and support of Angela Ruddock, neither the thesis nor this book would have been completed.

Chapter 1

Introduction

The opening of the postwar archives stimulated a number of studies in the 1980s which focused on the British role in what is now referred to as the 'first' cold war. Using newly available documentary sources, British and some American scholars argued persuasively that the cold war was not exclusively a Soviet–American affair; Britain, too, played a leading role.[1] This confirmation of a significant British role in the early postwar period, however, serves to highlight the absence of general analyses of the British contribution to East–West relations since 1945 and assessments of the British contribution to East–West détente in particular. To date, those scholars who have touched on Britain's contribution to moderating East–West conflict have tended to concentrate on the negative side of the record – on the alleged failure of Britain's enthusiastic advocacy of 'summitry' in the 1950s, for example. In general, British attempts to act as a mediator or 'honest broker' between East and West have been regarded as both ineffectual and pretentious, a rather desperate effort to prove that Britain could still wield influence on a global stage despite mounting evidence of a material 'descent from power'.[2]

The contention here is that Britain's contribution to détente cannot be so easily dismissed. If cold war studies have benefited from spotlighting Britain's role, it is at least arguable that an understanding of East–West détente might similarly benefit from a sustained analysis of the British contribution. Whether significant or not in terms of its impact on East–West relations, the promotion of détente has certainly been a recurring theme in postwar British foreign policy. To take the most recent illustration, the Thatcher government decided after its landslide electoral victory in 1983 to give the highest foreign policy priority to working 'for an improvement in East–West relations' (Howe, 1987, p. 559). To many commentators at the time, this conciliatory approach appeared to represent a fundamental reorientation of British policy given the implacably hostile approach to the East that had characterized the first Thatcher administration. Significantly, however, this overt attempt to steer East–West relations in a more cooperative direction has a number of antecedents in the postwar period, which indicates an important but neglected theme in British foreign policy.

One of the central objectives of this book is to trace this theme historically in order to make some assessment of the significance of the British contribution to East–West détente since the 1950s. This will facilitate, *inter alia*, the location of British policy in the 1980s within an important historical context. From a high point that roughly coincides with the premiership of Harold Macmillan, this historical account will involve charting the gradual decline of Britain's ability to play a central role in the détente process. However, this does not mean that the British contribution has been insignificant since the 1960s. A narrative approach is complemented by a more explicitly analytical objective. The object here is to offer an explanation rather than 'merely' to describe the apparent continuities in British détente policy. To this end, different analytical perspectives are deployed – though not necessarily given equal weight – in order to develop an explanation of British policy. Thus, what follows can more appropriately be described as an interpretative study rather than a detailed history of an important dimension of postwar British foreign policy. The approach taken is that of the foreign policy analyst rather than the historian.[3]

From an international system or a 'systemic' perspective, British détente policy can be explained in structural terms or in terms of adaptation to changing circumstances. A structural account starts from the premise that Britain, like the other allies of the superpowers, had become 'locked into' a bipolar international system by the early 1950s. This confrontational structure was not only highly dangerous but it gave British governments little room for manoeuvre. Persistent British attempts to mediate between the superpowers and to play a conciliatory East–West role can be explained as an attempt to create a more flexible and less threatening international system. A tight bipolar structure, after all, not only imposed rigidity and inflexibility on policy-making but also heightened the possibility of nuclear war, whether by miscalculation or design. If British policy-makers were to continue playing a significant global role in international relations, defending if not advancing distinctive British interests around the world, it was necessary to create some room for manoeuvre within a hegemonic Western system dominated by the United States. From this perspective, the prospect of a continuing East–West cold war, with the superpowers facing each other in an 'eyeball-to-eyeball' confrontation, was clearly inimical to British interests. It is interesting that this use of a détente policy as a vehicle to create a more flexible international structure was also adopted by the French and, to greater effect, by the West Germans, who, it will be argued, followed the British example by exploiting the potential of a quasi-independent high-profile East–West role.

The related adaptation explanation suggests that British policy in this context provides an important illustration of policy-makers pragmatically adapting to Britain's changed material circumstances after the Second World War by attempting to replace power, narrowly defined in material terms, with influence. If it is assumed that policy-makers, particularly after the Suez disaster in 1956, had an interest in manipulating the illusion rather than the substance of power, a significant East–West role promised to help to maintain Britain's position in the international hierarchy. This policy arena provided valuable opportunities to deploy what might be called the 'symbols of power'. Exploiting those opportunities enabled British leaders to display statesmenlike qualities on a global 'stage' and British governments to exert some independent leverage over the superpowers. In historical terms, British policy can be located within a tradition of adaptation to change, a tradition that can be traced back at least to the turn of this century.

From this analytical perspective, the gradual decline of British influence on East–West relations can be explained in terms of structural changes or changing patterns of East–West relations and the inability of successive British governments to reorientate policy to take account of those changes. With hindsight, indeed, British influence appears to have been dependent on the perpetuation of a bipolar international structure. As soon as that structure began to change, British influence began to wane, because those changes also transformed the bases of that influence. These bases included exploiting a 'special relationship' with the United States, using membership of an exclusive nuclear club to initiate or 'buy into' arms control negotiations, maintaining close if not always harmonious relations with the major West European allies and, whenever possible, keeping open direct contacts with the Soviet bloc. Thus, structural changes in East–West relations, which began in the 1960s, accelerated in the 1970s and became revolutionary in scope at the end of the 1980s, lie at the heart of this explanation of the decline of British influence in this policy arena.

A central problem which became more apparent towards the end of the 1980s than it had been before was the extent to which British influence was tied to maintaining – or, in the case of the Soviet Union, fostering – 'special' bilateral relations with the superpowers, rather than acting as a European power and relying upon various multilateral links with other West European states as a base from which to wield influence. This does not mean, of course, that British governments ignored these links; indeed there was a marked 'Europeanization' of British foreign and defence policy from the 1960s onwards. But these links never appear to have been as attractive to policy-makers as the pull of 'Atlantic' or, more accurately, non-European connections. Significantly, the revolutionary changes in Central and Eastern Europe, which ended the 1980s and began the 1990s, served to highlight more starkly than before the inherent weakness of the British orientation to the extent that they underlined a structural trend that had been apparent for twenty years or more – namely, that intra-European relations were becoming more and superpower relations less pivotal to East–West relations as a whole.[4]

From a state or political system level of analysis, on the other hand, a very different type of explanation of British policy can be developed. From this perspective, what might be called a 'domestic imperatives' hypothesis suggests that British efforts to promote more harmonious East–West relations can be explained in terms of the demands of the domestic political environment, whether these were manifested in expressions of public opinion, pressure group activity, opposition demands or bureaucratic pressures. Two particular ways of developing such an analysis are pursued here. Electoral analysis is used where appropriate in an attempt to correlate peaks of governmental interest in promoting détente with the build up to general elections, on the assumption that such a stance would yield electoral advantage. This assumption in turn rests, of course, upon establishing first, that détente was an issue in the context of a particular election and, second, that there was a demand for détente whether expressed in terms of popular attitudes or in terms of the opposition's electoral programme. Electoral analysis is limited for the purposes of this study, however, because even if a linkage can be established, it does represent a 'peak' of interest in promoting détente at a particular time rather than an explanation of policy over a longer time period. Alternatively, the salience of détente as a domestic political issue over longer time periods is considered. 'Salience' in this context can denote a variety of factors. It can refer to expressions of popular concern – about the destructiveness of nuclear weapons, for example. It might also indicate concerns within political parties about détente or détente-related issues. It certainly indicates a degree of sensitivity on the part of the political leadership to a popular mood or to party or opposition pressures. Clearly, the more salient an issue détente is, the more likely 'domestic imperatives' are to impact on the calculations of policy-makers. One major assumption here is that détente has been more salient as a domestic political issue at times of East–West tension than at other times. Therefore, what are generally regarded as the high points of cold war and 'new' cold war – the 1950s and the early 1980s in particular – are more closely scrutinized for evidence of the impact of domestic political factors on British policy.

It follows from this proposed analysis that domestic imperatives are unlikely to provide a consistently important explanation of British détente policy during the postwar period as a whole. But this does not mean that particular domestic factors are not relevant to an explanation of British policy at certain times. The factors of variable significance considered here include not only a high level of tension in East–West relations but also the proximity of a general election, the electoral threat posed by the opposition, the effectiveness of anti-nuclear sentiment expressed either through a political party or through pressure-group activity and, finally, the 'visibility' in domestic political terms of a nuclear deterrence strategy. The latter is a particularly interesting variable, given the indications that the promotion of East–West détente has on different occasions appeared to provide governments of both political persuasions with a convenient distraction from the 'naked' pursuit of a deterrence policy.

A third and final analytical perspective focuses on the attitudes of key decision-makers. The central issue from this perspective is whether a consistent set of attitudes towards détente can be elicited from the statements of policy-makers, which helps to explain the continuity of British policy during the postwar period. Can we indeed talk about a British approach to or conception of détente which underpinned that policy? The general argument developed here is that a characteristically British approach to détente can be identified and that the basic elements of that approach were in evidence by the end of the 1950s. What is significant is that fundamentally the same approach has been maintained with remarkable consistency for the last forty years.

This approach appears to be rooted in the traditional realpolitik assumption that the 'normal' condition of international relations is a mix of conflict and cooperation resulting from shared and divergent interests among states. To avoid conflicts of interest culminating in war, each state has two essential instruments, defence and diplomacy. A strong defence posture is necessary to deter a potential enemy from initiating warfare. If this is unsuccessful, however, the instruments of defence have traditionally provided a more or less effective war-fighting capability. The alternative response is to try whenever possible to resolve inevitable differences of interest by a continuous process of accommodation. For this diplomatic process to be effective, however, open contacts and regular negotiations with potential enemies are essential. It follows logically from these assumptions that an appropriate general strategy for maintaining a 'normal' condition of international relations is to balance military strength with a readiness to resolve differences by negotiation.

Relating these preconceptions to the real world of international relations, however, it is clear that British policy-makers faced an 'abnormal' situation after the Second World War in at least two important respects. First, the cold war confrontation between the superpowers served to minimize both the political will and the opportunities to resolve by negotiation what had become East–West differences. Second, the onset of the nuclear age meant that the consequences of war – of not resolving differences by negotiation – were incalculably more devastating to individual states and to the international system as a whole than in the pre-nuclear age. On the one hand, this new situation heightened the need to organize strategic relationships so as to deter war by developing appropriate security structures. But it also necessitated the initiation and development of a process of accommodation – reducing tensions and working towards a modus vivendi at least with potential enemies. Thus, defence (or deterrence) and détente were different dimensions of the same strategy designed to 'normalize' East–West relations.

If this brief account captures the essence of the British approach to détente, differences of priority and emphasis have been evident throughout the postwar period. Most important, the priority given to the pursuit of deterrence or the promotion of détente has changed over time, reflecting in part at least differing international circumstances. In general, since the establishment of an effective structure of deterrence in the form of the North Atlantic alliance, British governments have soon become uncomfortable whenever the West and, in particular, its principal ally the United States have appeared to pursue a policy of deterrence to the exclusion of détente – as in the early 1950s and the early 1980s, for example – and a policy of détente to the apparent neglect of the structure of deterrence – as in the early 1970s. In other words, whenever Western policy towards the East has, in the view of British policy-makers, been 'unbalanced' they have sought to use their influence to focus the attention of their allies on the dangers inherent in such a policy.

With respect to East–West détente itself, the British have consistently taken the view that détente is a process but a slow, piecemeal one where caution and limited expectations are appropriate. Nevertheless, progress is possible, and this is registered by agreements on specific areas of East–West tension. Each tangible agreement is important, because it helps to create the preconditions for further progress towards agreement on other areas of disagreement, and so on. Given the nature of international relations, there will inevitably be setbacks in any détente process, but this should not deter policy-makers from pursuing what might be called the politics of accommodation whenever possible.

British views about the appropriate mode of détente diplomacy between East and West have changed – in emphasis at least – in the postwar period. In the 1950s, there was an apparent preoccupation with arranging 'summit' meetings of the heads of government of the smallest possible number of states – ideally the 'Big Three' only – on the assumption that only heads of government could deliver the agreements that would punctuate progress. Thereafter, with Britain less likely to get an invitation to exclusive summit meetings, more emphasis was placed on regular diplomatic channels of communication. What has remained constant throughout the postwar period, however, is a belief in the importance of direct, high-level contacts between West and East on the assumption, rightly or wrongly, that personal face-to-face contacts between leaders help to foster understanding, build confidence in the détente process and promote discussion of outstanding problems. The preferred agenda of such discussions has been defined by the British in the broadest possible terms, though, again, the emphasis has changed to some extent. In the 1970s and 1980s, there was far more emphasis on human rights issues, for example, than was evident in the earlier period.

Certain potential problems with this study, both substantive and methodological in nature, can be suggested and it is appropriate that they should be raised at the outset. The most obvious substantive objection is that the focus of this study overstates the importance of East–West relations in postwar British foreign policy. Certainly, East–West relations have not consistently dominated the foreign policy agenda since 1945, and it is not the intention here to suggest that they have. Other issues such as decolonization, Anglo-American relations and the state of play with Britain's allies and partners in Western Europe have often provided far more pressing and time-consuming problems for British policy-makers. But, to the extent that East–West relations and the state of superpower relations in particular have defined international relations since 1945, this arena has provided the most important milieu within which British policy-makers have had to operate. So even when British interests have not been directly at stake in a particular East–West issue – as in the Conference on Security and Cooperation in Europe (CSCE) negotiations, for example – and governments have not been primarily concerned to influence the overall direction of East–West relations, the state of those relationships have, nevertheless, always been at least of indirect importance to Britain.

With respect to the proposed analytical framework, it might be argued that these different types of explanation are not necessarily separable or mutually exclusive. There is clearly a danger of artificially highlighting one type of explanation to the exclusion of others. Any explanation is contingent upon the level at which the analysis is pitched, an important methodological issue which is taken up in the next chapter. Even more important, perhaps, there is a danger here of imposing a design on British policy-makers with respect to détente policy that may also be artificial. Many scholars and, indeed, policy-makers themselves have argued that British foreign policy can *only* be explained as an ad hoc response to changing international circumstances. The notion that policy-making might be calculated or predetermined in terms of objectives is alien to the pragmatic ethos that allegedly dominates British policy-making. Joseph Korbel's case for effectively ignoring

British détente policy in his study and focusing on the French and West German contributions to East–West détente appears to rest on the argument that British governments have:

> seen détente as a pragmatic proposition that should serve and be served through a variety of processes that seem to alleviate tensions and contribute to peace in Europe. In contrast to France's concept of détente based on analytical assumptions, London has shunned away from grandiose schemes, spectacular state visits and eloquent phrases. It has given preference to the ways of quiet diplomacy and practical steps of rapprochement (Korbel, 1972, p. 61).

In more general terms, Geoffrey Goodwin located British foreign policy many years ago in what he called an 'empirical tradition'. Developing for an American audience the argument that policy-makers in Britain have traditionally been suspicious of 'large concerns or great schemes', Goodwin warned that:

> generalizations about the ends of British diplomacy need to be treated with special caution – we may easily fall into the trap of allowing hindsight to read a logic and coherence – a 'grand design' – into policies which in reality may have been little more than tentative gropings to meet bewilderingly complex situations (Goodwin, 1959, p. 31).

Any would-be analyst of British foreign policy has to give careful consideration to this caveat because the logical extension of the empiricist case is that British foreign policy cannot be analysed, it can only be described. In the absence of overarching principles and objectives, it might be argued, there is simply nothing to analyse. Indeed, this approach raises doubts about whether there is any policy even to describe, if by 'policy' is meant the purposeful pursuit of objectives.

In the context of this study, it suggests that the search for continuity in British attitudes and policy towards East–West relations in general and détente in particular will be fruitless if consistency in the pursuit of certain objectives rather than the most general historical trend is looked for. Similarly, from the empiricist perspective, it will be a pointless task trying to identify and establish a British conception of détente if it is assumed that policy-makers in Britain simply do not have analytical 'conceptions' or 'preconceptions' that relate to policy-making. Clearly, this raises important issues, which go to the heart of the nature of foreign policy-making in Britain. They will be addressed towards the end of the study after the analysis has been developed. The remainder of this introductory chapter offers an overview of the structure of this study. The analysis of British détente policy begins in the next chapter, with a review of the central concept of détente. A conceptual analysis of détente here is based on a critical survey of primarily 1970s literature on East–West détente. Literature from this period is chosen partly because of the sheer volume of commentary that was produced during what for many was *the* 'high point' of East–West détente, but also because this literature conveniently illustrates a variety of uses of the term. For the purpose of this study, a conceptual analysis of détente provides a useful analytical context within which to locate a British approach to détente, but, equally important, it helps to develop an evaluation of the impact of British policy.

The problem of assessing any state's contribution to détente is exacerbated by the ambiguities that surround the concept of détente itself. Indeed, one of the reasons why détente has been neglected by scholars as a significant theme in postwar British foreign policy is that 'détente' has been conventionally regarded as denoting tension-easing agreements between the blocs in the late 1960s and early 1970s. If this conception of détente is accepted, relatively little significance can be attached to the British role. Korbel, for example, assumes that détente was a feature of this particular historical period and is thus able to conclude that Britain's détente policy 'requires no elaborate discussion' because British governments have not 'at least by deeds, demonstrated any intensive interest in détente' (Korbel, 1972, pp. 60, 66).

Other scholars, however, have argued that détente is more appropriately conceived as a historical process of accommodation between the superpowers and their allies that has its origins in the 1950s. This process can be traced over time, highlighting the more 'visible' manifestations of détente such as summit meetings or arms control agreements. If this conception of détente is accepted, it can be argued that British diplomacy has made a significant contribution to an important process of change in postwar international relations and, in particular, that the role of Britain as a catalyst of détente in the 1950s and early 1960s has not received the attention it deserves. If the origins of détente are identified by reference to specific 'landmarks' or 'turning points', such as the four-power Geneva summit in 1955, the Eisenhower–Khrushchev summit in 1959 or the Partial Test Ban Treaty in 1963, linkages can be established between British policy and those key developments. If the British contribution to the détente process has been of declining significance since the early 1960s, locating détente as a process within a longer historical time frame enables us nevertheless to develop a more positive evaluation of British policy.

The origins of British détente policy can be usefully traced back to the late 1940s. Chapter 3 reviews the development of British policy by contrasting it with developments in American policy during the same period. The main thrust of this chapter is the argument that the evolution of British attitudes and policy towards détente has to be set within a cold-war context. The focus here is the development of divergent British and American attitudes to the cold war, the nature of the Soviet/communist threat and, most significant, appropriate responses to that threat. While American attitudes towards the Soviet Union and international communism perceptibly hardened, the more pragmatic British could not wholly accept the manichaeistic view of the world that emerged in Washington. For the Americans – as detailed in NSC-68 (see p.36) – the cold war by 1949–50 had come to mean political warfare between two monolithic power blocs, with negotiations between them effectively ruled out. The British, on the other hand, saw the cold war as a short-term necessity: the object remained the normalization of relations with the Soviet bloc. It became apparent as early as the Korean War that British policy-makers were committed to containing East–West conflict not by confrontation and political warfare but by a policy of military strength combined with diplomatic accommodation. After 1949, divergent Anglo-American attitudes were reflected in differences on policy, with the British more concerned than the Americans to secure a normalization of relations with the Soviet Union and its allies as soon as possible.

Having located British policy within both an analytical and a historical context, we deal at greater length in Chapters 4 and 5 with the high point of British influence between 1953 and 1963. These are the years in which British diplomacy was most effective in terms of its impact on East–West relations. The period begins with Churchill's initiatives, following the death of Stalin, designed to secure an early summit conference, and it ends appropriately with the signing of the Partial Test Ban Treaty, regarded by many as both a major achievement as far as the development of a détente process is concerned and the single most important contribution of British diplomacy during that period.

The second half of Chapter 4 applies the explanatory framework detailed earlier, beginning with an attempt to identify governmental attitudes towards détente that underpinned British policy in the 1950s. The apparent preoccupation with summitry in the early 1950s is located within a broader conception of conciliatory diplomacy and a piecemeal but developmental approach to the politics of accommodation with the East. By the end of the 1950s, the statements of British policy-makers make it clear that the objective of British policy was to establish at least a semi-permanent system of open contact and exchange between East and West, which would, in Foreign Secretary Selwyn Lloyd's phrase, 'avoid a constant atmosphere of crisis'. Central to this objective of re-establishing a 'normal' system of East–West relations was the development of a Western policy that would balance a structure of deterrence with a process of détente.

The attempt to explain British policy continues by reviewing the constraints upon Britain in the postwar international environment. From a systemic perspective, the promotion of East–West détente in the first half of the postwar period provided valuable opportunities for British leaders to create some room for manoeuvre within a tight bipolar structure, both to protect distinctive British interests and to maintain a leading position in the international hierarchy. The cultivation of alternative sources of influence during this period was the key to Britain's relative success in adapting to a new international structure in order to maintain a significant global role. The final section of this chapter looks at the domestic political context of British policy and concludes that 'domestic imperatives' in terms of the salience of the nuclear issue and the potential electoral consequences also provide an important explanation of British détente policy in the second half of the 1950s.

While Chapter 4 presents a detailed analysis of this important period, Chapter 5 offers a case study of British policy in relation to the test ban treaty negotiations. The assumption here is that a case study will highlight important aspects of a détente policy in action and will further clarify an understanding of the impact of that policy. This chapter, therefore, is less concerned with explanation per se and more concerned with evaluating British policy. It begins with a narrative account of the emergence of nuclear testing as an international issue and describes, from a British perspective, the development of the Geneva negotiations between 1958 and 1963. It continues by evaluating more explicitly the contribution of British diplomacy to the eventual achievement of a treaty and concludes with a brief assessment of the importance of the Partial Test Ban Treaty to détente.

The second half of this study charts the decline of British influence on the direction of East–West relations after 1963, but is equally concerned, in analytical terms, to highlight the persistence of a particular set of attitudes towards détente, which underpinned continuing efforts to play a distinctive role in the détente process. Chapter 6 focuses on the period from the early 1960s to the mid-1970s. The narrative sections of this chapter concentrate on three issues to illustrate British détente policy during this period: the abortive attempts to mediate in the Vietnam war; the British contribution to the negotiations which culminated in the Nuclear Non-Proliferation Treaty (NPT) in 1968; and, finally, the British role in European security affairs, with a focus here provided by the Conference on Security and Cooperation in Europe (CSCE). In terms of the impact of British policy, the conclusion drawn from a review of these issues is that, in contrast to the earlier period, Britain played essentially a supporting role in the important developments in East–West détente that emerged during this period.

An attempt to explain British policy again starts with a review of British attitudes. What is significant here is that, although there was continuing support for East–West détente during this period (in rhetorical terms at least), there was also evidence of a growing ambivalence towards détente, stemming from a concern that East–West accommodation, particularly at the superpower level, might undermine the structure of European security. Thus, in terms of a 'balanced' approach to defence and détente there was a perceptible swing during this period towards the defence rather than the détente side of the 'balance'. It was apparent by the late 1960s that a concern to maintain the cohesion and solidarity of NATO had become a higher priority for British policy-makers than pressing for East–West détente.

A more sceptical British approach towards détente was reinforced by important structural changes during this period, which effectively served to marginalize Britain as far as the détente process and, indeed, East–West relations as a whole were concerned. The development of direct negotiations between Soviet and American

leaders after the Camp David summit in 1959 inevitably limited the opportunities thereafter for Britain to play an effective
mediation role between East and West. Moreover, the downturn
in Anglo-American relations from the mid-1960s onwards, the
inability of British nuclear weapons to buy a seat at the 'top
table' of nuclear arms control negotiations after 1968 and the
increasingly high-profile role played by the West Germans during
this period, all detracted significantly from Britain's ability to
influence the direction of East–West relations. Last but not least,
the perceived necessity of securing membership of the European
Economic Community not only imposed constraints on Britain's
ability to act independently in the East–West arena but also ensured
that West–West relations were beginning to overshadow East–West
relations for British policy-makers during this period. The domestic
political context of British policy cannot be ignored, particularly
in the early part of this period, but domestic factors tend to be
overshadowed by the powerful impact of structural change and
the consequent problems of adaptation.

Chapter 7 takes the history of British détente policy from the
mid-1970s up to the end of the 1980s. The narrative account here
is punctuated by the electoral cycle and dominated, perhaps inevitably, by the policies of the three successive Thatcher governments.
The continuation through the Wilson and Callaghan governments
of a supportive but somewhat sceptical approach to détente was followed in 1979 by the election of a prime minister who was instinctively opposed to the politics of accommodation with the Soviet
bloc. Indeed, the posture of the first Thatcher government towards
East–West relations appeared to mark a radical break with the
traditional balanced approach. There was a gap, however, between
rhetoric and action. Although East–West relations were not a major
focus of this government, actual policies were more consistent
with the traditional approach than the hostile, anti-Soviet rhetoric
suggested. Nevertheless, there was a dramatic intensification of
policy after 1983, as the prime minister sought, in her second term,
to improve the then parlous state of East–West relations in an apparently conscious effort to follow in the footsteps of her Conservative
predecessors, Winston Churchill in particular. In the third Thatcher
term, there were some attempts to continue this active role, but
caution and a renewed concern about the dangers of détente in the
context of the changes that were beginning to take place in Central
and Eastern Europe came to characterize the British approach.

In terms of the impact of British policy, the second Thatcher government showed that Britain could still play a significant role in the détente process. But the effectiveness of British diplomacy in the mid-1980s rather bucked the trend. Given that Britain was being further marginalized by structural changes during this period – a development that became more apparent in Mrs Thatcher's third term – it may well be that the relative success of British policy fostered some illusions about continuing British influence which, in turn, made it more difficult to adapt to those changes. British efforts to promote détente, however, were also influenced during this period by traditional attitudes that continued to have an impact, even in Mrs Thatcher's first term, and by the domestic political salience of the nuclear issue.

The final chapter draws together the elements of British attitudes towards détente that are discussed in earlier chapters. Given the assumption that an essentially consistent view of détente has influenced British policy over an extended period, this raises important questions about the sources of those attitudes. This chapter takes up the proposition that an understanding of British détente policy requires some understanding of those sources. Thus, the longer-term historical antecedents of postwar British attitudes towards détente are sought in traditional attitudes to diplomacy, the relationship between diplomacy and defence, and what is called 'globalism'. The significant conclusion drawn from this historical detour is that an understanding of the conservative realpolitik tradition in British political thought is not sufficient to explain attitudes towards détente. The analysis here suggests that elements of a liberal as well as a conservative tradition have influenced British thinking about détente. The final part of this chapter deals with the important issue of whether British policy can be explained in terms of a pragmatic tradition or whether a distinctive British conception of détente can be established which challenges the pragmatic ethos. The analysis begins, however, with the central concept of détente.

Chapter 2

The concept of détente

Détente as a concept has been established in the vocabulary of political science since the early 1970s. The increasing use of the term since then, however, not only by scholars but also by policy-makers and journalists, has generated diversity of usage and connotation and, therefore, conceptual ambiguity. Hence, this chapter attempts to clarify the meaning of détente by posing the following questions. What does détente mean? How has the term been used? Can détente be used effectively as an analytical term?

The absence of conceptual clarity in the context of détente has linguistic and political consequences. If any word is used in different ways, there is a danger of misunderstanding what any particular usage signifies. This has always been a particular problem with détente. As Marshall Shulman noted in the early 1970s, 'the ambiguities of the word "détente" which has come into wide usage have led to much confusion' (Shulman, 1973, p. 35). If a word, such as détente, is used in political language, any confusion and misunderstanding may have more serious consequences. At the practitioner level, conceptual ambiguities may well compound political cleavages. As Graham Vernon commented with reference to the ideological rift between the superpowers, 'differences between the United States and the Soviet Union are both real and deep enough that neither side needs the additional burden of terminological ambiguity' (Vernon, 1979, p. 271).

There is a relationship, moreover, between meaning and expectations and particular concern was expressed in the 1970s about the expectations raised by the use of détente in political debate. The late Senator Frank Church, for example, in his evidence to the 1974 Senate Hearings on détente, voiced a prophetic warning about the propensity of the Nixon administration to oversell the idea of détente, risking disillusionment when the advertised benefits did not materialize (SFRC, 1974). From an analytical perspective, Philip Windsor made essentially the same point about possible confusion with the concept of *entente* when he argued that détente is a misleading term if 'it raises expectations of a developing relationship [between the superpowers] which will lead to a closer and closer understanding' (Windsor, 1971, p. 23). More recently, Ray Garthoff commented that 'much of the confusion in American understanding seems to have stemmed from a tendency to interpret détente as though it meant entente' (Garthoff, 1985, p. 25).

Nevertheless, it is part of the task of the political scientist to clarify concepts, and an appropriate starting point is to look at the derivation of the term. Détente is a corruption of the old French verb *de(s)tendre*, which originally denoted the releasing – the *de(s)tente* – of the strained string of the archer's bow (or crossbow) and the consequent discharging of the arrow (or bolt). Thereafter, it entered by analogy the lingua franca of traditional diplomatic language and signified either a policy of reducing tensions or a general lessening of international tensions. This general meaning was carried over into English around the turn of this century and, in translation, into other languages. The term re-emerged in the 1950s in an East–West context and became widespread in the 1970s. For a variety of reasons, the term acquired an essentially pejorative connotation in the West in the mid-1970s and Western leaders were loath to use the term thereafter.

Some understanding of the derivation of this term is helpful to the extent that it clarifies a dictionary definition. Following its French origins, détente has been conventionally defined as 'the easing of strained relations, especially in a political situation' (OED, 1972, p. 782). An extended etymological or linguistic investigation, however, would add little to an understanding of modern political use. As David Finley commented, détente is:

> a vague abstraction, useful in the traditional parlance of diplomacy, which has been infused with sometimes overlapping but distinct meanings in the rhetoric and grammar of different parties. The diversity stems from the differing premises, differing purposes, and differing expectations of the parties (Finley, 1975, p. 67).

Further clarification of this concept, therefore, requires an account of the range of meaning and connotation associated with modern use.

Before proceeding, however, and assuming albeit implicitly that use confers meaning, it is necessary to consider the fundamental objection that détente has no meaning. This charge can be levelled in various ways. It might be argued that détente does not denote any specific phenomenon other than 'wishful thinking' perhaps. George Ball put this point bluntly. 'Over time the "spirit of détente" has become such an overused phrase that the skin has worn off to disclose precisely nothing. Its constant flogging by political writers has made it as cheap and commercial as the "spirit of Christmas"' (Ball, 1976, p. 2). Several analysts have suggested that détente simply refers to such intangibles as 'attitude' or 'mood'; the implication being that 'atmospherics' are a substitute for substance or, at best, that détente is merely a synonym for traditional diplomacy. A variant on this theme is to suggest that détente is 'simply' a journalistic expression, a convenient but essentially meaningless shorthand. A more serious charge suggests that détente is an artificial construct, a product of academic analysis, mechanistic and simplistic but, more important, having no referent in political behaviour.

It is clear that the use of the word détente does pose major problems. George Kennan, for example, argued that 'no new word' is required to explain relations between the superpowers in the 1970s, as attempts to forge a new relationship with Moscow can be traced back to the reopening of the US embassy in 1933 (SFRC, 1974). George Wallace, standing as a candidate in the 1976 American presidential election, became exasperated by what he called that 'high fallutin' word. Why don't they just say gettin' together?', he asked (quoted in Bell, 1977, p. 2). In that same election campaign, President Ford decided to drop the word détente from his political vocabulary because of its controversial nature.

It is significant that a number of analysts and policy-makers have preferred to substitute a variety of other words or phrases for détente, including 'constructive dialogue' or 'constructive confrontation', 'adversary partnership', 'peaceful engagement', 'normalization of relations' and 'era of negotiation'. Whether these are synonyms – though with differing connotations – intended to clarify the meaning of détente or a way of avoiding the pejorative associations linked with the term, or even a way of making the point that détente has no meaning, their pervasive use is a clear indication of problems both with the word détente and its meaning. Similarly, it can be argued that the use of metaphors in this context is a further indication of a genuine problem. Walter Clemens, for example, referred to détente as 'a fragile flower . . . difficult to cultivate, complicated to nurture . . . easy to trample' (Clemens, 1974, p. 136). Coral Bell talked of détente as 'at best a kind of loose-planking which any ill-calculating manoeuvre can dislodge, temporarily at least' (Bell, 1971, p. 70). While metaphors can clarify the nature of some phenomena, in this context they merely serve to reinforce the impression of vagueness and ambiguity.

THE USES OF DÉTENTE

Despite the clear indications that the concept of détente is problematic, the fact remains that the term has been widely used by political analysts and policy-makers alike, albeit in different contexts and with different meanings intended. Some indication of the range of meaning and connotation must now be given if further clarification of this concept is to be sought. Pierre Hassner suggested that a broad distinction can be drawn between détente as a condition (or situation) and détente as a policy (Hassner, 1977, p. 251). A third important use, détente as a process, can be added to Hassner's formulation. At the risk of imposing a coherence on both the academic literature and the pronouncements of policy-makers that may be unwarranted, the 'overlapping but distinct' notions of détente as condition, as process and as policy will serve as a convenient structure for the next section of this chapter.

Détente as condition

Three different conceptions of détente as condition can be identified in the literature: détente as historical period; as prelude to entente; and as illusion. Détente as historical period has arguably been the most pervasive formulation here, with détente regarded as the antithesis of cold war and a historical period subsequent to it. The Cuban missile crisis is usually regarded as the key turning point historically and the period after 1962 is labelled accordingly. This use does not imply the resolution of cold war conflicts between East and West, but rather that, in the period of détente, conflict became less salient, one dimension only of a multilevelled relationship between the superpowers and their allies. The idea of détente as a temporary phase is central to this conception, and this was reinforced by references in the late 1970s to the 'end' of détente and the onset of a 'new' or 'second' cold war (see, for example, Chomsky, 1982; Halliday, 1983).

From this perspective, détente was the product of a temporary balance of forces, was built upon a nuclear stalemate and was buttressed by a series of tangible and intangible agreements across the East–West divide. Thus, the period of détente – broadly identified as the 1970s – can be characterized either by a specific set of agreements or less tangibly by a willingness to foster cooperative as well as conflictual relations. It can be defined as 'a stabilised interstate system whose balanced configuration is the reference datum for the rest of international behaviour' (Finley, 1975, p. 71). Coral Bell's analysis of détente as the product of a triangular relationship between Washington, Moscow and Peking fits neatly into this 'power' conception. She also stressed the ephemeral nature of détente as a historical phenomenon with a reminder that 'all détentes in history have proved perishable in due course' (see Bell, 1977, p. 71). These assumptions enable the prevailing balance of power to be used to explain a period of détente and a changing structure of power to account for its passing.

A second use identifies détente as a prelude to entente. Though related to the first to the extent that détente is seen as a function of certain structural factors, this conception identifies trends that push relationships beyond the 'stage' of détente to much closer ties, variously labelled entente, rapprochement or even convergence. From this perspective, détente is conceived as a sort of 'half-way house' between cold war conflict and entente: or, as Walter Clemens put it:

> a point on a logical spectrum of relations along which conflict either increases or decreases. If tensions mount, the parties may move towards cold and then hot war. If tensions diminish the parties move towards détente – from détente, they could move further towards rapprochement or even entente (Clemens, 1974, pp. 134–5).

What appears to distinguish this final stage from détente is the stability of the system. Richard Rosecrance, for example, concluded that nothing short of 'a partial Soviet–American entente will provide the necessary structure in which present destabilising currents can be contained' (Rosecrance, 1975, p. 481). Marshall

Shulman drew a distinction between an 'atmosphere of détente' and a 'rapprochement or real stabilization' (Shulman, 1966, p. 58). The idea that détente, whether lasting or ephemeral as a historical phenomenon, is essentially an illusion, a charade devoid of any reality, provides a final important use under the general heading of détente as a condition. This use houses those merely sceptical of the achievements of détente, together with a transnational lobby of critics, like the late Senator Jackson, Solzhenitsyn and Deng Xiao-Ping, who at various times accused Western leaders of appeasement towards the Soviet Union. The general argument here is to suggest that, because of important differences between the Western concept of détente and the Soviet notion of 'peaceful coexistence', the Soviet Union managed in the 1970s to increase its power at the expense of the West. Détente is a dangerous illusion which poses a grave threat to Western security because it refers to a situation in which one party gains unilateral advantages at the expense of the other, 'under cover' as it were of a relaxation of tensions. References by the first Reagan administration to détente as a 'one-way street' exemplify this conception of détente (see Pipes, 1981).

Détente as process

These notions of détente as a specific condition can be contrasted with détente as a process. Henry Kissinger, testifying as Secretary of State to the Senate Hearings on détente, insisted that détente is 'a continuing process, not a final condition that has been or can be realised at any one specific point in time' (SFRC, 1974). This conception had already been voiced before those same Hearings by former Secretary of State Dean Rusk. Détente, he maintained in his testimony, 'is not a condition in which all problems are solved, but a process by which all points in dispute are resolved, and potential crises are anticipated and avoided'. This conception can also be found in academic analyses. Dalton West, for example, described détente as 'a complex, necessary, long-term process of accommodation. The only measure of its success will be the gradual growth of mutual satisfaction' (West, 1978, p. 33). For Europeans, Joseph Korbel suggested, détente means a 'slow, undefined process of alleviation of tensions' (Korbel, 1972, p. 36).

Following the signing of the Helsinki Accords in August 1975 which concluded the Conference on Security and Cooperation in Europe (CSCE), references have been regularly made to the

'Helsinki process'. All the participating states who signed the Final Act committed themselves to 'broaden, deepen and make continuing and lasting the process of détente' (quoted in Alting Von Geusau, 1979, p. 1). The CSCE Review Conferences in Belgrade (1977–78), Madrid (1980–83) and Vienna (1986–89) can be seen as symbolizing that continuing process. As British Prime Minister James Callaghan commented in a message to the Soviet News Agency Tass in July 1976, 'the Final Act was the beginning rather than the end of the process' (F.C.O., 1977, p. 28).

This conception of détente as a process is interesting because it draws attention away from specific agreements and treaties, except as landmarks or perhaps 'turning points', and, to some extent, away from teleological concerns, and focuses attention on the processes of change over time and the underlying causes of that change. This conceptual route will be explored in greater detail in the last section of this chapter. One important point to note here, however, if only because it has been stressed in the literature, is the relationship between nuclear weapons and détente. Herbert Dinerstein, for example, differentiated between détentes in traditional diplomacy that were essentially temporary in nature and the more permanent necessity of détente in the nuclear age (SFRC, 1974). The simple imperative of avoiding nuclear war of itself ensures the recurrence of détente on the international agenda. Robin Edmonds also made this important point: 'the logic of strategic nuclear power is so inexorable that sooner or later the relationship between the superpowers – however much they may pursue their rivalry in other less dangerous fields – must become positive' (Edmonds, 1975, p. 5).

The idea of an unfolding historical process has, not surprisingly, tempted scholars to date the process, to say when détente 'started' and to identify who 'started' it. Starting dates have varied enormously between 1953 (the death of Stalin) and 1975 (the Helsinki Accords). Several scholars, however, choose the late 1960s, largely because they conclude that the coming to power of the Nixon and the Brandt administrations presaged important initiatives that linked together superpower and European détentes. The question of whether the first moves came from the West or the East also divides scholars. Theodore Draper, for example, implied the latter when he argued that there were in fact three separate détentes; between the Soviet Union and, first, France from 1965, then West Germany from 1970 and, finally, the United States from 1972 (Draper, 1974, p. 33).

Détente as policy

The idea of bilateral détentes between certain states takes us on to the third important use of this concept, détente as policy. Different states at different times during the period since 1945 have been described as pursuing a détente policy. British policy will be examined in detail in later chapters, but it would be useful at this stage to establish and illustrate the notion of détente as a policy by reviewing historically the détente policies pursued by the United States, the Soviet Union, France and West Germany.

Coral Bell argued that détente first emerged as an articulate 'Western aspiration' rather than a policy or a strategy at the time of Stalin's death in 1953, with Winston Churchill as the major spokesman (Bell, 1977, p. 6 ff). The elements of a distinctive détente policy pursued by both superpowers, however, can also be traced back at least to the early 1950s. To look at the United States first: Averell Harriman, in his testimony to the Senate Hearings on détente, took issue with those who thought that it was President Nixon who initiated the 'period of negotiation' with the Soviet Union. Harriman maintained that US détente policy goes back to the Eisenhower period and the signing of the Austrian State Treaty in 1955 (SFRC, 1974). Certainly, the rhetoric associated with détente stretches back to Kennedy's 'Strategy of Peace', through Johnson's 'Peaceful Engagement' and 'Bridge-Building' to the Nixon–Kissinger 'Structure of Peace'. Key developments at the level of declaratory policy prior to the Nixon period were Kennedy's speech at the American University in Washington (June 1963), outlining his 'Strategy of Peace', and Johnson's October 1966 speech, which called for a reconciliation with the Eastern bloc. The major achievement was clearly the signing of the Partial Test Ban Treaty in August 1963. The full flowering of US détente policy, however, took place during the Nixon presidency with the initiation of diplomatic relations with China and the signing of a major set of agreements with the Soviet Union in 1972–73 (see Garthoff, 1985).

Soviet détente policy has been traced back even earlier in the 1950s. Adam Ulam, for example, argued that a policy of détente began with the August 1953 speech by the new Prime Minister Malenkov, who declared that 'we stand as we have always stood for the peaceful coexistence of the two systems' (Ulam, 1976, pp. 149–50). Other declaratory landmarks here would include Krushchev's speech to the Twentieth Congress of the Communist Party of the Soviet Union (CPSU) in 1956 and Brezhnev's 'Peace Programme' speech to the Twenty-Fourth CPSU Congress in 1971. The major achievements of Soviet policy would include those common to the United States and also the Moscow (Soviet–German) Treaty of 1970. Discussions of French détente policy, on the other hand, have focused on the high-level ministerial exchanges during 1965–66, which culminated in De Gaulle's visit to Moscow. This attempt to revive France's historic links with the Soviet Union was part of De Gaulle's 'Grand Design' and had been an important policy objective since his visit to Moscow in 1944. The French refusal to recognize East Germany, however, and later the Soviet invasion of Czechoslovakia at a time of domestic instability in France finally ended this phase of French policy (see, for example, Bell, 1977, p. 12 ff; Urban, 1976, p. 203 ff).

Much more significant in terms of achievements was the détente policy or *Ostpolitik* of West Germany. This policy represented a reversal of the assumption that the reunification of Germany must precede any détente. The *Ostpolitik* rested on the premise that reunification, if it was to be achieved at all, would be a consequence of détente. While the uncompromising Adenauer line towards the East, enshrined in the Hallstein Doctrine (1955), was softened by the Erhardt and Kiesinger governments, it was the Brandt government (elected in October 1969) that implemented this policy. The formula of 'two states in one nation' was adopted and it was this which, as Theodore Draper puts it, 'finally enabled West Germany to give up the substance while saving the shadow of reunification' (Draper, 1974, p. 35). During the 1970–72 period, the *Ostpolitik* produced a number of treaties that, in effect, secured the territorial stabilization of Europe with the implicit acceptance of 1945 borders, and provided a temporary solution at least to the Berlin and the wider German problem.

If this brief review serves to establish the notion of détente as a policy in both declaratory and substantive terms, there is some debate about whether détente has constituted a policy instrument or a policy objective. One commentator, for example, has asserted that détente must be considered as 'an instrumental policy rather than a goal-state valuable in itself' and can only be evaluated in terms of the goals that détente is instrumental in achieving (Weede, 1977, p. 408). Certainly, the instrumental nature of détente is much in evidence in the policies considered here. Both superpowers have clearly seen détente as a useful strategy for managing adversary power. For the United States, a détente policy promised different things at different times, including the resolution of, or at least a distraction from, other problems such as Berlin and Vietnam, a means of exploiting the Sino-Soviet rift and, not least, commercial opportunities in the Soviet Union and China. For the Soviet Union also, détente promised and delivered crucial economic and technological assistance from the West, as well as the legitimization of the territorial and political status quo in Europe.

With respect to France, De Gaulle was preoccupied in the 1960s with the possible uses of a détente strategy. As Alfred Grosser comments, 'ever since De Gaulle's visit to Moscow in 1944, the aim of French policy [had] been to promote whenever there was an opportunity . . . constructive relations with the Soviet Union . . . not as an end in itself, but in order to strengthen the French hand in our dealings with the United States' (quoted in Urban, 1976, p. 265). Not only was détente regarded as a way of containing American (or 'Anglo-Saxon') influence in Europe and elsewhere, it was a potential vehicle for exercising restraint on the traditional enemy, Germany, and was therefore a central plank in the Gaullist plan to restore French power and *grandeur*. For West Germany, the *Ostpolitik* delivered more tangible benefits. Most important, from a German perspective, intra-German relations were much improved with freer travel and communication between the two Germanies. Also, the demise of the Hallstein Doctrine enabled the Federal Republic to broaden political contacts as well as trade and cultural relations. Perceptions in Bonn of the important benefits accruing from détente help, for example, to explain divergent NATO responses to the Soviet invasion of Afghanistan in 1979.

There are problems, though, with the assertion that the meaning of détente in this context is restricted to détente as a policy instrument. It is not always clear in practice whether the intention has been to pursue détente as an objective or 'merely' as a means to a variety of other ends. Moreover, different states at different times appear to have pursued détente as an end in itself, most obviously when it was perceived that a détente was needed but did not exist. The argument will be developed in later chapters that, by making diplomatic initiatives and playing a positive role in East–West negotiations in the 1950s, the early 1960s and the 1980s, British leaders sought to play a significant role in the 'creation' or re-establishment of an East–West détente. Similarly, initiatives by other states, particularly at the declaratory level, have also been geared to creating or at least establishing the preconditions for a détente.

DÉTENTE AND RELATED CONCEPTS

The last section has provided some clarification of the concept of détente by identifying and illustrating the most important ways in which the term has been used. Another way of trying to clarify the meaning of this concept would be to compare détente with related concepts – some of which have already been touched on in this chapter – such as diplomacy, appeasement and peaceful coexistence.

Détente, diplomacy and appeasement

Reference was made earlier to the possible objection that détente is merely a synonym for diplomacy or perhaps traditional diplomacy. If the cold war is taken to represent the absence of diplomatic activity across the East–West ideological divide, then détente can be related to the process of restoring diplomatic relations. Stanley Hoffman implicitly links détente to a notion of traditional or 'normal' diplomacy. Writing at the beginning of the 1970s, he looked forward to a period when:

> instead of relations of total enmity or total friendship, both inimi-
> cal to diplomacy, there would again be those fluctuating mixes
> of common and divergent interests characteristic of eighteenth
> and nineteenth century European diplomacy. Ideology would
> not disappear but its external effects would be neutralised:
> different political systems could coexist since beliefs would be
> disconnected from behaviour through voluntary or necessary
> restraint (Hoffman, 1972, p. 61).

The allegation that détente is synonymous with appeasement is another indication that the cold war represented in diplomatic terms an 'abnormal' period. Appeasement, denoting the attempt to conciliate by making concessions, was an integral part of traditional diplomatic practice, but it had acquired pejorative connotations in the 1930s. Thus, as Alexander George points out, what was still recent historical experience in the postwar period served to 'discredit more generally the traditional reliance on classical diplomacy, upon negotiation and reconciliation for adjusting conflicting interests and for reconciling change in the international system with the requirements for stability' (George, 1980, p. 225; see also Herz, 1964, pp. 296–320). Détente, diplomacy and appeasement are clearly related concepts in terms of traditional diplomacy but, from a cold war perspective, it can be argued that détente has a distinct meaning (see also Craig and George, 1983).

Détente and deterrence

The contrast between the cold war and earlier historical periods in terms of traditional diplomatic practice also provides a context for discussing the relationship between détente and deterrence. The issue here in conceptual terms, however, is not one of synonymity but of compatibility. Critics who equate détente with appeasement in a pejorative sense argued that détente is also undesirable because it undermines the structure of deterrence, which is crucial to the maintenance of peace in the nuclear age. From this perspective, détente and deterrence are incompatible strategies.

A related but less critical position stresses the primacy of deterrence over détente. President Carter, for example, in a speech to the World Affairs Council in Philadelphia in May 1980 designed to signal a more hard line direction in US foreign policy, declared that 'détente with the Soviet Union remains our goal. But détente must be built upon a firm foundation of deterrence' (*Guardian*, 10 May 1980). This view of détente as desirable but essentially subordinate to deterrence has its antecedents in the 'negotiation from strength' strategy associated with former US Secretary of State Dean Acheson in the late 1940s.

A third position stresses the complementarity of deterrence and détente in the nuclear age. This view starts from the premise that deterrence is a negative, reactive strategy that may prevent nuclear war in certain circumstances but at a cost of freezing the sources of conflict. The argument here is that deterrence must be balanced by détente – with the latter conceived as a positive strategy of incentives – so that some progress might be made in resolving or at least ameliorating the differences of interest that produce conflict (see Luard, 1967, pp. 167–89). The Harmel Report of December 1967 on the future tasks of the NATO alliance explicitly adopted this 'stick and carrot' view that détente and deterrence are complementary and, indeed, mutually reinforcing rather than contradictory strategies, and advocated that both should be part of a long-term process to promote better relations. It is interesting that Helmut Schmidt in 1983 called for a return to the 'Harmel approach' and warned the Reagan administration that an exclusively military strategy would fail unless the president understood the need for a wider political strategy in the context of East–West relations (*International Herald Tribune*, 5 December 1983).

Détente and peaceful coexistence

It is clear from the earlier discussion of détente as illusion that apparent similarities between the concepts of détente and peaceful coexistence obscure differences of use and connotation. A Soviet preference for using 'peaceful coexistence' rather than 'détente' in political language suggests the possibility of conceptual ambiguity here, which has major implications with respect to perceptions and expectations about East–West relations. Although peaceful coexistence and détente have essentially the same meaning from a Soviet perspective, two questions need to be asked in the quest for conceptual clarity. What do Soviet leaders mean by peaceful coexistence? Is their concept consistent with a 'Western' concept of détente? Given the radical developments in Soviet thought outlined in President Gorbachev's remarkable speech to the United Nations General Assembly in December 1988, this discussion deals with the Soviet position up to 1985.

Peaceful coexistence emerged as a concept in the Soviet Union after the 1917 Revolution and referred to the tactical necessity of avoiding war – an imperative, given the vulnerability of the new Soviet state. As Graham Vernon explains, 'peaceful coexistence as a Soviet policy was developed by a leadership which perceived it needed time to prepare for an "inevitable" war' (Vernon, 1979, p. 274; this section draws extensively upon Vernon's discussion). In the nuclear age, however, this policy ceased to be a tactic devised to gain time and became a long-term strategy, a 'fundamental principle of Soviet foreign policy' as Khrushchev put it in his speech to the Twentieth CPSU Congress in 1956. Khrushchev's speech was the first clear statement of the new priority to be attached to peaceful coexistence in Soviet policy. This principle was linked explicitly to the rejection of the Leninist doctrine on the inevitability of war between states with different social systems. According to Khrushchev, war was no longer a 'fatalistic inevitability' (*Pravda*,

15 February 1956; see also Marantz, 1975, pp. 501–27). In a later speech to the Supreme Soviet in October 1959, the Soviet leader declared that peaceful coexistence had become:

an objective necessity, deriving from the present situation in the world, from the contemporary stage in the development of human society . . . the question now at hand is not whether or not there should be peaceful coexistence. It exists and will continue to exist, unless we want the lunacy of a nuclear-missile war (*Izvestia*, 1 November 1959).

As noted earlier, critics of both détente and Soviet policy argued that peaceful coexistence does not have the same meaning as the Western concept of détente. Specifically, they rejected the argument that peaceful coexistence had become a principle of Soviet policy rather than a tactical expedient. Peaceful coexistence, it was argued, does not mean 'ideological coexistence'; if anything, it implies that the 'class struggle' has intensified. For the Soviet Union, détente or peaceful coexistence is merely a tactical ploy designed to lessen the dangers of nuclear war. Thus, the 'new' policy simply represents a change of methods to achieve the same revolutionary goals that were established in 1917 (see, for example, Conquest *et al.*, 1974).

There is substance to this critique to the extent that Soviet leaders neither suggested that adopting a policy of peaceful coexistence signals the end of the ideological struggle nor that the policy would not be used to advance the interests of the Soviet Union and/or international socialism. Indeed, Soviet leaders stated precisely the opposite on numerous occasions. Leonid Brezhnev, for example, in his speech to the Twenty-Fifth CPSU Congress in February 1976, made it clear that 'détente and peaceful coexistence refer to relations between states. This means above all that disputes and conflicts between countries must not be settled by means of war or by means of the use of force or the threat of force'. But, he continued, 'détente does not in the slightest abolish, and it cannot abolish or alter, the laws of the class struggle. We don't conceal that we see in détente a way to the creation of more advantageous conditions for peaceful socialist Communist construction' (*Izvestia*, 25 February 1976).

It can be argued that the Soviet Union always had a coherent and a consistent conception of peaceful coexistence/détente which, ideologically, has to be understood in terms of the interrelationship between peaceful coexistence and 'proletarian internationalism' (see

Vernon, 1979). Whether this distinctive Soviet view is inconsistent with a Western conception of détente is, however, a moot point. First, that position assumes that there is an agreed 'Western' understanding of détente that might be used for comparative purposes. Secondly, this position is itself ideological to the extent that it assumes that Western states do not also use détente to advance their politico-ideological interests. Finally, it assumes that there are no common interests other than the avoidance of nuclear war that might be advanced by détente.

DÉTENTE AS AN ANALYTICAL TERM

The discussion so far in this chapter has established clearly different if overlapping uses of the term détente. Some additional clarification has been provided by comparing détente with other related concepts. Nevertheless, the problem remains that any overall agreement on meaning is limited to a simple dictionary definition, and this only serves to paper over the variety of use and connotation. The absence of an agreed meaning, however, raises the important question of whether détente can be legitimately used as an analytical term. The problem of establishing an agreed meaning of détente, as this discussion has illustrated, is exacerbated by the fact that the term has been suffused over time with ideological content. The 'politicization' of détente is indicated by attempts to rescue the concept by the use of qualifying adjectives, as in references to 'real', 'genuine' or even Richard Nixon's 'hard-headed' détente (Nixon, 1984): but such devices merely sidestep the issue of the ideological use of this concept. References to détente as a 'political shibboleth' or a 'portmanteau slogan' are further illustrations of this problem (Draper, 1976, p. 34; Leopold Labedz, quoted in Urban, 1976, p. 283).

Indeed, it was clear by the mid-1970s that détente had acquired almost theological connotations, with the capacity to excite passions either for or against it. At one extreme, détente was regarded as the only alternative to cold or even 'hot' war; at the other extreme, it was regarded as little more than a euphemism for appeasement. In policy terms, one side's strategy was another side's stratagem. Thus, while US and specifically Henry Kissinger's détente policy could be described as 'a mode of management of adversary power' (Bell, 1977, p. 1), Soviet détente policy could be viewed as 'a stratagem of subterfuge propagated by a determined adversary to

gain an advantage in a continuing contest for hegemony or power'
(Finley, 1975, p. 75).

From this perspective, détente was and is an 'essentially contested
concept' (Gallie, 1962). As Barry Buzan has commented with
reference to the concept of security, 'such concepts necessarily
generate unsolvable debates about their meaning and application
because (quoting Richard Little) . . . they contain an ideological
element which renders empirical evidence irrelevant as a means
of resolving the dispute' (Buzan, 1983, p. 6). In this sense, there
can be no agreement on the meaning of détente. And yet, this
cannot rule out the use of détente for analytical purposes. If that
followed, many of the core concepts in social science would also
be rendered unusable. It does, however, underline the point that
the concept must be carefully specified within an explicit analytical
framework.

In pursuit of such a framework, it is appropriate at this stage to
reflect on the existing uses of the concept rather more critically.
While all the uses considered here highlight recognizable aspects of
détente to a greater or lesser extent, the various notions of détente
as a specific condition pose most problems from an analytical
perspective. Détente as historical period is simple and attractive
but most vulnerable to the charge of being an artificial construct
or journalistic shorthand. There are too many elements of 'détente'
in periods labelled 'cold war' or 'new cold war' and vice-versa to
make the cyclical account wholly convincing. Where the conception
is located (usually implicitly) within a 'power' framework, the focus
tends to be too restrictively military-strategic to account for the
recurrence of détente at different times. This suggests that a broader
framework, which also highlights political and economic factors, is
needed. Détente as prelude to *entente* is also rather contrived but,
more important, like détente as illusion, it is explicitly normative
in orientation and therefore problematic for analytical purposes.

Détente as policy and process

If détente as condition is difficult to use effectively for analytical
purposes, the existing uses of détente as policy and as process
provide a basis for developing and applying this concept at two
conventional levels of analysis: the international system and the
state. At the system level, détente can be analysed in the broad
context of a changing international system and conceived as a

process of accommodation generated by dynamic structural changes in the system over time. At the state level, on the other hand, détente can be conceived as a policy issue and analysed from the perspective of individual states rather than the system as a whole. At this level of analysis, similarities and differences between détente policies will be highlighted and can be compared.

This broad approach addresses the thorny problem of competing interpretations of détente by suggesting that the meaning of détente is contingent upon the level at which it is analysed. At the system level, the analytical task is to identify a process of accommodation and the relevant 'change' factors, and then to try and establish a causal relationship. At the state level, the task is to identify détente as a policy issue in the foreign policies of particular states. An account of détente as policy will highlight the perceptions of policy-makers, the 'uses' of détente, in domestic as well as foreign policy, and the policy objectives sought through détente. The explanation is likely to focus on both domestic factors and the international determinants of state behaviour.

This study is primarily concerned to investigate détente at the state level by analysing British détente policy since the 1950s. But one of the central objectives of the study, as stated in the introductory chapter, is to identify a British role in an East–West détente process and to offer some evaluation of that role. It is appropriate, therefore, to conclude this chapter by specifying the notion of détente as process rather more explicitly. There are broadly two ways of approaching this, which may be interrelated in any particular analysis. One approach would be to use a his-torical–descriptive methodology and attempt to trace the outlines of a process of East–West accommodation over time. The other approach would be to focus more on the causes than the evidence of détente by locating a détente process within changing structures of international relations and resulting patterns of behaviour.

The first approach, it might be argued, would be predisposed to highlight the more 'visible' manifestations of a process of accom-modation. Historically, 'phases' or 'periods' of détente might be described and associated 'landmarks' or 'turning points' identified as signposts along the way. A study of East–West détente by Richard Stevenson (1985) will serve to illustrate this type of approach. Stevenson bases his analysis on 'four periods of easing tension in contemporary US–Soviet relations': the 'spirit of Geneva' (1955); the 'spirit of Camp David' (1959); the post-missile crisis détente

(1963–64) and the 'Moscow détente' (1972–75). The objective of Stevenson's study is to reveal the 'factors working for and against détente'. To that end, he describes for each period what he calls the 'setting, occurrence and aftermath' of détente. He concludes that 'certain basic factors making for conflict between the superpowers have continuously asserted themselves to impose limits on the extent to which a relaxation of tension can change the relationship' (Stevenson, 1985, p. 202). Thus, détente has 'proved to be a limited process with limited potential'. Nevertheless, détente is identified as a process in the sense that 'the legacy of détente has been cumulative in US–Soviet relations'. While progress has not been linear or cyclical, Stevenson argues that each period of détente has built upon the legacy of the previous period. 'Since the 1950s, significant agreements have been reached, US–Soviet dialogue has been re-established, and the process of negotiation has been firmly entrenched as the means to deal with conflicting issues' (Stevenson, 1985, p. 201).

Though useful in descriptive terms, it can be argued that this sort of analysis is limited as an explanation of détente. The idea of recurring periods of détente since the 1950s and the notion of a cumulative process suggests that there is an underlying dynamic in the system that is not captured by a historical–descriptive analysis. A major problem with Stevenson's analysis from this perspective is his conception of détente as essentially a product of an evolving US–Soviet relationship – a 'type of maturation process' he calls it at one point – rather than a result of broader changes in the international system over a period of time which themselves might be said to undermine the ability of the superpowers to control the system. If the cold war is identified in structural terms with a bipolar distribution of power and the primacy of ideological and military-strategic alignments, a détente process can be related to challenges to that structure of rigid bloc differentiation.

A structural analysis might be developed around four interrelated 'change' factors that weakened East–West ideological and military alignments and gradually eroded a bipolar structure: the general impact of nuclear weapons and the specific impact of a nuclear stalemate; the growth of economic interdependence; the diversification and diffusion of power; and the changing interests and attitudes of international actors. The impact of these changes, it might be argued, was to produce if not a recognizably multipolar system, then at least a multi-levelled international system with interactions at different levels of activity on a variety of issues, not wholly constrained by an East–West ideological structure or limited to security politics.

The explanation of détente with reference to these changes, however, is still dependent upon the approach and the perspective adopted by the analyst. From a superpower perspective, for example, détente might be explained as an attempt to manage a process of change, the pace of which in some respects at least was being set by their allies. From the perspective of the allies, on the other hand, détente might be explained as a vehicle for exploiting those changes in order to create some freedom of manoeuvre within their respective hegemonic systems. As Richard Barnet observes, détente 'proved to be a time for subordinate nations on both sides of the ideological divide to rediscover their political past' (Barnet, 1983, p. 345).

It is not necessary in the context of this study to pursue further the various explanations of a détente process. The concern in this chapter has been to clarify the concept of détente and, more specifically, to establish the notions of détente as process and as policy, thus providing a useful conceptual framework for an analysis of British détente policy. This begins in the next chapter by locating British policy after 1953 within a historical context.

Chapter 3

Britain, the cold war and détente

British détente policy has its roots in the early postwar period and can most effectively be located within a historical context by comparing British and American attitudes to the cold war, differing perceptions of the Soviet/communist threat and, most important, different views about appropriate responses to that threat. If the period from 1945 to 1953 is viewed from this perspective, what emerges is a significant divergence of attitudes, particularly after 1949 when American attitudes perceptibly hardened.

By the end of 1946, differing perceptions of Soviet intentions towards the West had been replaced by an apparent congruence of Anglo-American perspectives on East–West relations. Certainly, both the Truman and Attlee governments now shared the view that the Soviet Union posed a direct threat to Western interests and were agreed on the pressing need to modify Soviet behaviour (Ovendale, 1982, pp. 217–36; Bullock, 1985, p. 239). The Attlee government fully supported the American response to this problem – the policy of containment that owed much to the ideas of George Kennan. The containment of the Soviet Union while the economic and military strength of Western Europe was rebuilt was regarded in London, as in Washington, as the only viable strategy for normalizing relations with the Soviet Union in the longer term. If containment was essentially a negative way of modifying Soviet behaviour, more positive inducements could be employed at a later stage as part of an overall strategy.

But, it should be remembered, containment itself was initially conceived in Washington as a strategy designed to facilitate a normalization of relations as quickly as possible. Cutting off diplomatic contacts and ceasing to negotiate with Moscow was not part of the original concept of containment. As Gaddis notes, 'Kennan took the position that modifying Soviet behaviour required both positive and negative reinforcement – this meant being prepared to engage in such negotiations as seemed likely to produce mutually acceptable results' (Gaddis, 1982, p. 71; see also Kennan, 1982, pp. xii–xiii). As implemented by the Americans, however, the policy of containment moved away from the original conception in important respects during the 1947–49 period. These policy changes produced friction in Anglo-American relations and can be seen with hindsight to reveal underlying differences of approach not only to East–West relations but also to international relations as a whole. It is necessary, therefore, to look at these changes in some detail.

The rationale behind these policy changes in Washington was clearly set out in a planning document drafted by a small ad hoc committee of State and Defense Department officials chaired by Paul Nitze, Kennan's successor as Director of Policy Planning at the State Department. Though it was not drafted by the National Security Council, this document became known as NSC-68 when it was produced in May 1950. NSC-68 made the case that the assumptions which underpinned the containment doctrine had changed and that, therefore, the policy itself must change. Most important, it was argued that the nature of the Soviet threat had changed. The Soviet Union, strengthened by recent developments – the imposition of a monolithic communist rule in Eastern Europe, the revolution in China, the successful testing of an atomic bomb – was now regarded as a much more formidable threat, particularly in military terms. Moreover, the source of the threat was assumed to have shifted from the Soviet Union per se to the international communist movement directed from Moscow.

Given these new assumptions in Washington, the object of containment, for the United States and also for the fledgling North Atlantic alliance, was to build, in Secretary of State Dean Acheson's phrase, 'situations of strength' to match and counter the threat. Despite talk of eventual 'negotiation from strength', this objective in practice excluded negotiation with the new implacable enemy, international communism. For the Americans, containment and the cold war had now come to mean political warfare between two monolithic power blocs: on the one hand, strengthening the cohesion of the Western bloc and, on the other, taking positive steps to undermine the cohesion of the communist bloc.[1] Negotiations with the Soviet Union, which had been an important though not a central component of the original strategy of containment, became the victim of this policy review document. Gaddis provides a convenient summary of the new American posture:

This approach was not intended to preclude eventual negotiations with the Russians, but it did seek to defer them until requisite levels of 'strength' had been reached. It left little room for efforts to alter the Soviet concept of international relations through positive as well as negative reinforcement. Rather, 'strength' came to be viewed almost as an end in itself, not as a means to a larger end; the process of containment became more important than the objective that process was supposed to attain (Gaddis, 1982, pp. 82–3).

Thus, American hostility to and fear of negotiations was based upon an entrenchment of cold war attitudes to the communist threat. The adopted image of 'Hitler in the Kremlin masterminding global subversion' ruled out negotiations and normal diplomatic relations: a regime bent on world revolution would simply regard a willingness to negotiate as a sign of weakness (Barnet, 1977, pp. 29, 86). By employing 'salami tactics', any concessions made would simply become the starting point for the next series of demands. Thus, as Adam Ulam puts it, 'next to all-out war, the prospect of negotiating with the communists inspired the most fear in the bosom of American diplomats' (Ulam, 1968, p. 536). Only a change in the Soviet system and the renunciation of global ambitions could lead to negotiations. As things stood in what was now conceived as a zero-sum game, there was simply nothing to negotiate about.

The British reaction to these changes of attitude and the policy consequences of these changes in the United States was one of growing concern. The central point to be developed here is that the British could not wholly accept what had become a manichaeistic view of the world in Washington. Certainly, the Attlee government played a major role in helping the Americans to construct a 'situation of strength' in Europe and elsewhere and this will be discussed later, but the underlying conception of containment and the cold war remained close to the original ideas of Kennan. The cold war, from a British perspective, could not be an end in itself; the object of policy on East–West relations remained the normalization of those relationships: cutting off diplomatic contacts would fundamentally undermine that objective. Simply 'talking' to the Soviet leadership in the language of military power would harden attitudes and serve to prevent a modification of Soviet behaviour.

As suggested above, divergent attitudes in London and Washington reflected fundamental differences of approach. The British conception of the cold war and the Soviet threat was rooted in a traditional realpolitik approach to diplomacy and international relations. Conflicts were the natural product of differences of interest between states. Differences of interest could and, whenever possible, should be resolved by a process of diplomatic accommodation. This necessitates communication, negotiation and the seeking of a modus vivendi with other states. Breaking off contacts and being unwilling to negotiate seriously is an aberration from the norm of traditional diplomacy and should be avoided. The greater the threat posed by other states, the more necessary is the maintenance of diplomatic intercourse. As Northedge and Wells argue, this almost constituted an 'elementary rule – the more dangerous to peace a state is, the more important it is to be in diplomatic contact with it' (Northedge and Wells, 1982, p. 127). From this perspective, the nature of the regime being dealt with, however odious, is irrelevant. In the words of a former British ambassador to Moscow, 'in intergovernmental relations, we cannot confine ourselves to dealing with states whose general policies we approve' (D. Wilson, 1974, p. 391). It is clear that there was a serious conflict between these normative principles and the approach to East–West relations set out in NSC-68.

The application of these principles to policy was evident in Churchill's 'spheres of influence' arrangement with Stalin in October 1944. For Churchill, a working relationship with Stalin and preventing the spread of communism to Western Europe and the Mediterranean were more important than the political arrangements within the Soviet 'sphere' (Carlton, 1982, p. 178). American policy at this time, on the other hand, was proceeding on quite different premises consistent with Roosevelt's 'Grand Design'. As Alexander George explains:

> instead of a new balance of power system – and instead of secret agreements and spheres of influence, he [Roosevelt] hoped that new governments would emerge in the occupied states of Europe through procedures or policies that were consistent with the principle of national self-determination and independence (Holsti, Siverson and George, 1980, p. 243).

Even before the end of the Second World War, then, there were indications of implicit differences of approach and the potential for future conflict between London and Washington.

When the control of British foreign policy passed to the Attlee government in 1945, these underlying principles were maintained. Although Ernest Bevin's prime concern as Foreign Secretary was, like Churchill's, to bind the Americans to the fate of Britain and Western Europe, he was also concerned to keep open the door to the East in the hope of a better understanding. As Elisabeth Barker puts it, Bevin saw the 'alliance with the Americans not as a preparation for an inevitable war against Russia, but as an essential foundation for future efforts of détente [sic]' (Barker, 1983, p. 185; see also Baylis, 1982). Barker documents the skilful way in which Bevin, allegedly the coldest of cold warriors, firmly resisted domestic pressures: from the Foreign Office in 1946 to mount an anti-communist crusade; from the Chiefs of Staff in 1948 to set up a political warfare machinery (the Information Research Department that was set up was not what the Chiefs had in mind); and again in 1949 from the Russia Committee of the Foreign Office for an interdepartmental committee with Ministry of Defence representation to be concerned with political warfare (Barker, 1983, pp. 47, 103–9, 177).

For Bevin, the cold war was not about subverting communism but essentially about normalizing relations with the East as soon as possible, although, it must be said, he became increasingly sceptical about that prospect the longer he was in office. He told the Cabinet in November 1947 that 'we have been scrupulously careful not to encourage subversive movements in Eastern Europe or anti-Russianism, or to lead the anti-communists to hope for support that we cannot give' (quoted in Barker, 1983, p. 109). The only significant blot on this record was British participation in the abortive CIA attempt to subvert Albania in 1949.

It was in 1949, however, that differences of approach between London and Washington became overt policy clashes, the precipitating issue being China. For the Americans, the 'loss' of China reinforced the notion of a monolithic communist bloc with whom negotiations were impossible. The British, for their part, infuriated the Americans not only by recognizing the new Peking government in January 1950, but by insisting that negotiations should be held with Mao. Mao was another Tito, they argued, and should at least be talked to: the Chinese would not long remain under the tutelage of the Soviet Union. For the West to negotiate with Mao would at least put pressure on the Russians to ameliorate their hostility (Barker, 1983, pp. 169–74; see also Boardman, 1976). The significance of British policy on China after the revolution is that it was in line with the principle of keeping contacts open and, moreover, it was an explicit rejection of the American conception of a monolithic international communism.

With the outbreak of the Korean War in June 1950 and the very real possibility of direct conflict between the superpowers, the dangers of the NSC–68 version of containment became apparent to the Attlee government. A new policy line of conciliation, consistent with the tenets of traditional diplomacy, was now required. As Arthur Cyr puts it, 'the directness of the confrontation between the superpowers encouraged efforts to pursue a mediating role' (Cyr, 1979, p. 147). While the British loyally backed the American line on Korea – even if they baulked at references to a 'centrally directed communist imperialism' – and immediately put British ships in Japanese waters at the disposal of the American naval commander, the need to defuse the crisis persuaded Bevin to risk further American displeasure by attempting to mediate.

In July 1950, Bevin suggested to the Soviet government that they put pressure on the North Koreans to withdraw north of the 38th parallel. This attempt to mediate was an embarrassing failure, however, and military support for the war effort was increased thereafter (Bullock, 1985, p. 795). But this initial failure did not signal the end of British attempts to mediate. The most significant diplomatic initiative was the November 1950 proposal to establish a demilitarized buffer zone in North Korea to separate the opposing forces (see Farrar, 1983, pp. 327–51). The immediate context for this initiative was provided by the entry of Chinese 'volunteers' into Korea in the last week of October. With General MacArthur determined to exploit his victory at Inchon by conquering the whole of North Korea – an ambition that had at least the tacit support of his president – the dangers of escalation suddenly became apparent to a British government which had given its support to the crossing of the 38th parallel. The attention of the government now focused on trying to avoid a major war in the Far East.

The British proposal emerged from a Cabinet meeting on 13 November 1950, at which the Chiefs of Staff issued a clear warning that a continuation of the military compaign to unify Korea under UN auspices would risk a major war with China. They recommended the establishment of a demilitarized zone, consisting of the whole of North Korea to the north of the 'neck' of Korea. This plan was accepted by the Cabinet. Bevin supported the Chiefs not only because he wanted to prevent the Americans from provoking further Chinese intervention, but also because he wanted to allay Chinese fears that the Western powers might occupy large tracts of Asian territory (Farrar, 1983, pp. 330–5; but see also Bullock, 1985, p. 820). During the next few days the government endeavoured to attract support for the plan, from the Americans and from other governments. The British representative in Peking was also instructed to explain to the Chinese what the government was trying to do. Some progress was made on all diplomatic fronts, but it proved impossible to delay MacArthur's planned offensive. Indeed, the plan was eventually overtaken by events, as MacArthur began his advance to the Yalu River only to be repelled by a massive Chinese counterattack.

In the context of an even more dangerous military situation, British attention switched from the demilitarization plan to trying to forestall a precipitate American response. The immediate concern was that MacArthur might press for authority to launch air attacks on China. But this concern was soon replaced by the fear that Truman might authorize the use of atomic bombs to resolve the Korean crisis. Hints that this was being contemplated were sufficient to send Attlee rushing to Washington at the beginning of December 1950, seeking assurances that atomic weapons would not be used (see Bullock, 1985, pp. 820–4). Attlee's visit may not have been crucial in preventing a nuclear war in Asia, but it did dramatically illustrate the extent of British concerns about both the direction of American policy and the state of East–West relations as a whole.

This concern was not restricted to the Labour government. By 1950, Bevin was beginning to despair about the possibility of a diplomatic solution to East–West problems. But the general election campaign at the beginning of that year brought Winston Churchill to the stump on this issue, sensing perhaps that Bevin was becoming too identified with the Acheson line (Barker, 1983, pp. 240–1). In an important speech in Edinburgh on 14 February, Churchill made the first of several appeals in the first half of the 1950s for what he called an East–West 'summit' meeting:

> I cannot help coming back . . . to this idea of another talk with Soviet Russia upon the highest level. The idea appeals to me of a supreme effort to bridge the gulf between the two worlds, so that each can live their life, if not in friendship, at least without the hatreds and manoeuvres of the cold war. . . . It is not easy to see how things could be worsened by a parley at the summit if such a thing were possible (Carlyle, 1953, p. 50).

This speech was a direct response to a press conference given by Dean Acheson on 8 February, in which he rejected the calls of some senators for a direct approach to Moscow and repeated his faith in the policy of building situations of strength (Calvocoressi, 1953, pp. 15–17). Churchill picked up the summit theme in a number of speeches through 1950 (see Gilbert, 1988, pp. 520–1, 571–4). In the first foreign policy debate of the new parliament at the end of March, for example, he argued that time was not on the side of the West. It was all very well and indeed necessary to build up 'situations of strength' and then 'negotiate from strength' at some unspecified time in the future but, as Churchill put it, 'time and patience . . . are not necessarily on our side' (quoted in Bell, 1962, pp. 13–14). It is interesting to note that this debate in Britain preceded the outbreak of the war in Korea, when the dangers of confrontation became apparent.

This debate also touched on an important theme that was to recur throughout the 1950s. One of the major themes in NSC-68 was the argument that the Russians were likely to risk going to war as soon as their military capabilities reached a point where they could reasonably expect to win. Thus 1954 was identified as the 'year of maximum danger' (Gaddis, 1982, pp. 96–7). The British, on the other hand, were much less pessimistic about the potential for Soviet risk-taking in the future, but much more concerned about the present dangers of war. This appeared to reflect their view that war was more likely to be caused by miscalculation or misunderstanding than by design. Thus, communication and negotiation were necessary now, rather than in the future, to create the sort of political climate in which either miscalculation or misunderstanding were less likely to occur. For the British, therefore, the Korean War underlined the urgency of the need for East–West negotiations.

The bipartisan nature of British concerns was confirmed after a Conservative government under Churchill was returned in October 1951. The new prime minister, stung perhaps by the 'warmonger' label that had been attached to him during the election campaign, immediately returned to the issue of negotiations with the Russians. In a major speech on 9 November at the Guildhall in London – to become a favoured venue for speeches about détente – Churchill talked in characteristically Olympian terms about the need to keep the giants from colliding.

The Americans, for their part, remained unmoved and 'uninfected' by what was becoming known as the 'British disease' (Northedge and Wells, 1982, p. 124). Calls for negotiations with the Russians were, after all, only to be expected from the man who had negotiated the 'spheres of influence' deal with Stalin. By the end of 1951, existing American antipathy to direct negotiations had been reinforced by Soviet attempts to set up 'peace movements' in Europe. This of itself served, in Coral Bell's words, to 'endow the whole notion of diplomatic bargaining with a disreputable fellow-travelling air' (Bell, 1962, p. 96). Soviet calls for peaceful coexistence were simply a ploy to divide the West and to lull it into a false sense of security. Churchill was naively playing into Soviet hands and eroding the cohesion of the Western bloc. The 1952 presidential election campaign was to add further inhibitions to the idea of East–West negotiation. Hitherto regarded as dangerous, negotiations were now to acquire explicitly moral connotations, akin to doing deals with the devil.

Nevertheless, there is some evidence that the Truman administration recognized that Churchill's oft-stated position on the desirability of East–West negotiations posed a threat to American policy. The extensive preparations taken in Washington for Churchill's first visit as the new prime minister in January 1952 show how seriously this threat was taken. An interdepartmental steering group was set up to review all aspects of policy with the Soviet Union.[2] The object was to enable the administration to justify its policies and, if possible, to persuade the Churchill government to align its policies more effectively. The specific concern was to show that there were no grounds for supposing that negotiations, particularly in a summit format, would achieve any positive results, although care was taken to 'avoid creating in the British mind any implication that we had abandoned the principle of negotiation with the Soviet Union'.

These preparatory papers reveal, though admittedly from an American perspective, the gulf between British and American approaches to East–West relations and the extent of British fears about the longer-term direction of American policy. It is interesting that the papers list the questions that the prime minister was expected to raise: Were the Americans looking forward to an 'unlimited period of Cold War'? Were they building up their forces to a point where they 'may desire to force a showdown'? Was it their objective 'to bring about revolt in the USSR and the Satellites'? The prepared responses to these hypothetical questions are also revealing. The administration was determined to 'go ahead and build our strength so that we will be in a position to continue the cold war on terms increasingly advantageous to the West'. But there was no intention 'of forcing a showdown with the USSR at some future time'. The response to the last question clearly illustrates the different attitudes to political warfare that had emerged. The administration was not unaware of the dangers of political warfare, but was committed to it as a strategy. On the other hand:

> The British will tend to question the necessity or desirability of political warfare operations. They are inclined to accept the present *status quo* in Eastern Europe and do not desire to engage in activities which they consider not only will be calculated to increase East–West tension but which might even provoke the Kremlin to acts of aggression. The British, in short, appear to believe that the immediate dangers of provocation overbalance the long-range deterrent results of political warfare carried on within Moscow's own orbit (Steering Group Negotiating Papers TCT D-1/5a, 6 January 1952. *Harry S. Truman Papers*).

Stalin's offer in March 1952 to open urgent negotiations on a German peace settlement provided another opportunity for Anglo-American differences to surface. There is some evidence that, in Richard Barnet's words, 'Churchill thought the moment was right for a deal on reunification, but neither Adenauer nor the Americans would consider it' (Barnet, 1983, p. 138). Stalin's offer envisaged a unified, rearmed but neutral Germany, and he followed it up with an invitation to Western businessmen to discuss trade in Moscow. Whether these Soviet moves were genuine bargaining bids or merely attempts to delay the military integration of the Federal Republic into the Western camp – or both

– cannot be ascertained with any certainty. But some commentators have argued though that this was an important opportunity for initiating an East–West détente that was missed by the West. Adam Ulam argues this case:

> It is tempting to postulate that the West could have secured a united, non-communist – if neutralised – Germany. [While] it is impossible to say with certainty that in 1952 the West could have traded West German rearmament for a Soviet surrender of East Germany . . . the fear of a German army backed by the United States and on the borders of the Soviet empire was a real fear felt by the Soviet policy-makers . . . and to conjure away his real fears Stalin was ready to pay highly (Ulam, 1968, pp. 506, 537).

As far as Churchill's position is concerned, it is clear that he had no room for manoeuvre at this time. The Western states had created West Germany and they would not seriously negotiate reunification despite the continuing rhetoric to the contrary. After the Summer of 1950, the United States, if not yet the allies who continued to wrangle over the European Defence Community project (EDC), was committed to the rearmament of West Germany in order to strengthen NATO's conventional defences. Not even lip-service could now be paid to the idea of a neutral Germany. Indeed, the talk during the 1952 presidential campaign in the United States was of 'liberation' and 'rollback', the sort of language that was consistent, of course, with a political warfare approach to East–West relations.

Richard Barnet provides a useful summary of the American position with respect to East–West diplomacy at the end of 1952:

> By the closing months of the Truman administration the Americans feared negotiation more than confrontation. An inconclusive negotiation with the Soviets would delay forward movement within the alliance, but a successful negotiation leading to an East–West thaw could have more serious consequences. The danger Acheson saw was that a US–Soviet deal would encourage neutralism, imperil the unity of the West and dilute American influence in Europe (Barnet, 1983, p. 138).

As the Eisenhower administration took office, the prospects for détente looked distinctly unfavourable. Churchill himself was concerned about the new president. 'For your private ear', he confided to Colville, 'I am greatly disturbed. I think this makes war much more probable' (Colville, 1985, p. 654). It was precisely 'such fears', Martin Gilbert comments, that 'gave Churchill a new sense of mission: to stay on as Prime Minister until he could bring about, by his own exertions, a reconciliation of the two Great Powers. This aim, more than any other consideration, was the underlying motive of his remaining years of power' (Gilbert, 1988, p. 774).

Having summarized the American position, it is appropriate to review British policy and attitudes at this point. It has been argued here that serious reservations about the direction of American policy began as early as 1949. Restraining the Americans became almost as important an objective as taking action to counter the Soviet threat. From a structural perspective, the rigidities of a bipolar confrontation between East and West not only imposed an inflexible structure on relationships within and between the rival blocs, but also froze at least a semi-permanent state of confrontation, heightening the possibility of world war. Given traditional British attitudes outlined above, it was not surprising perhaps that British governments would attempt to play a mediating role both to retain flexibility and to offset the dangers of war.

What is significant in the broader context of this study is that the British did not appear to see this position as being 'for' détente as opposed to being 'for' cold war, or as being in any sense disloyal to the Americans and the other NATO allies. The contention here is that it was the Americans who came to adopt the position implicit in NSC-68 that détente was the antithesis of cold war and, therefore, was automatically suspect. For the British, the pursuit of détente was not perverse or deviant, it was simply normal diplomacy, to be sought almost instinctively the more 'abnormal' the times became.

And yet it might be argued that this British posture was disingenuous. Surely, Britain had made a major contribution to establishing the very cold war structures that made effective nego-tiation with the Soviet bloc extremely difficult, if not impossible? Hadn't Churchill's 1946 'Iron Curtain' speech, for example, set the pace for the Americans in metaphorical bloc-building? Certainly, the developments in Europe that so concerned George Kennan, the creation of the Federal Republic of Germany and the establishment of NATO, as well as the instrument of containment that Kennan positively welcomed – Marshall Aid – owed a considerable debt to British diplomacy. As Northedge and Wells suggest, it does seem paradoxical that Britain, arguably the 'architect' of détente in the early 1950s, should also have been a major architect of the cold war in the late 1940s (Northedge and Wells, 1982, p. 128).

An explanation of British policy lies partly in basic attitudes to international relations, a theme that will be developed in later chapters. But it also lies in two other imperatives that governed British foreign policy after the Second World War. The first of these was Britain's economic plight. Such were the economic problems that faced the Attlee government, particularly evident after the harsh Winter of 1946–47, that the burden of supporting the British zone in Germany had become intolerable. The agreement of December 1946, which fused together the British and American zones, can be seen with hindsight to have been the first important move towards the establishment of a separate, independent Federal Republic of Germany in September 1949.

Similarly, the desperate need to ensure a massive influx of American dollars to fund both industrial recovery and a welfare state in Britain is crucial to an explanation of Bevin's role in organizing the European response to the Marshall Plan through the mechanism of the Organization for European Economic Cooperation (OEEC). This role was also significant in terms of the second imperative: binding the United States to Britain and Western Europe. As early as 1946, much to the growing concern of the Labour Left, the Attlee government had decided that British security as well as economic recovery necessitated a close alliance with the Americans. As Barker explains,

> the British tended to see the Soviet threat more and more in terms of the problem of Anglo-American relations: if the British and the Americans stood together, the threat would recede; if they did not, it would become more and more formidable, in the first place to British interests but ultimately to the Western world as a whole (Barker, 1983, p. 46).

The Dunkirk Treaty with France in 1947, followed the next year by the Brussels Treaty with the Benelux countries, though nominally directed against Germany, laid firm foundations for the North Atlantic Treaty of April 1949.

An independent West Germany, the OEEC and NATO were the important structures that severed West from East in political, economic and military terms. These were the developments in Europe that Kennan thought would be 'certain to reinforce Soviet feelings of suspicion and insecurity and, hence, to narrow the opportunities for negotiations' (see Gaddis, 1982, p. 71). However genuine were British attempts to create some measure of détente from Korea onwards, and however pressing and immediate were the imperatives that conditioned policy-making in the late 1940s, British policy prior to 1950 did much to help the Americans to construct the very cold war structures that in turn necessitated, as the British saw it, the search for accommodation.

This brief survey of British attitudes and policy towards East–West relations during the period 1947–53 provides a useful historical context for analysing British policy in the period thereafter. The comparison with American attitudes and policy reveals important differences of approach, which can be explored in more detail in later chapters. So important is this period, however, in terms of understanding the British approach to East–West relations in the postwar period as a whole, that it would also be useful to conclude by summarizing the argument that has been developed so far.

This chapter began by suggesting that, in 1947, British and American governments appeared to share basic attitudes towards the Soviet threat. Containment was regarded as an appropriate short-term strategy for modifying Soviet behaviour, but the longer-term objective was the normalization of East–West relations. By 1949–50, however, the Truman administration appeared to have lost sight of that objective. Containment had in effect become an end in itself, with the construction of a 'situation of strength' now regarded as the only viable strategy for the foreseeable future to meet the heightened threat of a monolithic international communism. The cold war had become synonymous with 'political warfare' between ideologically opposed blocs. Normal relations, including negotiations, were effectively ruled out.

The more pragmatic British, however, found it very difficult to accept this overtly ideological approach to East–West relations. They continued to view containment as a short-term strategy and the cold war as a temporary, 'abnormal' phase in relations. The longer-term objective of policy continued through this period to be the normalization of relations with the Soviet bloc. The British could neither accept the NSC-68 definition of the threat nor the prescribed response. Indeed, they became concerned that if the West tried to counter the Soviet threat by 'strength' alone, the result would be to rigidify East–West divisions, produce confrontation and possibly war. To avoid this, the appropriate response to the threat, from a British perspective, was to combine 'strength' with diplomacy, a structure of deterrence with a process of accommodation.

Thus, while British and American governments appeared to be united in a common purpose at this time, underlying attitudes had begun to diverge and this was becoming apparent in policy terms by 1950. While the Americans were only prepared to 'negotiate from strength' with the Soviet bloc – if at all – the British were beginning to push for a Western policy which combined 'strength' *and* 'negotiation'. For the Americans, cold war and détente had become antithetical approaches to East–West relations, whereas for the British they appeared to be different aspects of the same strategy – two sides of the same coin, as it were – designed to normalize relations across the East–West divide.

This analysis provides an explanation for what otherwise seems to be the paradox that successive British governments in the immediate postwar period could be 'architects' first of cold war, then of détente. In the late 1940s, the Attlee government was concerned to counter the Soviet threat by actively building structures that would deter possible aggression. After 1949, however, and the signing of the North Atlantic Treaty, the Labour government followed by the Churchill government sought to augment a deterrence posture with some degree of accommodation with the Soviet bloc. The more dangerous East–West relations became, the more urgently accommodation was sought and the more predisposed British governments were to assume a mediating role. If an embryonic British détente policy can be dated from 1950, the next chapter looks in more detail at the development of this policy in the decade after 1953.

Chapter 4

Britain as a catalyst of détente

Following his unsuccessful appeals for a summit meeting in 1950 and 1951, Churchill took up the call for a détente or, in his phrase, an 'easement of relations' between East and West, in a major speech to the House of Commons in May 1953. In contrast to earlier failures to initiate a process of accommodation, some progress was made thereafter in the form of East–West negotiations on a number of issues during 1954–55. The international context in 1953 had been transformed by changes of leadership in the United States and the Soviet Union and by the approaching end of the Korean War. In particular, the death of Stalin in March 1953 seemed to herald a new era, and President Eisenhower, despite resistance from the State Department, made a speech the following month in which some conciliatory gestures were extended to the new Soviet leadership. He asked for positive signs that the Soviet leaders recognized the opportunity for a new start in East–West relations. This cautious American response to Stalin's death was reinforced by the arrival in the United States of Dr Adenauer. In a series of speeches across the United States, the West German Chancellor expressed scepticism about a change in Soviet policy. He, like the Americans, required convincing evidence of a new direction in Moscow.

By the end of April, the impact of Eisenhower's speech had been effectively neutralized and there was a distinct possibility that the hopes raised by Stalin's death would come to nothing. It was at this point that Churchill made his timely intervention. While the Americans and the West Germans were adopting a 'wait and see' approach, Churchill thought the time was right to press for a 'conference on the highest level [which] should take place between the leading Powers without long delay'. From his description of the proposed summit, the prime minister clearly had in mind a revival of the 'Big Three' wartime pattern of conferences, with himself doubtless playing a leading role. Churchill was under no illusions that all problems could be resolved immediately, but he was encouraged by recent Soviet restraint. If some issues could be settled, Korea and Austria for example, this could create a political atmosphere that would enable other issues to be resolved and would certainly lessen the possibility of world war. In an important section of the speech, he explicitly recognized the reality of Soviet power and the legitimacy of Soviet interests, particularly in the security sphere. 'We all desire that the Russian people should take the high place in world affairs which is their due without feeling anxiety about their own security. I do not believe that the immense problem of reconciling the security of Russia with the freedom and safety of Western Europe is insoluble' (Folliot, 1956, pp. 57–65).

Churchill's speech was greeted enthusiastically by the House of Commons and press reaction in Britain, Europe and the Commonwealth was broadly favourable (Gilbert, 1988, p. 832). Even *Pravda* quoted with approval Churchill's 'realistic approach' to the problem of reconciling Soviet and West European security and the need to tackle East–West problems in a piecemeal fashion (Folliot, 1956, pp. 66–71). The reaction in Washington, however, echoed the sentiments of Eisenhower's April speech: evidence of Soviet sincerity in terms of deeds rather than words must precede a summit conference. Churchill's speech and the positive reactions to it were, however, an embarrassment to the Americans and could not be dismissed lightly. It was all very well to question the prime minister's motives, but not even Senator McCarthy could accuse Churchill of being soft on communism. Indeed, as Coral Bell suggests, 'perhaps the most important function of [Churchill's] speech was that it changed the political colour attributable to the idea of such negotiations' (Bell, 1962, p. 100). If, as the president was advised, an East–West summit was likely to take place sooner or later 'with or without Churchill's pushing', it was important for the administration to make some concessions in order to retain control of the situation, preserve the unity of the West and prevent Churchill from taking all the credit.[1] The major concession came in the form of American agreement to a Western summit to be held in Bermuda in July 1953. Churchill was not happy about the proposed inclusion of the French, but he assumed that the Bermuda meeting would be a prelude to a four-power summit thereafter (HC Deb, 5th Series, Vol. 515, Coll. 2262, 21 May 1953).

Towards the end of June, however, Churchill suffered a stroke and was unable to sustain the momentum he had created. This was significant because, in his absence, a meeting of Western foreign ministers could only agree to invite the Russians to a foreign ministers' conference on the issue of German reunification. Neither the level nor the agenda of such a conference was what Churchill had in mind, but at least the possibility of a summit remained open. By the Autumn, the prime minister had recovered sufficiently to be pressing again for a summit in the new year, preceded by a Western summit in Bermuda. He returned to the theme at the Conservative Party Conference in Margate and the Guildhall again provided the venue for a major speech on détente in November. As Martin Gilbert comments, despite Churchill's age and poor health, securing a summit had now become 'the predominant reason for his wishing to remain as Prime Minister' (Gilbert, 1988, p. 869).

If, by the end of 1953, Churchill had failed to achieve his objective, he was at least keeping negotiations on the political agenda although he was having difficulty carrying along the other allies and his own Cabinet (Carlton, 1981, pp. 333–4). American agreement to negotiations, albeit at foreign minister level, was a clear indication that the administration, persistently prodded by Churchill, was becoming sensitive to being thought excessively rigid on East–West relations. In October 1953, for example, NSC-162/2 'acknowledged that the United States should keep open the possibility of negotiations with the Soviet Union, both to pursue whatever opportunities for settlement might arise and *to convince allies of American good faith in seeking them*' (Gaddis, 1982, pp. 190–1; emphasis added).

The four-power foreign ministers' meeting in Berlin in January 1954 represented the first attempt since 1949 to reach a negotiated agreement between East and West. No progress was made on Germany, but the conference did reach an agreement to include China in a five-power conference on Korea and Indo-China, to begin in Geneva at the end of April. Hitherto, the Americans had been resistant to the idea of an international conference that included the Chinese, but Eden played an important role at Berlin in helping to persuade Dulles to agree. If the Berlin conference served to confirm an East–West stalemate in Europe, the cold war in Asia had reached another dangerous phase. The prospect of a French defeat in Indo-China had again highlighted the possibility of a general war. Dulles's 'massive retaliation' speech at the beginning of the year foreshadowed an attempt to get congressional and allied support for military intervention in Indo-China. The British, however, took the view that this attempt to internationalize the war was not only dangerous but would prejudice the chances of the Geneva Conference before it had begun. Eden refused to back Dulles and skilfully guided the Conference over the next three months to a negotiated settlement of the Indo-China problem (Carlton, 1981, pp. 338–9).

But it was against the background of heightened fears of war in Asia in the Spring of 1954 that Churchill, in a letter to Eisenhower, returned to the issue of summit talks. Once again, however, the idea was spurned. In a follow-up letter to the president and in speeches to the House, the prime minister made it clear that his determination to promote détente had been reinforced by recently published reports of the dramatic increase in destructive potential demonstrated by American hydrogen bomb tests. For Churchill, as Coral Bell notes, the dangers of thermonuclear war had now become a 'brooding preoccupation', which necessitated renewed efforts at reaching an accommodation with the Soviet Union (Bell, 1962, p. 109).

While Churchill was concerned about the effect of the Soviet Union's acquiring hydrogen weapons in terms of increasing the threat to the West, he was also worried, like Attlee before him, about the possibility of the Americans initiating a nuclear war. The possible use of nuclear weapons in Indo-China was the immediate concern, but basic Anglo-American differences on the subject had surfaced at the Bermuda meeting the previous December in the context of Korea. The Americans had taken the view that if the Korean truce broke down, they felt free to use atomic bombs, and Eisenhower was planning to declare this intention in a speech to the United Nations. The British were horrified and managed to persuade the president to water down the threat (see Colville, 1981, p. 106).

With regard to Indo-China, Eden, as noted above, headed off Dulles's attempts to internationalize the war. Churchill, less involved with the specifics of Indo-China, devoted his attention to attempting to increase the flow of nuclear information from the United States, without which there could be no effective consultation on the use of nuclear weapons. To pursue this objective as well as to discuss other pressing problems, Churchill and Eden flew to Washington at the end of June. The significant development here, as far as Churchill's continuing summit aspirations were concerned, was Eisenhower's remarkable volte-face on this issue. The prime minister again raised the topic, but this time, to his undoubted astonishment, the president agreed to participate in a summit. Later in the visit, Eisenhower, under pressure from Dulles, modified his position. He would not attend a summit and the United States would not play an active role, but if Churchill wanted to take the initiative by meeting Malenkov 'the United States would raise no objection nor do anything to damage the chance of success' (Colville, 1976, p. 242).

Churchill left Washington elated and determined to take advantage of Eisenhower's more amenable mood by visiting Moscow at the first available opportunity for an exploratory meeting with Malenkov. Mindful that Eden and perhaps other members of the Cabinet would oppose or seek to delay such a visit, however, the prime minister tried to forestall domestic opposition by presenting the Cabinet with a *fait accompli*. On the voyage back from Washington, after furious rows with Eden, Churchill managed to browbeat the foreign secretary into agreeing in principle to the idea of a direct approach to Moscow. He then sent a draft telegram to Rab Butler, the acting prime minister, marked 'private and personal': Butler in turn sent it on to Moscow with only minor changes (Carlton, 1981, pp. 353–4).

On his return to London, Churchill faced a storm of protest. Lord Salisbury and at least one other member of the Cabinet were threatening to resign. Eden had returned to Geneva, but was sending telegrams insisting that there must be full Cabinet discussion about the visit. A domestic crisis which might have brought the government down was averted at the last minute by a shift in Soviet priorities. Molotov had expressed interest in Churchill's proposal at the beginning of July, but by the end of that month he was issuing invitations to thirty-two states to meet and discuss a European security plan. He had clearly lost interest in the Churchill initiative. Whether the prime minister would have pursued the matter if the Soviet leadership had maintained interest is an open question: the domestic political costs would undoubtedly have been high (see Young, 1988, pp. 67–70). But if the domestic constraints were critical, the international context in the second half of 1954 cannot easily be discounted.

The refusal of the French Assembly in August to ratify the European Defence Community Treaty (EDC) was certainly significant. It had the effect of bringing the German rearmament issue to a climax and putting the question of negotiations with the Russians onto the 'back burner'. Until the end of 1954, Western attention as a whole focused on the problem of bringing a rearmed West Germany into NATO within a framework that would satisfy Allied and particularly French fears. The ingenious solution put together by Eden, to extend the Brussels Treaty machinery to include West Germany and to pledge a permanent British military presence on the Continent, was incorporated into the Paris agreements in October. The Federal Republic would be recognized as a sovereign state (as outlined in the 1952 Bonn agreements) and would simultaneously join NATO and a revised Brussels Treaty Organization, to be renamed the Western European Union (WEU). German forces would be controlled politically by the WEU and operationally by the Supreme Allied Commander, Europe (SACEUR) (on Eden's role, see Carlton, 1981, pp. 360–3).

At the beginning of 1955, Eden was also centrally involved in resolving the Formosa Strait crisis which, like the German rearmament issue, had to be dealt with before a four-power summit meeting could take place. The British, unlike the Americans, were less concerned with the legal niceties of whether Peking or the Government of Chiang Kai-Shek had sovereignty over Formosa and the offshore islands, than with the issue as a potential *casus belli* that might suck in the Americans and possibly the Russians (Eden, 1960, p. 309). Bellicose statements from Washington and Peking in January 1955 heightened fears of another Far Eastern imbroglio. Patient British diplomacy during the following months gradually helped to bring about a reduction of tension in the area and the end of sporadic fighting. The government used its good offices with Washington, Moscow and Peking to work towards a settlement (see Boardman, 1976, ch. 7).

THE GENEVA SUMMIT

A four-power Geneva summit was eventually held in the Spring of 1955, to which there were two significant British contributions: Eden's proposals for German reunification and his continuing diplomacy on the Quemoy and Matsus issue. Not content simply to offer again the proposals for German reunification that he had presented to the Berlin Conference, the new prime minister put forward a revised 'Eden Plan' at Geneva. The objectives of this plan were to establish a military balance and to widen the area between opposed forces in Europe. But, most important, it sought 'to establish a sense of security in Europe and begin the process of reducing tension there' (Barraclough and Wall, 1960, p. 156). Shorn of its link to German reunification, the plan was an important contribution to détente, and it provided a positive response to the evident Soviet concern with security and a lessening of international tensions. The Eden Plan was also significant in another détente-related sense. Despite the prime minister's best efforts to present the plan in the context of German reunification, it was strongly opposed both by the Federal Republic and the Americans, precisely because it implicitly accepted and sought to stabilize the existing status quo in Central Europe and implicitly recognized the division of Germany.

Eden's diplomacy at Geneva on the Quemoy and Matsus issue, however, had a much more positive outcome. Though hostilities in the Formosa Strait had ceased in May 1955, the continuing fear of war spurred on diplomatic efforts to conclude a settlement. The breakthrough finally came in July when Washington proposed to Peking, through Britain, the commencement of Sino–American talks. Eden took the opportunity of the Geneva summit to press the matter informally with Eisenhower and Khrushchev (Eden, 1960, p. 310). Shortly after Geneva, the State Department announced that 'as a result of communication between the United States and the People's Republic of China (PRC) through the diplomatic channels of the United Kingdom' talks at ambassadorial level between the two countries would begin in August (Boardman, 1976, pp. 128–9). British diplomacy had thus been instrumental in helping to resolve a dangerous crisis and in setting up the first bilateral talks between the USA and the PRC.

The opening of Sino–American talks was not, however, an indication of a dramatic breakthrough in East–West relations as a whole in 1955. Both sides took up fixed positions at Geneva and no progress in the form of substantive agreements was possible. These positions were a reflection of the fixed positions taken up all along the line dividing East and West. The Paris agreements and the establishment of the Warsaw Pact had completed a neat, symmetrical pattern of division in Korea, Indo-China, Germany and Europe as a whole. The geography of the cold war at least was now more sharply defined than ever. But it would not be appropriate to regard the Geneva conferences as simply a continuation of the cold war by other means. The absence of a dramatic breakthrough in East–West relations did not mean that there were no important outcomes related to the détente process. That a first East–West summit since 1945 could be held at all without apparent rancour was a reflection of a new atmosphere, which, in turn, was underpinned by tangible settlements. The most significant outcome of Geneva was the general perception that a world war involving nuclear weapons had become less likely. 'There ain't gonna be no war', said Macmillan laconically as he left Geneva (Bell, 1962, p. 130). 'Geneva has given this simple message to the world: it has reduced the dangers of war', concluded Eden's report to the House of Commons (Eden, 1960, p. 311). These perceptions were reinforced by the fact that the summit produced the tentative beginnings of an East–West accommodation. Both sides tacitly recognized the territorial status quo in Europe, and to that extent, Soviet control of Eastern Europe had ceased to be a *casus belli*. Thus, the 'summitry' of 1955 was a landmark in the détente process, although, paradoxically, it also served to highlight the limitations as well as the potential of détente. The 'Spirit of Geneva' continued to affect the general climate of international relations in 1956, but the process of accommodation had gone as far as it could at that stage.

This account suggests that Britain deserves most of the credit on the Western side for the diplomatic activity culminating in the Geneva conferences. There was a striking continuity through the governments of Churchill and Eden in the British voice calling for a normalization of relations with the Soviet bloc, and for much of this period that voice belonged literally to Winston Churchill. While the Americans were doing everything possible to avoid East–West negotiations, the French were preoccupied with Indo-China and the EDC, and Adenauer with securing sovereignty for the Federal Republic, Churchill contributed his international stature and his anti-communist credentials to the call for negotiations.

Given the constraints on his freedom of action, it would be difficult to suggest what else Churchill could have done to promote détente. With his speeches and his threats to meet Malenkov, with or without the Americans, he repeatedly risked a rift with Washington despite the fact that the Anglo-American alliance had long been the cornerstone of his foreign and defence policies. He unashamedly used his wartime friendship with Eisenhower to press for a meeting with the Russians on every available opportunity. On at least one occasion prior to 1955, he almost persuaded the president to attend a summit. If Churchill was frustrated by American intransigence, he was also constrained by the limits imposed on Western diplomacy as a whole by the German reunification issue, so adroitly promoted by Adenauer. What was undoubtedly the most galling constraint for Churchill, however, was the unwillingness of his Cabinet colleagues, and Eden in particular, to provide a united governmental front. This could not but weaken his position and detract from his efforts to press for a summit.

But if the question of the desirability of a summit bitterly divided Churchill and Eden (until the latter became prime minister), their common fears about the dangers of nuclear war linked Churchill's efforts and the more practical contributions of Eden. To the extent that the 1955 détente was built upon the foundation of tangible agreements that resolved certain East–West conflicts that might have resulted in nuclear war, Anthony Eden made a significant contribution. The settlements in Indo-China and the Formosa Strait owed much to his diplomatic skills. Moreover, his contribution to the signing of the London and Paris agreements was crucially important, because these agreements resolved the status of West Germany. This, in turn, stabilized the lines of division in Europe and undermined American arguments against the holding of a summit. It may also be argued that, however unwittingly, the Eden Plan presented at Geneva, with its implicit acceptance of a divided Germany and the territorial status quo in Europe, was an important contribution to the process of East–West accommodation. The plan certainly constituted a major link to the détente process in the second half of the 1950s, to the extent that it stimulated several arms control proposals that were collectively labelled 'disengagement' schemes (see Howard, 1958).

Thus, both Churchill and Eden in their different ways played an important role in setting in train the diplomacy of détente, which culminated in the Geneva conferences and the ensuing 'Spirit of Geneva'. By 1955, it must be said, Britain was no longer alone in pressing for a détente, but no other Western state matched the British commitment to a normalization of East–West relations in the first half of the 1950s.

MACMILLAN AND DÉTENTE

The contribution of the Macmillan government to the next phase of détente was even more distinctive. By the late 1950s, no other state on either side of the Iron Curtain was pursuing détente with the persistence and the determination shown by Britain. During the Macmillan period as a whole, the centrepiece of British efforts to ameliorate East–West tensions was the patient diplomacy between the end of 1957 and the Spring of 1960, which culminated in the Paris summit. In terms of continuity, this policy echoed Churchill's efforts between 1953 and 1955, although Paris unlike Geneva, of course, did not produce significant results. Of more practical and immediate significance, as in the earlier period, were British efforts to play a conciliatory role in East–West crises. British policy in the Middle East, Berlin and Laotian crises between 1958 and 1961 illustrates the contribution of British diplomacy to reducing the possibility of military conflict between East and West.

Macmillan's memoirs suggest that he came into office in January 1957 determined to play an active role in the détente process. Although he felt compelled to postpone an arranged visit to Moscow because of Soviet threats over Suez and the intervention in Hungary, he nevertheless records his hopes that he 'might at some time attempt an improvement in the relations between Eastern and Western blocs [although] it was clear that for such an adventure the time was not now propitious' (Macmillan, 1971, p. 289). Conciliatory initiatives in the East–West sphere were effectively ruled out for the time being by the need generated primarily by the Suez débâcle to re-establish good relations with NATO allies and the USA in particular, and to establish a credible deterrence strategy in the context of a new British defence policy.

It was not until the latter part of 1957 that Macmillan had the opportunity to play a significant role. The Geneva summit, which he had attended as foreign secretary, was never far from his thoughts and, in September, he began 'to consider means by which a new effort could be made' towards another summit, although he was under no illusions that progress would be speedy. 'Clearly more preparations both personal and diplomatic would be required, and patience as well as a bold initiative would be necessary' (Macmillan, 1971, p. 305). But the constraints that had frustrated Macmillan's détente aspirations were now beginning to look less pressing. Relations with NATO allies had improved enormously during the twelve months since Suez. Most significantly, the rupture in Anglo-American relations that followed Suez was healed during Macmillan's visit to Washington in October. This meeting appears to have been crucial to the prime minister's perception of his freedom of manoeuvre. He now felt sufficiently confident both of the relationship with the United States and of Britain's nuclear status to be able to play a more active East–West role (Macmillan, 1971, p. 330 ff).

At the December NATO Council meeting in Paris, Macmillan took the lead in proposing what would now be called a 'dual track' approach. He suggested that the meeting should consider two separate agendas, one military and the other political. The object was to facilitate agreement on two issues: the stationing of American Intermediate Range Ballistic Missiles (IRBMs) in different European member countries, to be balanced by some political gesture to the Soviet Union. In the event, the 'military' meetings could only deliver an agreement in principle to establish missile sites in Europe, but the 'political' meetings were much more satisfactory. Following an intervention by Macmillan with the Americans, the final communiqué offered the Russians a meeting at foreign minister level to resolve outstanding differences.

That NATO meeting, in fact, heralded the revival of a persistent British advocacy of an East–West summit which, given the restored Anglo-American relationship, could scarcely be ignored in Washington. But the prime minister had to remain patient for most of 1958. Nevertheless, he tried a variety of tactics in the early part of the year to get East–West talks going. He responded positively to Bulganin's proposal for a nuclear-free zone in Europe. He wrote to Eisenhower suggesting a joint policy on disengagement based on Eden's demilitarized zone plan. He even floated for the first time the idea of his visiting Moscow in an attempt to break the diplomatic deadlock. Any momentum that was developing towards a summit, however, was ended by the unilateral Soviet suspension of nuclear tests at the end of March. This had the effect of focusing attention on the narrower issue of test ban negotiations as a more promising alternative to a summit. With more British tests planned in the Autumn and the MacMahon Act still not amended, this new turn in East–West relations was something of an embarrassment for the British government. Indeed, it was not until the summit issue was revived in a different form, following the crisis in the Middle East in July 1958, that Macmillan again had some opportunity to play a more positive role. But if Britain was effectively precluded from contributing to the first tentative stages of what became the test ban negotiations, direct (albeit limited) military involvement in the

Middle East crisis also made it difficult to play a conciliatory role in that context.

Nevertheless, that crisis, and an equally unpredictable crisis in the Far East in the Autumn of 1958, appeared to strengthen the prime minister's determination to work towards a general summit and, thereby, a détente (Macmillan, 1971, p. 557). Patience was about to give way to initiative in the form of a Macmillan visit to Moscow. This idea was not discussed in detail until the beginning of 1959, by which time a new East–West crisis centred on the status of Berlin was confirming the prime minister's worst fears of the consequences of not securing a relaxation of tensions.

THE BERLIN CRISIS AND MACMILLAN'S VISIT TO MOSCOW

With the onset of the Berlin crisis, British détente policy entered one of its most influential phases. In the next twelve months, British diplomacy played a major role in relieving the tensions of the crisis and, in so doing, paved the way to the Paris summit. The achievement of British diplomacy during this period was to develop and sustain a momentum that transcended the immediate crisis and carried Britain's allies towards a summit meeting that none of them wanted. British policy linked the chain of developments – Macmillan's visit to Moscow, the four-power foreign ministers' meeting in Geneva and the Eisenhower–Khrushchev summit at Camp David – that culminated in Paris in May 1960.

From this perspective, Macmillan's trip to Moscow was crucial. At the heart of the Berlin crisis was Khrushchev's ultimatum. Until that was lifted, it was difficult to see how there could be a negotiated resolution of the crisis. Such blatant coercion could only produce a united but negative Western response: meanwhile, tensions mounted as the Soviet deadline approached. Mikoyan's visit to the United States in January 1959 may have eased tensions somewhat and may even have put negotiations at some level back on the agenda, but the time-limit remained operative. It was Macmillan's dramatic initiative the next month that produced the lifting of the ultimatum by persuading Khrushchev to accept the idea of an interim foreign ministers' meeting to discuss Berlin. Macmillan still had the difficult task of persuading his allies to agree to that meeting, but the Moscow visit had succeeded in setting in train a process of negotiation and had effectively stabilized a very dangerous and unpredictable situation (see Macmillan, 1971, pp. 605–25; Barraclough, 1964, pp. 19–22).

Having secured general agreement to the foreign ministers' meeting, Macmillan wanted the allies to regard that meeting as a preliminary to a summit. Eisenhower made an important concession to this view by agreeing publicly to this sequence of events, although he insisted on making his agreement to attend a summit conditional upon progress at the foreign ministers' meeting. Little of substance was in fact achieved at the Geneva meetings and a diplomatic stalemate soon prevailed, but the fact that high-level talks were taking place seemed to make a further contribution to a reduction of tensions. More important in terms of the impact of British policy, sufficient progress was made towards an interim Berlin settlement to enable Macmillan, in his correspondence with Eisenhower, to maintain the pressure on the president to follow through on his commitment to a summit. The unexpected response to this build-up of British pressure was Eisenhower's invitation to Khrushchev to a Camp David summit.

The Eisenhower–Khrushchev meeting in September 1959 restored the momentum of the negotiating process: the two leaders agreed to continue negotiations about Berlin without a specific time-limit hanging over the proceedings, and sufficient progress was made for Eisenhower to declare that many of his objections to a four-power summit had now been removed. Thus, the meeting resolved the question of whether or not a summit would take place, even if important issues of timing and agenda remained to be discussed. The Macmillan government could claim much of the credit for this crucial meeting, not least because the prime minister's Moscow trip had provided a recent precedent for a heads of government meeting. As Macmillan himself succinctly put it, 'the British broke the ice' (Macmillan, 1972, p. 81). It can also be argued that the February meeting encouraged Eisenhower to send and Khrushchev to accept the invitation to the United States. However, to the extent that British pressure on Washington was responsible for Camp David, the government had been almost too successful.

The significance of Camp David went beyond the fact that it led to another temporary improvement in the international atmosphere. From an American perspective, as Gaddis notes, that meeting 'served to legitimize the idea that negotiations were an appropriate means of dealing with Moscow, and that they could be undertaken without risking the unravelling of alliances or the appearance of appeasement' (Gaddis, 1982, pp. 196–7). This 'legitimization' of direct negotiations between the superpowers at heads of government level provided an important legacy that Eisenhower's successors could build upon and was a crucial development in the détente process. But it also marked a turning point for Britain: thereafter, British diplomacy as a major influence on the direction of East–West relations began to assume less significance. Thus, it was the Camp David meeting rather than the oft-cited failure of the Paris summit six months later that marked the important turning point for Britain.

'DAMAGE-LIMITATION' AFTER THE PARIS SUMMIT

But if Macmillan had lost the initiative several months before the Paris summit, his government still managed to play a significant role in reviving and sustaining the détente process after the collapse of the summit. The prime minister personally played a statesmanlike role in keeping open East–West contacts in the last six months of 1960, as dangerous and unpredictable a period in East–West relations as any since 1956. If Macmillan had little choice after Camp David but to look to the United States for Western leadership, it was clear that no lead could be expected from Washington in the last months of the Eisenhower presidency. In the absence of leadership from elsewhere, the prime minister had both the opportunity and a pressing context in which to make a more significant contribution to East–West relations than had been possible in the previous twelve months. Nowhere was British and Macmillan's personal leadership more valuable than at the United Nations in the Autumn of 1960.

Following essentially polemical speeches to the Assembly by Eisenhower and Khrushchev, it was left to Macmillan to rise above cold war rhetoric and make a speech that genuinely transcended the ideological divide. He began by censuring the efforts of both superpowers to cajole the non-aligned into siding with one bloc or the other. Both East and West, he argued, had become 'obsessed' by their own ideologies. The ideological rift, he continued, was neither 'inevitable' nor 'irreconcilable' and, in a broader historical perspective, was less important than what would later be called the 'North–South' issue. Underdevelopment was identified as the major international problem that could be tackled only when cold war tensions had been abated. As he put it, 'the emergent and under-developed countries would be the beneficiaries of a political détente between the great rival forces of East and West' (Gott *et al.*, 1964, pp. 52–5).

Macmillan's detractors could argue that his speech contained nothing new in terms of concrete proposals and was couched in terms calculated to appeal to an Assembly whose ranks had recently been swollen by new Afro-Asian members. But, as the prime minister was aware, the tone and presentation of his speech were more important than its content (Macmillan, 1972, pp. 275–9). The impact of the speech was heightened by Macmillan's evident willingness, in contrast to Eisenhower, to meet Khrushchev in New York. Little was achieved of a substantive nature in these discussions, but at least the thread of contact was maintained and the possibility of future progress left open (see Barraclough, 1964, p. 562).

Continuing British efforts to promote East–West détente extended into the Kennedy period and can be illustrated by the attempts to bring the 1961 crises in Berlin and Laos to a diplomatic solution. It is interesting that the Laos crisis was analogous to the 1954 Indo-China crisis, with the USA again trying to 'collectivize' a commitment to military intervention to stem the communist tide. This time, the British stalled on the military option, while mediating more overtly from the position of joint chairman of the 1954 Geneva Conference. Mediation was difficult and delicate in this context, however, because it was necessary not only to head off a military intervention and set up a process of negotiation supported by both superpowers, but also to persuade Washington to switch its support to the faction in Laos that had already been adopted by the Soviet Union.

British policy operated at two levels. In public, the government worked with the Soviet Union to reconvene the Geneva machinery. Once established, this served to relieve the pressures for external intervention and created an extended pause while the various factions in Laos actually negotiated a solution. But this eventual outcome was not achieved without patient diplomacy at Geneva and much private lobbying of both US and Soviet governments. Much of the credit for the success of British policy has been given to the patient diplomacy of Foreign Secretary Lord Home (see, for example, Kilmuir, 1964, p. 313). But he was undoubtedly helped by the fact that Kennedy, unlike Dulles in the earlier Indo-China crisis, was predisposed to accept a negotiated solution in Laos. The thrust of British policy, therefore, was to reinforce the views of the more conciliatory elements in the new administration.

British policy played much the same sort of role in relation to the Kennedy government during the 1961 Berlin crisis, although from a weaker position. As the American posture on Berlin hardened in the Summer of 1961, the British attempted to inject some flexibility into the situation. The now routine pressure on Washington to adopt a more forthcoming attitude to negotiations was accompanied by 'lip-service only' to pressures in the opposite direction to reinforce the conventional strength of NATO. While it can be argued that British policy helped a more conciliatory American view on Berlin to prevail, a brief comparison with the impact of British policy in the earlier phase of the Berlin crisis shows how limited British influence had become. The government was forced to take a tougher and less independent line on Berlin in 1961, and it was the Rusk–Gromyko talks rather than any British initiative that encouraged the Russians to lift the later ultimatum on Berlin. Indeed, it was the British contribution to the test ban negotiations between 1959 and 1963 that provides the best illustration of the catalytic role of British diplomacy during this period, and this is discussed in some detail in the next chapter. The focus of this chapter now moves from an evaluation of the impact of British détente policy towards an explanation of that policy. This begins with an attempt to identify general attitudes towards détente, which appear to have underpinned British policy during the 1950s.

BRITISH ATTITUDES TOWARDS DÉTENTE

It was suggested in the last chapter that divergent British and American approaches to cold war and détente reflected different attitudes to the idea of negotiations with the Soviet Union and international communism. Kennan's precepts notwithstanding, the development of US containment policy, after NSC-68, came to preclude negotiations until such time as a position of 'strength' had been attained: to negotiate prematurely would simply demonstrate weakness. The semblance of negotiations might be offered but only as a tactical ploy to expose the weakness of the other side. Under Dulles, existing inhibitions acquired explicitly moral connotations, as if the moral superiority of the West would somehow be undermined by contact with the communist states. The famous symbol of this attitude was

Dulles's refusal to shake hands with Chou En-Lai at Geneva in 1954.

Other indications of American attitudes emerged during the first half of the 1950s. After Stalin's death, Eisenhower's April 1953 speech called for the new Soviet leaders to demonstrate 'sincerity of purpose attested by deeds' (Folliot, 1956, p. 48). Twelve months later, when Chou En-Lai offered to negotiate directly on the Formosa issue, the American response was cool, to say the least. As the Chatham House Survey puts it, 'Dulles characteristically asked for tangible evidence of China's sincerity and good intentions' (Barraclough and Wall, 1960, p. 13). That 'sincerity' and 'good intentions' should be a precondition for, as it were, 'conceding' negotiations suggests that negotiations were regarded as some sort of special reward for good behaviour rather than as a normal part of international relations. American attitudes towards 'summitry' were, if anything, even more antipathetic. Personalized diplomacy between heads of government had long been regarded with suspicion in Washington as a practice associated with the absolutist European tradition and, therefore, one that was incompatible with a constitutionally constrained presidency. The guiding assumption was that the United States had never gained advantage from summit conferences; thus, they were an inappropriate mechanism for the maintenance of American interests.

The greater British willingness to negotiate across the East–West divide during the 1950s reflected a different set of attitudes towards negotiations and, more broadly, towards diplomacy. Negotiations, particularly with states whose interests directly conflicted with those of Britain, were regarded as a normal part of international relations. Indeed, the basic premise appeared to be that negotiations were an integral part of the fabric and the dynamic of international relations. It was not a question of 'conceding' negotiations or setting preconditions, but rather of using negotiations whenever possible as part of a regularized process of allaying tension and working towards an accommodation. This attitude, it can be argued, lay at the heart of the British conception of détente; it was simply regarded as normal diplomacy.

It is tempting to see British attitudes towards summitry as merely an exercise in Churchillian nostalgia, but they were an extension of basic attitudes to diplomacy. Personalized diplomacy was regarded as a natural supplement to regular diplomatic channels. Harold Macmillan's final speech to the Geneva foreign ministers' meeting in November 1955 seems to capture the essence of a British view. The 'Geneva spirit', he argued, 'was really a return to normal human relations. It meant a readiness to discuss and to negotiate. It meant a reversion to some of that flexibility without which the conduct of human affairs becomes almost intolerable. It meant "give and take" in international life' (Frankland, 1958, p. 73). From this perspective, summits were not to be regarded as exceptional occurrences but as regular affairs. Before Geneva, Macmillan had suggested that the summit should be designed 'not to settle problems, but to inaugurate a long period of negotiations' (Bartlett, 1977, p. 138). Even Anthony Eden, for so long opposed to a summit, made the same point at Geneva. He told Eisenhower that he looked upon that summit as 'the first of a series' (Eden, 1960, p. 291).

It is interesting that the Macmillan period sees a development of these attitudes and a clearer picture of a British conception of détente begins to emerge. The idea of regular summits develops into what might be called institutionalized summitry as an explicit policy objective during this period. Summit meetings were regarded as essential for two reasons, both related to the reduction of tensions. First, it was assumed that personal meetings between leaders would foster mutual understanding and build confidence. It was also assumed that only heads of government meetings could produce the major agreements that would register progress towards the resolution of outstanding East–West differences. Macmillan returned from Moscow more convinced than ever that only Khrushchev had the power to deliver substantive agreements (Macmillan, 1971, pp. 633–4). Agreement on at least one major issue would, it was thought, stimulate agreement on other issues in a 'step by step' process. Summit meetings were the key, then, to the piecemeal approach that had also been fundamental to Churchill's view. While agreement on Korea and Austria had served as symbols of progress for Churchill, a Berlin settlement and, later, a test ban treaty served the same function for Macmillan. Hence, Macmillan's determination to secure at least an interim settlement on Berlin at the Paris summit (see Macmillan, 1972, p. 94).

Significantly, however, Macmillan was less committed than either of his immediate predecessors to the idea of a summit for its own sake. He was certainly convinced that such meetings required adequate preparation. His memoirs make it clear that he conceived of summit meetings as the pinnacle of a more or less continuous cycle of negotiations between East and West. Lower-level meetings of ambassadors or perhaps foreign ministers would explore positions, identify common ground and prepare specific issues for agreement by heads of government. Periodic summits would follow, and then the cycle would begin again.[2] There was nothing automatic or inevitable about this rather idealized process, however, and this was where Macmillan, like Churchill before him, spotted the opportunity for a distinctive British contribution. As the experience with the Americans had shown, states in the real world of international relations were not always prepared to negotiate with each other. It was often necessary for one state to take an initiative that would, as it were, 'kick-start' the negotiating process. Once that process was initiated, conciliatory diplomacy was still needed to keep the momentum going and reach agreements.

Thus, summit meetings were regarded as essential, but they were not the sole objective of British détente policy during this period. Indeed, as the Paris summit approached, both Macmillan and Foreign Secretary Selwyn Lloyd began to worry about popular expectations of what a single summit meeting could achieve (Macmillan, 1972, pp. 105, 114). The danger of frustrated expectations became another reason for identifying Paris as the first of a series of summits located, conceptually at least, within a regularized cycle of negotiations at various levels.

The prospect of Paris also elicited indications of an even broader conception of détente. Two important speeches by Selwyn Lloyd in August 1959 and February 1960 linked together the idea of regular summits, a broad process of negotiations and, significantly, a more permanent system of open contact and exchange between East and West as the ultimate objective of détente. In both speeches, Lloyd reviewed the British contribution to détente not simply in terms of helping to establish East–West negotiations but also in terms of promoting other sorts of contacts with the Soviet Union. In his final speech to the 1959 foreign ministers' meeting in Geneva, he referred to action taken in concert with the Soviet government that had contributed to producing 'the kind of atmosphere in which agreements are possible'. He talked of 'specific measures with regard to the expansion of mutual trade, the development of mutual contacts and the facilitation of communications'. In a later speech to the House, he further specified 'an increase in our cultural arrangements' and cited the ending of jamming of BBC broadcasts as 'one by-product of better understanding'. In this view, the development of political, economic and cultural contacts were all interrelated and part of a coherent strategy. The object of British détente policy, according to Lloyd, was nothing less than 'evolving a system of regulating international affairs', which would 'avoid a constant atmosphere of crisis'.[3]

Détente and deterrence

An important insight into the British approach to détente is provided by the clarification of the relationship between détente and deterrence that emerged during the 1950s. An indication of Churchill's approach, it will be recalled, was apparent as early as 1950 with his objection to Acheson's 'negotiation from strength' principle. The concern was that American policy tended to be less balanced than this aphorism would suggest: certainly, in the first half of the 1950s, 'strength' always seemed to have a higher priority than 'negotiation'. By implication, the British view was either that negotiations were more important than strength or that both were equally important. The analysis of British policy developed so far suggests that the second option characterized the British position. Persistent though British efforts to conciliate were, the continuing perception of a Soviet threat was such that those efforts were located within and closely related to the institutionalized structure of deterrence that British policy had done much to create. Serious threats to that structure produced a British response designed to shore up the foundations. Only when that structure was perceived to be in good order was policy oriented towards the promotion of détente. A brief résumé of British policy in the second half of 1954 will serve to illustrate a central element of the British approach.

Between August 1954, when the French Assembly refused to ratify the EDC, and the ratification of the Paris agreements in May 1955, the continued existence of the Atlantic alliance was in some doubt. The problem of how to bring a rearmed West Germany into NATO within a framework that would allay the fears of the other allies produced an unambiguous British response. Eden worked hard and successfully to repair the damage: meanwhile, Churchill's attempts to get the major powers to a summit conference had to be temporarily shelved.

A clear indication of Churchill's position had already emerged from his discussions with Eisenhower at Bermuda in December 1953. According to Colville's account, the prime minister advocated a policy that linked together simple notions of détente and deterrence and seemed to go to the heart of Churchill's conception of détente:

> Both at the Plenary Conferences and in private Churchill advocated what it amused him to call his policy of 'Double Dealing'. This he described as a policy of strength towards the Soviet Union combined with holding out the hand of friendship. He said that only by proving to our peoples that we should neglect no chance of easement, could we persuade them to accept the sacrifices necessary to maintain strong armed forces (Colville, 1976, p. 240; see also Gilbert, 1988, pp. 944–5).

Such was the apparent continuity of the basic conceptions that underpinned British policy that, exactly four years later, Macmillan was expounding a similar theme. Having returned from the NATO Council meeting in Paris, where he had successfully carried through a 'dual track' policy, he summed up the British position to the House of Commons. 'Our policy . . . is really two-fold, and I think in essence simple. It is a firm and powerful NATO, from the military point of view, but always ready to discuss and to negotiate on a practical basis to obtain practical results.' In his memoirs, the prime minister adds, 'in a single phrase it could be described as "arm and parley"' (Macmillan, 1971, p. 340).

In a Party Political Broadcast at the beginning of 1958, Macmillan gave a most explicit account of the relationship between détente and deterrence. Not only did they, in his view, constitute the 'only two ways to preserve the peace of the world' but he regarded them as 'parallel, indeed complementary' approaches (Macmillan, 1971, p. 463). This consistent view of détente and deterrence as, in effect, two sides of the same coin was a major influence on British policy during this period. A viable structure of deterrence in political as well as military terms was required to balance a policy of détente, and vice-versa. If that structure was fundamentally undermined, as was the case with NATO in the twelve months after Suez, priority was given to strengthening the alliance. Once the effectiveness of the alliance had been re-established, to the satisfaction of the British government, priority was given to the promotion of détente. The six months after the Paris summit, with both deterrence and détente undermined, sees perhaps the clearest illustration during this period of 'double dealing' or a 'two-fold' policy in action.

ADAPTING TO BIPOLARITY:
FROM POWER TO INFLUENCE

Having identified some of the important sets of attitudes that appear to have influenced a policy of promoting East–West détente during the 1950s, the attempt to explain that policy continues at a systemic level of analysis with a broad review of the international 'power' context of postwar British foreign policy. The constraints that faced successive British governments after 1945 were outlined in the last chapter, but Elisabeth Barker provides a useful summary here of the essential foreign policy problem in London: 'Britain's power to influence world events or even to pursue an independent foreign policy . . . was strictly limited. Skilful manoeuvring was required if the British were to retain some freedom of choice and the capacity to take initiatives' (Barker, 1983, p. 69). British policy towards détente and East–West relations more generally during this period can be interpreted as a remarkably successful attempt to adapt to the realities of declining material power in order to remain at least a quasi-independent actor with global interests. In power terms, this could only be done by manipulating the symbols of power – by, as it were, substituting 'influence' for 'power'. In structural terms, the requirement was to increase the scope for action and to exert leverage within a bipolar system.

Even before the end of the Second World War, as Ritchie Ovendale has commented, 'Britain's position at the conference tables of world diplomacy . . . obscured the reality of Britain's diminished power' (Ovendale, 1984, p. 3). By 1947, it was clear that the 'Big Three' concept was dead. Thereafter, the political task was to maintain as equal a relationship as possible with the remaining superpowers, despite the increasingly evident material disparities. In many ways, as this study has already shown, the Anglo-American relationship proved to be the more problematic. No Western government worked harder than the Attlee government, spearheaded by Ernest Bevin, to create a hegemonic system under American leadership. But the relationship with Washington was also suffused, not surprisingly perhaps, with elements of doubt, suspicion, fear and even jealousy. For all the anti-colonial rhetoric that poured out of Washington in the early postwar years, the suspicion persisted in London that the Americans wanted to undermine if not destroy the British Empire simply in order to take over those interests themselves, particularly in the Middle East and Asia (see, for example, Barnet, 1983, pp. 25, 101–4; Epstein, 1954, chs 3, 4). As a 1954 Department of State memorandum put it, the British had 'doubts as to our capacity for considered leadership and doubts as to our true purposes in the Far East'.[4] From a British perspective, however, the Empire was crucial initially to survival and, later, the Empire–Commonwealth was conceived as an important vehicle for the maintenance of Britain's role as a global power (see Ovendale, 1984, ch. 5).

The significance of this perceived American threat to British interests was that it sharpened an awareness of differences of interest and the need to defend those interests. This, in turn, meant that British governments could not automatically follow an American definition of the acceptable parameters of action in relation to the Soviet bloc. Anglo-American differences of interest with respect to the recognition of China after the Revolution provides a good example. Not only did Britain have extensive economic interests in China, Hong Kong and elsewhere in South East Asia, but the Attlee government felt compelled to take account of Commonwealth views on this issue, in particular that of India, whose leader Nehru strongly favoured recognition. As Goodwin notes, 'Labour leaders were particularly attentive to the views of these Asian members of the Commonwealth . . . and were apt to regard relations with India as symbolising hopes placed in the Commonwealth' (Goodwin, 1972, p. 42). Quite simply, Britain had special interests in South East Asia not shared with the United States, and British recognition of the Mao government was in part a reflection of this.

Conciliatory British diplomacy during the Laos crisis was also influenced by a perception of British interests that complicated a simple application of cold war images. The more pragmatic British response to changes in that area was to support governments that were judged not to constitute a threat to British politico-economic interests, rather than in terms of the acceptability or otherwise of their apparent ideological stance. For the United States, on the other hand, until the Kennedy administration began to modify American attitudes to some extent, an unambiguous commitment to anti-communism was required to elicit support (see Watt, 1965, p. 323).

Serious differences of interest with the United States were, of course, dramatically highlighted by the Suez crisis. Despite Macmillan's successful attempt to heal this major rift in Anglo-American relations, the 1956 crisis further sharpened an awareness of those differences and the continuing need to be vigilant in the protection of distinctive British interests. As a traumatic illustration of Britain's 'descent from power', Suez provided an important stimulus to a détente policy in other ways. By underlining economic vulnerability and the difficulty of defending interests by traditional politico-military methods, Suez hastened the search for alternative ways of maintaining global influence.

The perceived linkage between a détente policy and Britain's position in the international hierarchy became most explicit when the United States directly challenged Britain's leading role in East–West relations. Macmillan's understandable concern, as he faced the prospect of an Eisenhower–Khrushchev summit at Camp David, was that direct superpower contacts might diminish the status that had accrued from a mediating role and reveal Britain as a 'second-rate power' (Macmillan, 1972, pp. 80). Twelve months later, Macmillan was telling Harold Evans that a letter sent to Khrushchev in July 1960, ostensibly written to maintain contacts during a very difficult period in East–West relations, had in fact been written 'to get back the initiative for our country and for myself' (Evans, 1981, p. 118). This interesting admission reveals a concern with the impact of the Paris disaster on Britain's international standing and the prime minister's own reputation.

From this perspective, the 'damage-limitation' strategy pursued in the second half of 1960 can be interpreted as an attempt to minimize the damage done to collective and individual reputations. Indeed, the prime minister's evident preoccupation with the presentational aspects of his speech to the UN in September suggests that he saw the UN General Assembly as the perfect forum in which to rectify any damage done (Macmillan, 1972, pp. 275–9). Through his masterful speech, qualities of independence, leadership and statesmanship befitting the representative of a major global actor could be displayed to the widest audience possible – though, it has to be said, New York was a poor substitute for Paris and the series of three or four summit meetings that Macmillan had worked so hard to achieve. Institutionalized summitry, the prime minister surely hoped, would have offered regular opportunities for such dazzling displays and would certainly have secured a more permanent vehicle for maintaining great power status and wielding global influence.

To draw this section to a conclusion: British governments during this period were not unaware of the potential benefits of actively pursuing détente in terms of the status that might accrue to

Britain. Significantly, the promotion of East–West détente provided opportunities for policy-makers to deploy the types of influence that Britain still possessed, in order to demonstrate leadership and, occasionally, statesmanship on a global stage. In that sense, détente can be regarded as a convenient policy instrument. Conciliatory initiatives and persistent attempts to mediate on East–West issues not only helped to divert attention from material decline but also helped to maintain the appearance at least of Britain as a great power. As Britain's decline became more evident, particularly after Suez, and the search for alternative ways of maintaining global influence more pressing, the identification of détente as an appropriate instrument became more explicit. Macmillan's determination to take a dramatic initiative by visiting Moscow and, thereafter, to retain for Britain and himself a leading role in East–West negotiations, offers the clearest evidence of the perceived importance of a détente policy in terms of adapting to a bipolar structure and maintaining Britain's position in the international hierarchy.

But, if détente as a policy instrument can be explained in terms of the need to manipulate the symbols of power, détente as a policy objective also served Britain's global interests. There are indications of an awareness as early as 1949 that the perpetuation of a bipolar confrontation between East and West was inimical to Britain's global interests to the extent that it imposed an inflexible structure on relationships within as well as between the rival blocs. Such a structure was bound to limit Britain's freedom of action and increase dependence upon the hegemonic leadership of the United States. However important a close Anglo-American relationship was to Britain's international influence, major differences of interest and perspective required British policy-makers to work towards creating a more flexible international structure, in which Britain's remaining global interests could more easily be protected. Most evidently in terms of Anglo-American relations, it may be argued, the promotion of East–West détente was both a policy instrument and a policy objective, representing a vehicle for demonstrating independence and a continuing attempt throughout this period to broaden the scope for independent action.

THE DOMESTIC IMPERATIVES HYPOTHESIS

This final part of the analytical framework looks at the extent to which British détente policy during this period can be explained in domestic political terms. Evidence is sketchy here, but there is some linkage between calls for East–West negotiations and potential electoral advantage. It will be recalled that Churchill's original call for a summit was made in the closing stages of the 1950 General Election campaign, and it may well be that he spotted the opportunity to make a decisive intervention. The Attlee government had a large majority, and it was clear that something dramatic was required if the Conservatives were to have any hope of victory. In the event, Labour was returned with a much reduced majority, but there is no evidence that Churchill's intervention either won or lost seats for the Conservatives (Nicholas, 1968, pp. 102–7). Churchill's November 1951 speech at the Guildhall can also be viewed in the context of the Election the previous month. During that campaign the Conservative opposition had been accused by the government of adopting a belligerent foreign policy stance with respect to the Iranian crisis. Churchill himself had been branded a 'warmonger' and was sufficiently disturbed by the accusation to sue the *Daily Mirror* after the election. Though the Conservatives were returned, David Butler estimated that the 'warmonger' smear cost them as many as a hundred seats (Butler, 1952).

Of the three elections held in the first half of the 1950s, the 1955 Election provides the clearest indication of a positive link between a détente policy and perceptions at least of electoral advantage. In particular, the timing of Eden's conversion to the idea of a summit, only two months before the election, more than hints at an element of opportunism. As Coral Bell puts it, 'with an election projected and the opinion polls showing a close contest likely, [Eden] had firmly adopted the summit idea' (Bell, 1962, p. 114). Moreover, an East–West summit was an issue in the 1955 campaign. Indeed, negotiations with Moscow had to a greater or lesser extent been an issue since the previous election. Originally adopted by the left wing of the Labour Party in the early 1950s as an alternative to German rearmament, the call for negotiations and specifically for a high-level meeting became more insistent and emanated from the Party as a whole after 1953. Butler argues that the narrowness of the Conservative victory in 1951 made the government sensitive to Labour opinion on, *inter alia*, the issue of negotiations with Moscow. He goes on to suggest that the success of Churchill's 1953 speech and the 1954 Geneva Conferences strengthened opposition demands for an East–West summit (Butler, 1952, pp. 6, 8). There were clearly important electoral reasons for the government to push hard on the summit issue. In an electoral context, the Western invitation on 10 May and the informal acceptance by Molotov on 15 May effectively stole Labour's thunder. The firm prospect of the Geneva summit can only have helped the government to increase its majority substantially.

There are limits, however, to the domestic imperatives hypothesis in the first half of the 1950s. The picture of the Labour opposition constantly goading the government to set up East–West negotiations rather overstates the overall impact of a party rent by internal dissension and disunity during this period (see Pelling, 1968, especially p. 105; Brand, 1974, ch. 14). Indeed, there were countervailing domestic pressures that were equally significant. Opposition from within the Cabinet to Churchill's initiatives has already been noted. There are also indications that the Foreign Office was ambivalent on this issue. According to John Colville's accounts, the Foreign Office objected to the section of Churchill's 1953 speech that dealt with the summit proposal, and disapproved of the prime minister's subsequent attempts to promote détente (Colville, 1976, p. 238; Colville, 1981, pp. 107, 165).

Sir Duncan Wilson records that Foreign Office attitudes to summitry remained very cautious even after Khrushchev's 'secret speech' in 1956. He maintains that senior Soviet experts in the Foreign Office took the view that 'summit meetings with Soviet leaders were at best a political necessity. At worst these could commit us to a lot of unnecessary discussions from which the public, in "euphoric" mood, would expect results. And so unnecessary concessions might be made' (D. Wilson, 1974, p. 384). There is some reason, though, to question whether there was a monolithic 'Foreign Office view' on this issue. Sir William Hayter, the ambassador in Moscow, who claims in his memoirs to have originated the idea of the Bulganin–Khrushchev visit to Britain in 1956, appears not to have shared the views of the 'senior Soviet experts' about heads of government meetings as described by Wilson (see Hayter, 1966, p. 134).

Domestic factors are more important as an explanation of policy in the second half of the 1950s, certainly in the period up to the general election in October 1959. The significance of the domestic context derives essentially from the sensitivity of Macmillan's political antennae. As he recounts in his memoirs in characteristically dramatic terms, Macmillan suddenly became aware of the salience of the nuclear issue in the Spring of 1957, and he relates his determination to push for a détente directly to the need 'to satisfy public opinion at home' (Macmillan, 1971, p. 297). Not only were growing fears about nuclear weapons being exploited by the Russians, in Macmillan's view, but more important in electoral terms, they were being exploited by a Labour Party strengthened by the return of Aneurin Bevan to the fold (see Brand, 1974, p. 283). The new shadow foreign secretary, armed with the nuclear issue, was clearly regarded as a potent threat. It is of interest that Bevan himself was regarded by Macmillan as a special threat because he represented a radical rather than a socialist tradition, which the prime minister saw as still occupying the important middle ground of British politics (Macmillan, 1971, pp. 298–9).

It was the Labour Party, however, rather than any broad left-of-centre coalition built around unilateralism that had become the identifiable threat by the end of 1957. Macmillan's confident expectation in June that Bevan would 'go violently anti-bomb . . . and outmanoeuvre Gaitskell' proved to be unfounded. At the Labour Party Conference in September, Bevan renounced unilateralism and stood side by side with his leader symbolizing reconciliation and presenting a picture of a party enjoying greater solidarity than at any time perhaps since the war. Bevan, unlike Macmillan, saw East–West negotiations as the best way of getting rid of nuclear weapons, but his views on an appropriate British role in those negotiations were uncomfortably close to the prime minister's own thoughts. It is significant that Macmillan should choose a Party Political Broadcast less than four months after the Labour Party Conference to present a detailed rationale for a policy of détente combined with a continued policy of deterrence. This public justification of a balanced policy can be seen as a response both to an increasingly vocal section of largely unilateralist opinion in the country (the Campaign for Nuclear Disarmament was formed in February 1958) and to a unified Labour leadership that now appeared capable of exploiting any indication that the government was not doing all it could to promote East–West negotiations.

The twin threats posed by public opinion and the Labour Party provided an even more pressing context for government policy in the twelve months that began with Khrushchev's ultimatum on Berlin and ended with the 1959 Election. Berlin was, after all, the classic example of an East–West crisis that could trigger a nuclear war, and it reinforced popular fears of nuclear weapons (see Barraclough, 1964, p. 6). After the Berlin crisis had begun, pressure mounted on the government to do something to lessen the possibility of nuclear war in Europe. On 20 January 1959, Macmillan was criticized in the House for a policy statement on Berlin that followed the inflexible line agreed at the NATO Council meeting the previous month. The prime minister was urged to take the lead in offering positive proposals to the Soviet government (Barraclough, 1964, p. 17, fn. 5). On the same day, Macmillan sent a telegram to the State Department, informing Dulles of his plan to visit Moscow. The Moscow decision had already been taken, but opposition pressure can only have reinforced Macmillan's determination to go and seems likely to have influenced the content of the proposals he took with him (see Macmillan, 1971, pp. 582–3).

A high-profile détente policy in 1959, starting with the Moscow trip – a natural 'media event' – can clearly be explained, in part at least, in terms of the expectation of electoral advantage. It promised to neutralize the opposition threat on the nuclear issue and it had obvious popular appeal. Macmillan could look the part of a statesman of world stature and the Conservative Party could claim the mantle of the 'party of peace'. Like previous Conservative administrations in the 1950s, the Macmillan government was very concerned about the prospect of an election and particularly sensitive to the charge of bellicosity. The electoral potential of getting the major powers to a summit meeting was not lost on the leadership (Macmillan, 1972, pp. 80, 92).

But if perceptions of electoral advantage help to explain a policy of détente in 1959, whether in fact that policy helped the Conservatives almost to double their majority in October is less clear. Despite the prime minister's apparent belief that elections are usually won on foreign policy issues (see Evans, 1981, p. 190), analysis of the 1959 Election suggests that, while the détente policy did the party no harm at the polls, no aspect of foreign or defence policy was crucial. Butler and Rose argue that the swing back to the Conservatives began in the Summer of 1958 and was clinched by the economic upturn and the hot Summer of 1959 (Butler and Rose, 1970, p. 198).

Nevertheless, it can be argued that electoral and domestic political pressures as a whole were significant determinants of a détente policy in the first half of Macmillan's period of office. After October 1959, however, domestic considerations appear to be less central to an explanation of policy. The Labour Party was certainly a less threatening force to contend with, having lost a third successive election. The landslide defeat in 1959 signalled another bout of internal feuding, which undermined the solidarity of the party and the precarious unity of the leadership. One important result of the recriminations was that the Scarborough Conference in 1960 voted in favour of unilateral nuclear disarmament. The 'capture' of the Labour Party by CND, albeit shortlived, may have compounded that party's problems but, as a demonstration of the strength of unilateralist sentiment in the country, it served as a reminder to the government that the popular mood could not be ignored. Indeed, there were clear elements of a domestic consensus that was reflected in the government's continuing attempts to promote détente. Conciliatory diplomacy during the 1961 Berlin crisis, for example, drew support from popular attitudes in so far as they were articulated through the press and in opinion polls (see Watt, 1965, pp. 233, 275; Richardson, 1966, pp. 316, 318–19).

Such was the extent of this consensus that it is difficult to identify any significant domestic opposition to a détente policy. Macmillan, unlike Churchill, appears to have encountered little opposition from within the Cabinet or the Conservative Party. Had there been any serious opposition, it can be assumed that it would have been overcome by the prime minister's personal commitment to détente and his 'presidential' style of government (see Watt, 1984, p. 141). Until 1960, Macmillan in effect acted as his own foreign secretary, with Selwyn Lloyd as his deputy. Lord Home had more independence as foreign secretary, but his views on, *inter alia*, détente were very close to those of the prime minister. According to Anthony Sampson, this domestic consensus did not include the professional diplomats in the Foreign Office to the extent that they were opposed to summitry. After the collapse of the Paris summit, 'the critics of "summit diplomacy" – including a large part of the Foreign Office – were full of "I told you so"' (Sampson, 1967, p. 141). There were certainly diplomats who were sceptical of summitry: Gladwyn Jebb, the Ambassador in Paris at the time of the summit, is a good example (see Gladwyn, 1972, pp. 276–7, 321–2). But, as in the earlier period, there is little evidence that the Foreign Office as a whole was opposed to détente during this period. Indeed, the broader 'philosophy' of détente, as articulated through Selwyn Lloyd in particular, would indicate that the Office took a cautious but broadly supportive view of governmental efforts to promote détente.

To summarize the conclusions here: domestic political factors do not constitute a significant explanation of British détente policy in the first half of the 1950s, although there is some linkage between a détente policy and potential electoral advantage, particularly in the context of the 1955 Election. On the other hand, domestic political imperatives in terms of the salience of the nuclear issue and its potential electoral consequences offer a much more potent explanation of policy in the 1957–59 period. If a sweeping Conservative victory at the polls and the consequent weakness of the Labour Party made domestic factors less imperative after 1959, there remained a broad domestic consensus that provided support for a continued policy of détente.

Chapter 5

Britain and the Partial Test Ban Treaty

The last chapter analysed British détente policy in the 1950s and early 1960s. This chapter complements that overview chapter, by developing a detailed case study of British policy in action during the latter part of this period. With the object of throwing further light on the nature and the impact of British policy, it describes and evaluates the significance of the British contribution to the negotiations between 1958 and 1963, which culminated in the signing of the Partial Test Ban Treaty in August 1963. The test ban issue rather suggests itself as a case study here, because many commentators have argued that British diplomacy, and Prime Minister Harold Macmillan in particular, played a crucial role in the negotiations. Harold Evans, for example, argues that:

> [the treaty] will surely merit a place in the history books – and rank as a true Macmillan achievement. It was he – with his sense of history – who read the signs aright in Russia and saw the opportunities: who coaxed and prodded the Americans: who argued the case with Khrushchev: and finally took the initiative which led to the Kennedy–Macmillan approach. He had persisted, moreover, despite the collapse of the Paris summit (Evans, 1981, p. 285).

Anthony Sampson suggests that 'Macmillan had succeeded, through the years of distrust, in keeping the lines open, and keeping the object in sight; and he had argued the case passionately and effectively' (Sampson, 1967, p. 235). Nigel Fisher goes as far as to conclude that 'without his [Macmillan's] earlier initiatives, the 1963 Test Ban Treaty might never have been signed' (Fisher, 1982, p. 292). To the claims of this trio of biographers can be added the testimony of Lord Hailsham, the minister who represented Britain at the final negotiations in Moscow:

it is clear that, if nothing else stood to his credit, Harold Macmillan's influence in bringing about the negotiation of the partial test ban treaty would entitle him to be treated as one of the great benefactors of his generation . . . He it was who saw that the time was ripe, and the parties were willing, and I do not myself believe that, if Britain had been absent from that table, a viable agreement would at that time have been negotiated, since Russian relationships with the United States were far less relaxed then than now (Hailsham, 1975, p. 217).

Sir Michael Wright, who was chief British negotiator at the Geneva negotiations until 1962, claims that the British contribution to the test ban negotiations consisted of important initiatives at critical stages, with more sustained pressure 'behind the scenes' during the whole period of the negotiations. He argues that the significance of British diplomacy was heightened by the fluctuating postures adopted by both superpowers towards the issue. As he puts it, 'British policy showed none of the vacillations of Moscow or the hesitation of Washington; and the single-minded purpose behind it was of significant influence in the shaping of Western attitudes and the course of the negotiations' (Wright, 1964, p. 135).

From a non-British perspective, Glenn Seaborg, the chairman of the Atomic Energy Commission under President Kennedy and a close observer of the negotiations, was clearly impressed by the influence of Britain on the United States:

In matters of testing and test ban negotiations, from the Eisenhower period forward the British consistently endeavoured, often with success, to exercise a moderating influence on US policy . . . Considering their relative unimportance as a military force, particularly in nuclear weapons, it is remarkable to consider how much influence the British had over US arms and arms control policies during this period (Seaborg, 1981, pp. 113, 114).

These illustrative comments from participants and commentators alike give a clear indication of the potential of the test ban issue as a case study of British détente policy. More important, they provide a focus for an evaluation of the British role. Three major questions structure the analysis in this chapter. What was the British contribution to the negotiation and final achievement of a test ban treaty? How significant was that contribution? How important was the treaty to the process of East–West détente? The analysis begins, however, with a brief account of the emergence of nuclear testing as an international issue.

THE TEST BAN ISSUE: FROM BRAVO TO GENEVA

Nuclear testing became a significant international issue in March 1954, after an American thermonuclear test at Bikini Atoll, codenamed Bravo, produced unexpectedly widespread radioactive fallout. A sudden awareness of the health hazards associated with nuclear testing in the atmosphere led to an immediate public outcry and the beginnings of an international opposition to the continuation of testing. The Soviet Union proposed a nuclear test ban as a separate arms control measure in the Spring of 1956, but the United States and Britain were resolutely opposed to separate test ban negotiations (Jonsson, 1979, p. 25).

The British position on this issue stemmed from the decision announced in February 1955 to develop a hydrogen bomb, a decision that required the continuation of testing to develop appropriate warheads. In January 1957, the government announced a series of tests to be held during the course of that year. The British concern at this time was that mounting international pressure might weaken American opposition to a test ban. This concern led Prime Minister Harold Macmillan to fly to Bermuda in March 1957 to discuss the problem with President Eisenhower. At that meeting he received the reassurances that he sought, the final communiqué stating their agreement that 'continued nuclear testing is required, certainly for the present' (Divine, 1978, p. 114).

Despite an evident commitment to nuclear testing, the British government was, nevertheless, involved in the chain of events which resulted in the opening of test ban negotiations at Geneva in October 1958. The test ban issue was first debated between the Western powers and the Soviet Union at the United Nations Disarmament Sub-Committee meetings which began in March 1957. The Zorin proposals introduced at the first session included a separately negotiated test ban. The British counterproposals of 6 May included the idea of setting up a committee of technical experts to study the possibility of devising an effective control system. Undoubtedly, these proposals were intended to be a delaying device, designed specifically to head off the test ban proposal until a credible British thermonuclear deterrent had been developed. But, from the perspective of the later Geneva negotiations, the important thing was that 'the idea of technical talks was introduced and gained currency' (Jacobson and Stein, 1966, p. 18).

In April 1958, the unilateral suspension of Soviet nuclear tests presaged a change in American policy on the test ban issue. President Eisenhower proposed a technical conference to work out the details of an inspection system for a future test ban. Khrushchev accepted this proposal, and a Conference of Scientific Experts met in Geneva in July 1958. At Geneva, agreement on methods of detecting nuclear tests was reached without too much difficulty, but problems emerged with regard to the size of the proposed inspection system. The Soviet delegation suggested a relatively small network of 110 control stations, while the Americans countered with a much more extensive system of 650 stations. After several sessions it became clear that neither proposal could provide the basis of an agreement. At this point, one of the two British representatives, Sir William Penney, introduced a compromise proposal: a network of 170 land stations, supplemented by as many as 10 shipboard posts. This proposal was eventually accepted and built into the final report of the conference.[1] The important conclusion of that conference was that 'a workable and effective control system' to detect violations of an agreement to suspend nuclear tests was 'technically feasible'. This opened the way for test ban negotiations to take place (see Jacobson and Stein, 1966, ch. 3; the proposed control system became known as the 'Geneva System').

Before the final report of the conference was officially released, Eisenhower issued a statement calling on the three nuclear powers to negotiate a permanent end to nuclear testing. Moreover, as a sign of good faith, he offered to suspend US tests for one year from the date when negotiations began, on condition that the Soviet Union did not resume testing in the meantime. Macmillan objected strongly to Eisenhower's initiative and to the suspension of tests in particular. Eisenhower would not be moved, however, and the British finally went along with the proposal.

THE TEST BAN NEGOTIATIONS 1958–60

Much apparent progress was made in the early stages of the Geneva negotiations. The Soviet Union agreed that the basic provisions of the Geneva system could be included in the text of a treaty and, by the time the first Geneva session was concluded in December, agreement had been reached on four articles of a test ban treaty. When the second session began in January 1959, however, the Americans informed the Russians that they now had new seismic information derived from their 'Hardtack' series of tests, which convinced them that the Conference of Experts had 'greatly overestimated the ability of seismic instrumentation to detect underground tests and to distinguish them from earthquakes' (Seaborg, 1981, p. 17).

The main implication of the new data, certainly as far as the Americans were concerned, was that many more control stations were now required for effective verification, and that many of these stations would need to be on Soviet soil. The result was that the conference became deadlocked on the inspection issue. The Americans were now insisting that all suspicious explosions must be inspected, and the Soviet Union was demanding a veto on voting by the proposed Control Commission, which in practice meant a veto on all on-site inspection on Soviet territory.

This deadlock provided the context for an intervention that, Jacobson and Stein suggest, was 'the first of a series of British initiatives designed to keep the negotiations alive and to stimulate progress in them' (Jacobson and Stein, 1966, p. 167). A Soviet representative at Geneva had suggested to David Ormsby-Gore, the British minister responsible for the negotiations, that if a finite annual quota of such inspections could be established, it would be easier for the Soviet Union to accept a treaty under which it would be subject to on-site inspection. When Macmillan visited Moscow, he picked up this suggestion and floated the idea of what Wright calls 'a small annual deterrent quota of veto-free inspections' (Wright, 1964, p. 93). Khrushchev showed interest in this compromise solution and the prime minister enthusiastically put the same proposition to Eisenhower when he and Selwyn Lloyd visited Washington in March. The president was unwilling to pursue the quota idea at this stage (although it became official US policy by the end of the year), but the two leaders, nevertheless, agreed the outlines of a more flexible negotiating posture.

In April, they sent similar letters to the Soviet leader proposing a phased agreement that would not, initially at least, require on-site inspection. Khrushchev rejected the idea of an atmospheric ban, but took up Macmillan's quota proposal and built it into a formal submission to the conference. The Western response was equivocal, however, and the negotiations focused for the rest of 1959 on the technical problems involved in detecting and identifying nuclear explosions. The size of the annual quota of inspections was to become a recurring stumbling block in the negotiations until 1963, but the Macmillan initiative had at least broken the deadlock and restored some momentum to the negotiations.

It is worth noting here that this initiative demonstrated at an early stage of the negotiations different British and American attitudes to scientific/technical questions and also the greater British determination – certainly until the Kennedy period – to secure a treaty. While the Americans had already become immersed in the welter of scientific, mainly seismological, data that poured forth from early 1959 onwards – and this almost paralysed decision-making in Washington – the British government was less concerned with the findings of seismological research and more concerned with the political requirement of securing a treaty. To this extent, they were closer to the Russians than to the Americans: the size of the annual quota of inspections was essentially a political rather than a technical decision. The Americans, on the other hand, found it extremely difficult to separate science from politics. Michael Wright provides a useful summary of the British approach:

> The underlying and consistent theme on the British side was that the West should be at least as forthcoming in political negotiations as the scientific and technical assessment of the risks warranted, since the contrary risks of the continuation of the arms race and of the spread of nuclear weapons were so great (Wright, 1964, p. 139).

Twelve months after Macmillan's trip to Moscow, the Geneva negotiations had again reached a 'critical state'. In February 1960, the United States tabled a new proposal, which provided for a phased treaty under which testing nuclear weapons would be prohibited in those environments where, in the American view, control was feasible (Jacobson and Stein, 1966, p. 236). This time, the Soviet Union accepted the idea of a phased treaty as long as it was accompanied by a moratorium covering those tests that were not banned. But the reaction in the United States to the Soviet counterproposal was hostile, largely because it would involve a continuation of the unpoliced moratorium.

Macmillan regarded the Soviet proposal favourably, however, and viewed the American response with growing concern. 'We must now bring tremendous pressure on the Americans to agree', the prime minister noted in his diary on 20 March (Macmillan, 1972, p. 185). Thus, he readily accepted an invitation to visit the United States to discuss the problem. The impact of Macmillan's visit was to strengthen the hand of those inside and outside the administration who were pressing for a positive response to the Soviet Union (see Divine, 1978, pp. 300–2). The result of his meetings with the president was a joint declaration, which embodied at least a conditionally favourable response to the Soviet plan.

A British intervention had again contributed to restoring momentum to the negotiations. Indeed, on this occasion, it promised a much more positive outcome. Seaborg describes the situation: 'While some differences remained, the two sides seemed at this point to be drawing together, and an agreement appeared in the offing. The momentum seemed so strong that those who were opposed to a test ban came forward in haste to make their positions known.' Nevertheless, 'the anticipation was that final agreement might be reached at the forthcoming Four-Power summit meeting in Paris' (Seaborg, 1981, pp. 23–4; Wright, 1964, p. 137. For a more sceptical view, see Jacobson and Stein, 1966, pp. 259–61). This 'hopeful atmosphere' was shattered, however, by the collapse of the Paris summit. The negotiations continued in Geneva, but nothing of substance was achieved. For the remainder of 1960, British efforts on the test ban issue, as on other aspects of East–West relations, were directed at 'damage-limitation'.

Michael Wright summarizes the British contribution to the test ban negotiations up to the end of 1960: 'If it had not been for [Macmillan's] active interventions, the test ban negotiations would almost certainly have broken down early in 1959, and again in the Spring of 1960, and testing by the West might have been resumed late in 1960' (Wright, 1964, p. 136). David Nunnerly quotes an American source who claims that Macmillan 'kept the talks going through the last dreary years of the Eisenhower Administration, when it was feared that the Americans might lose interest in a treaty' (Nunnerly, 1972, p. 94). If little of substance other than the avoidance of breakdown had been achieved, this needs to be set within the context of the negotiating postures of the superpowers and the record of the Eisenhower administration in particular.

Determined British efforts to push the negotiations towards a successful conclusion during this period were in effect neutralized by the absence of a similar commitment in the United States. As Schlesinger puts it, 'while the British earnestly sought agreement, the American government remained divided within itself on the desirability of a treaty' (Schlesinger, 1965, p. 451). The influence of a powerful lobby in the United States that opposed a treaty was maximized by the setting up of a cumbersome machinery in Washington called the Committee of Principals, which was given responsibility for policy decisions. Although this structure was designed to give equal weight to different agency views and interests, it was often deadlocked by opposed views (see, in particular, Jacobson and Stein, 1966, pp. 470–3). Only strong executive leadership could have cut through this slow-moving, bureaucratic structure and this, in stark contrast to the situation in Britain, was absent.

As a direct consequence of this decision-making structure in Washington, the American delegation at Geneva was far less effective than it might have been. According to Wright, it was 'left for lengthy periods temporarily incapable of negotiating, like a yacht with no wind in the sails. It is no exaggeration to say that for months on end instructions were doled out to them from Washington much as a Victorian workhouse might dole out the gruel' (Wright, 1964, p. 120). Schlesinger confirms that the result was a delegation which 'played a weak and inglorious role in the negotiations' (Schlesinger, 1965, p. 452). Naturally this, in turn, handicapped the British delegation's efforts to establish common positions and negotiate effectively with the Soviet Union.

From a British perspective, the frustrations inherent in this situation can only have been exacerbated by the fact that the Soviet delegates were much more willing to negotiate seriously during the Eisenhower period – certainly until May 1960 – than was the case after Kennedy assumed office. But, as the British representative put it:

> Soviet sincerity in [1958–60] was never put to as searching a test by the Americans as it ought to have been . . . Had the energy and drive brought to bear on the problems of a test ban and disarmament in 1961 and later been available during the two preceding years, the issues would almost certainly have been clarified earlier, and there might have been more progress earlier (Wright, 1964, p. 125).

When set in the context of the postures adopted by the other negotiating parties, the British contribution up to the end of the Eisenhower period emerges as a less modest achievement than simply helping to prevent the breakdown of talks would suggest.

THE TEST BAN NEGOTIATIONS 1961–63

With the arrival of President Kennedy in the White House in January 1961, however, the prospect of a test ban treaty looked much brighter. The resumption of the Geneva conference was postponed until March so that the new administration could undertake a thorough review of policy. Significantly, new appointees such as John McCloy, Jerome Wiesner and Glenn Seaborg strongly favoured a test ban, and a technical group – the Fisk Panel – was immediately set up under McCloy to investigate how the United States might move closer to the Soviet position by making concessions on, for example, the quota issue. The new president himself took a close personal interest in the issue from the start (Seaborg, 1981, pp. 30–7).

During this preparatory period, there was close liaison with the British. Before the Fisk Panel reported to the Committee of Principals, a British delegation led by Ormsby-Gore and Wright visited Washington to coordinate US and British positions in preparation for the resumption of the Geneva talks. According to David Nunnerly's account, the visitors 'found to their surprise the extent to which the Americans gave favourable consideration to long-held British positions. Indeed the modifications to the American position which the British had urged for two years were now more or less accepted' (Nunnerly, 1972, p. 94).

The involvement of Ormsby-Gore now became of particular importance for British influence as a whole, because he was a close personal friend of the new president. Arthur Schlesinger claims that it was Ormsby-Gore's commitment to détente that 'had steadily reinforced Kennedy's scepticism about the clichés of the cold war' and it was he who had 'renewed Kennedy's interest in the [test ban issue] in 1959 and [had given] him a detailed memorandum on the British and Russian positions and the American non-position' (Schlesinger, 1965, pp. 424, 453). Ormsby-Gore was able to provide a convenient and valuable communication link between Macmillan and Kennedy, particularly after he became Ambassador in Washington later that year (see Nunnerly, 1972, ch. 4).

When the Geneva conference reconvened, however, it soon became clear that the problem lay not with the Americans but with an intransigent Soviet Union. In April, a complete draft treaty was tabled for the first time by both Western delegations, which included some important concessions to the Soviet position. This draft was summarily rejected by the Soviet delegation. Despite the careful preparation, it was becoming evident that the first stage of the negotiations under Kennedy was floundering. But the British could at least take heart from the fact that the Americans were now adopting a much more positive attitude. Soviet intransigence, however, raised again the question of whether or not the United States would resume testing. As early as February 1961, with the possibility of an early agreement with the Soviet Union disappearing, pressures within the United States began to grow. The British response, as in 1960, was to endeavour to dissuade the Americans from pursuing that course of action. This helped to reinforce Kennedy's own predisposition not to resume testing, at least until the Soviet Union resumed testing in September 1961. Then, after a rather desperate attempt by the two Western leaders to get the Soviet Union to agree to an atmospheric ban with no inspection, the president ordered the resumption of underground testing.

Having failed to prevent the resumption of underground testing, Britain turned its attention to atmospheric tests. If the Americans could be dissuaded from testing in the atmosphere, this still left open the possibility of negotiating at least a partial test ban. By September 1961, however, the United States was already beginning to make contingency preparations for atmospheric tests. As part of these preparations, it was decided that Christmas Island in the Pacific was needed as a test site. As this was a British possession, the question of its use provided an excellent opportunity for the British government to influence American decision-making.

Macmillan began the process of trying to stall an American decision to go ahead with atmospheric testing by proposing that Britain and the United States should jointly announce a six-month moratorium on atmospheric testing. Kennedy eventually turned down this proposal, but 'it presaged further interventions by the British prime minister' (Seaborg, 1981, p. 113). From a bargaining perspective, the British position was complicated at this stage by a request at the beginning of November to use the Nevada site to conduct a British underground test. McGeorge Bundy, Kennedy's Special Assistant for National Security Affairs, spotted the opportunity for a simple trade-off, but the president rather missed the point. In a letter to Macmillan, he readily acceded to the request for the use of Nevada on the assumption that the British would allow the Americans to use Christmas Island. Macmillan's reply on 16 November must have rather shocked the president. Glenn Seaborg describes the impact. 'Any hopes that we may have had that Christmas Island would fall into our laps . . . were quickly dispelled . . . it was evident that Macmillan meant to use our need for Christmas Island as leverage in an attempt to dissuade us from atmospheric testing' (Seaborg, 1981, p. 118). Macmillan managed to put off a decision about Christmas Island until his meeting with Kennedy at Bermuda in December.

By the time the Anglo–American summit convened, the American government had got itself into a difficult situation. Although the decision had now been taken to resume atmospheric testing in the Spring of 1962, the Americans felt that they still needed British support to go ahead. As Schlesinger explains, not only was Christmas Island regarded as the 'ideal site' for testing, it was thought to be 'politically difficult for the United States to resume [atmospheric testing] without British concurrence' (Schlesinger, 1965, p. 489). The scene was set for an interesting confrontation.

Macmillan started off the talks in Bermuda by declaring that the failure to secure a test ban treaty the previous year had been 'an historic opportunity to make progress towards a détente', which had been missed. He made it clear where he felt the blame lay: 'It was the fault of the American "big-hole" obsession and the consequent insistence on a wantonly large number of on-site inspections' (Schlesinger, 1965, p. 452).[2] Referring to the desperate need to break the cycle of the arms race and to prevent the proliferation of nuclear weapons, the prime minister developed the theme that a major new disarmament effort must be made. Kennedy, on the other hand, argued that recent Soviet behaviour had demonstrated that they were not interested in agreements: therefore, preparations for atmospheric testing must go ahead.

It soon became clear that the Americans could not be deflected from resuming atmospheric testing, although Kennedy did agree to postpone an announcement to that effect for as long as possible. Macmillan then rather surprised the Americans again by saying that a decision on Christmas Island would need Cabinet consent. The prime minister was determined to secure a worthwhile quid pro quo from Kennedy for the use of the island. A long letter to

Kennedy at the beginning of January 1962 set out the price of Christmas Island in scarcely veiled terms. In essence, the proposal was that the impending Eighteen-Nation Disarmament Conference (ENDC) should be converted into a forum for relaunching the test ban negotiations.

Despite some anger in the State Department at these blatant tactics, Secretary of State Dean Rusk took the view that the response to Macmillan 'should not be perfunctory' and the president became committed to a dual track approach: continuing preparations for testing coupled with the launching of another arms control initiative. By February, agreement had been reached on the use of Christmas Island, but Macmillan had achieved his limited objective. The joint Anglo-American statement issued was 'consistent with the position taken by the British at Bermuda – that any agreement on Christmas Island must be coupled with a further major effort to reach an arms control agreement with the USSR' (Seaborg, 1981, p. 134).

Transferring the negotiations to the new ENDC forum, however, brought no immediate breakthroughs and, with an impasse in Geneva yet again, the US atmospheric test series began in April 1962. As the year proceeded, however, the arguments for national means of verification and against the requirements for compulsory on-site inspection were strengthened by two developments. First, the eight neutral states represented at the ENDC presented a joint memorandum that stressed the importance of national means of verification and provided for the possibility of on-site inspection by invitation only. Second, some preliminary findings of the US Defense Department's seismic research programme, Project Vela, suggested that improved methods of detection and verification were technically possible without international control stations and on-site inspection. The political impact of these developments was to undermine the American position with respect to on-site inspection.

The result was an intensive review of the whole US position. Once again, a well-timed letter from Macmillan to the president sought to influence the direction of American policy. The prime minister stressed again the urgent need for a test ban and the British view that a ban could be effective with fewer controls. The letter also indicated that the United States would have to renegotiate the use of Christmas Island, should it be needed for a further series of tests. Thus, as Seaborg notes, the British 'retained their small amount of leverage over US policy' (Seaborg, 1981, p. 167).

Following the review, two alternative treaty drafts – one comprehensive and one limited – were jointly presented by the Western delegations at Geneva at the end of August. The Americans conceded that fewer control posts were acceptable but 'some' on-site inspection was still a requirement. It should be noted that the comprehensive draft left blank the size of the inspection quotas for future negotiation. Kennedy and Macmillan both expressed a 'strong preference' for the comprehensive treaty, but they announced that they would be willing to accept the limited treaty. The Soviet delegation, however, rejected both proposals. Thereafter, nothing of substance was achieved at Geneva until the following Spring, when the final breakthrough was made.

THE MOSCOW TALKS

In March 1963, the situation again looked unpropitious. The ENDC was deadlocked and the president was being asked to approve a new series of atmospheric tests. The Soviet government had agreed in principle to on-site inspection, but refused to discuss the technical details. Kennedy was coming under great pressure from Congress not to accept a treaty without adequate verification. It was at this point that Macmillan made arguably his most decisive intervention. As Glenn Seaborg explicitly concedes, 'much of the credit for the next, and ultimately decisive step, must be given to the British' (Seaborg, 1981, p. 208).[3]

When news of the stalemate in Geneva reached him early in March, the prime minister lunched with the Foreign Secretary Lord Home and Minister of State Joseph Godber to discuss a plan to break the deadlock. Macmillan then consulted Ormsby-Gore to find out what sort of initiative would be most acceptable to the Americans. The ambassador counselled against proposing another summit meeting and the use of normal diplomatic channels. He suggested instead the sending of two special emissaries, one from Washington and one from London. This prompted the sending of another long Macmillan letter to Kennedy which, the prime minister later claimed with some modesty, 'helped to start the ball rolling' (Macmillan, 1973, p. 464). Having suggested various ways of bringing the negotiations to a successful conclusion, including the familiar call for a three-power heads of government summit at Geneva, the letter concluded with the ambassador's idea. In his reply, Kennedy suggested that they send a joint letter to Khrushchev along the lines suggested in Macmillan's letter. It is worth noting Macmillan's comments in his diary at this time: 'for me the tension was very great. I was desperately anxious to achieve a modicum of success, and I felt instinctively that at least some agreement was within our grasp' (Macmillan, 1973, p. 465).

Khrushchev's reply was belligerent in tone and content, but he did agree to receive the emissaries. The Americans and Kennedy in particular were downcast, but, encouraged by Ormsby-Gore to ignore the rhetoric and take up the offer, a reply was sent suggesting that the emissaries go to Moscow at the end of June or the beginning of July (Schlesinger, 1965, p. 899; Horne, 1989, pp. 509–10). Khrushchev's reply set the date for 15 July. Macmillan and Ormsby-Gore between them had succeeded in setting up the Moscow talks.

The first meeting in Moscow ended any lingering possibility that remained of securing a comprehensive test ban treaty. Khrushchev himself made it clear that he was prepared to increase the number of 'black boxes' (automatic seismic stations) that would be permitted, but he was no longer prepared to accept any on-site inspections (Jacobson and Stein, 1966, pp. 454–5). He did, however, table two draft treaties, one for a limited test ban and one for an East–West non-aggression pact. In return, Harriman gave Khrushchev a copy of the limited test ban treaty draft the West had introduced at Geneva in August 1962.

Soviet insistence on discussing a non-aggression pact was an important issue that had to be resolved before substantive discussion of the limited test ban drafts could proceed. The British delegation was not averse to discussing this issue, but Harriman's instructions were quite explicit. Such an agreement could not be discussed because it involved other allies, and the French and the Germans were known to be opposed. When Harriman made this position clear to the Russians, there was a strong adverse reaction. Indeed, Harriman was afraid that 'the Soviets might even withhold agreement on the test ban in order to have their own way' (Seaborg, 1981, p. 243).

Although Hailsham is said to have taken the view that the Soviet Union would not insist on linking a non-aggression pact to a test ban treaty, he came up with a compromise solution. He suggested that reference could be made to the desirability of a non-aggression pact in the final communiqué after the talks, which the Western parties would then commend to their allies for sympathetic consideration. The Americans in the person of the president agreed to this compromise and it was put to the Russians. At first, Gromyko said that this was not sufficient to meet his requirements, but he finally relented.

Having disposed of this issue, the discussions then turned to the fine print of the test ban treaty drafts. The Soviet Union agreed to much of the language of the Anglo-American draft but took issue with two of the provisions, those relating to peaceful nuclear explosions and withdrawal from the treaty. An American offer to give up the right to continue peaceful nuclear explosions in return for the retention of a procedure for withdrawal from the treaty was accepted by the Russians, but hard bargaining ensued on the precise wording of the withdrawal clause. At one point, Harriman threatened to terminate the discussions if agreement could not be reached on an acceptable clause. As these rather semantic arguments dragged on, Hailsham became concerned that there was a possibility of losing the whole treaty. He sent a telegram to the prime minister complaining of excessive American rigidity. Macmillan, in turn, expressed his concern to the president through Ormsby-Gore. Meanwhile, irrespective of Hailsham's intervention, a compromise on wording had been agreed in Moscow and the treaty was initialled on 25 July (Nunnerly, 1972, p. 197). Macmillan and Khrushchev wanted the treaty to be formally signed at a summit meeting, but Kennedy was resistant to the idea and the treaty was signed in Moscow by the three foreign secretaries on 5 August.

THE BRITISH CONTRIBUTION TO THE TEST BAN TREATY

Having presented a detailed narrative account of the test ban negotiations with some commentary in an attempt to highlight the British role, it is appropriate at this stage to offer a more explicit evaluation of the British contribution to the treaty. In this section, therefore, the contributions of the major parties to the negotiations are compared and set within the situational context in which the treaty was eventually signed. The object here is to consider whether the claims noted at the beginning of this chapter stand up to a close examination of the events.

It is clear from this account that the claim, of Sir Michael Wright in particular, that Britain took the lead in setting up the Geneva negotiations cannot be substantiated.[4] The continuing British commitment to nuclear testing, in the context of developing a credible thermonuclear deterrent and, more important in political terms, restoring close Anglo–American nuclear cooperation, meant that the government was ambivalent at best towards the test ban issue. This ambivalence was not resolved until the Geneva negotiations were actually under way. There was an important contribution by British scientists to the events leading up to those negotiations, but the British government scarcely deserves the credit for making them possible.

Once the negotiations were in progress, however, a series of British initiatives between 1959 and 1963 played an important role in keeping them going, eventually arriving at a successful conclusion in the form of a partial treaty. These initiatives, however, were less significant than the sustained pressure on both superpowers, and the Americans in particular, over an extended period. After all, the 1959 initiative served to break one deadlock, but, as David Nunnerly argues, 'ultimately, it was to have no practical effect on the outcome of the negotiations' (Nunnerly, 1972, p. 93). The 1960 initiative, however promising, was stymied by the collapse of the Paris summit.

What the Macmillan government did manage to do remarkably successfully was to influence domestic political processes in the United States and, to a lesser degree, in the Soviet Union. As noted in the narrative, there were powerful lobbies in Washington and Moscow, who were actively opposed to any sort of test ban treaty, however limited. This meant that the respective leaders, however well disposed to a treaty, had very little room for manoeuvre. Either a well-timed visit or a letter from the prime minister were only the most obvious manifestations of a sustained attempt to reinforce the embattled positions of those who were fighting for a test ban agreement. This often included bolstering the personal predispositions of the other leaders, whether it was Eisenhower, Khrushchev, or Kennedy in particular.

More successfully on the test ban issue perhaps than on any other issue in the postwar period, the British shamelessly exploited a 'special relationship' with the Americans. David Nunnerly describes the relationship:

> [it] did not mean that there were channels of communication of a different order to those open to all governments in diplomatic negotiations. It simply represented . . . a willingness to use the channels available more frequently, more thoroughly and often at a higher level than is usual in diplomacy (Nunnerly, 1972, p. 13).

Leadership links, personal friendships, ministers, diplomats and scientists on the ground in Geneva were all used to maximize British influence. The fact that open disagreements were usually avoided and the semblance at least of a unified Anglo-American negotiating position maintained at Geneva only served to increase the effectiveness of the British voice.

Henry Kissinger has described how the special relationship worked during the Nixon period, but, for reasons that will become clear in the next chapter, his description is arguably more appropriate in the period covered here. He writes of 'a pattern of consultation so matter-of-factly intimate that it became psychologically impossible to ignore British views. [The British and the Americans] evolved a habit of meetings so regular that autonomous American action somehow came to seem to violate club rules.' He notes in particular 'the degree to which diplomatic subtlety overcame substantive disagreements' (Kissinger, 1979, pp. 40, 90).

The value of a Washington 'insider' like David Ormsby-Gore for such 'intimate consultation' was crucial. The complexities of American decision-making on this issue were such that an input had to be made, preferably by someone who knew how the system worked, at an early stage of the domestic deliberations. Once the policy process had produced a result, and it was adopted as policy, it was extremely difficult to get it changed. According to one American official, 'Ormsby-Gore had a knack of getting in the British views at the early stages so we took them into account before we came to a final conclusion' (Nunnerly, 1972, p. 47).

It must be said, of course, that the absence of any significant lobby in Britain which was opposed to a test ban treaty put the government in a highly advantageous position vis-à-vis its negotiating partners in Geneva. As Lord Zuckerman has noted, 'there was no sophisticated debate about the test ban in the

United Kingdom' which compared to the one which raged in the United States (Zuckerman, 1982, pp. 114–15). Indeed, as discussed in the last chapter, the domestic political imperatives in the late 1950s were such as to raise the problem for the analyst of trying to disentangle the motives of Macmillan the statesman and Macmillan the politician (see Freeman, 1986, ch. 3). But if the prime minister's perceptions of the mood of public opinion in Britain help to explain his determination to get a test ban treaty, the absence of any widespread popular support for a test ban in the United States provides a starting point for a brief evaluation of the American contribution to the treaty. Clearly, that absence of support, combined with an informed and powerful lobby opposed to a treaty, put Eisenhower and Kennedy in a very different domestic situation to Macmillan.

The account offered here has stressed the deficiencies of the Eisenhower administration with respect to the test ban negotiations. On the credit side, however, Eisenhower's initiative in halting nuclear tests and his role in setting up the Geneva talks should also be noted. Moreover, it was his administration's April 1959 proposal for a test ban limited to the atmosphere that eventually became the basis for the partial treaty in 1963 (see, in particular, Divine, 1978, pp. 228–31, 318). It should also be remembered that it was the Eisenhower administration that first grappled with the intricacies of the test ban issue (Jacobson and Stein, 1966, p. 490). Despite the evident inadequacies of the Eisenhower contribution to the negotiations, he bequeathed a not insignificant legacy to his successor.

The Kennedy administration brought a much higher level of commitment to the search for a treaty, however, and can claim much of the credit for the eventual outcome. Kennedy was more prepared than Eisenhower to give time and attention to the issue and to master the technical intricacies involved (Wiesner, 1965, p. 11). Moreover, he was more convinced than Eisenhower ever was of the desirability of a test ban treaty and, therefore, was more prepared to take risks to achieve that goal. Most significantly perhaps, he was prepared to use the influence of his office to advance the chances of success. He chose new personnel who were committed to a test ban to head the relevant agencies in Washington, and he appointed Arthur Dean, a more effective chief negotiator in Geneva. He altered the balance of institutional power by establishing the Arms Control and Disarmament Agency in September 1961 and bringing it into the decision-making process (Jacobson and Stein, 1966, pp. 473–5).

Kennedy's famous speech at the American University in Washington in June 1963 is an excellent example of the president's skill in managing the policy process and the wider domestic and international political environment. The timing of the speech was critical. At the end of May, Senators Dodd and Humphrey had introduced a resolution into the Senate which called for a partial test ban treaty. The thirty-two other senators who signed this resolution were a long way short of the necessary two-thirds majority required to ratify a treaty, but, at least, as Norman Cousins comments, 'for the first time, President Kennedy could feel some momentum behind him on the test ban fight' (Cousins, 1972, p. 123). Two days before Kennedy's speech, Khrushchev had finally agreed the dates for the Moscow talks. A major speech by the president at this time could not only build on a degree of domestic support but also affect the political atmosphere in which the talks were held.

The speech was a classic example of the power of presidential initiative. Prepared without consulting the bureaucracy – for fear, presumably, of having the message watered down – it gave a clear signal to the Russians that Kennedy genuinely wanted a test ban treaty. The speech was an impressive *tour de force*, later described by Sorensen (who helped to write it!) as 'the first presidential speech in eighteen years to succeed in reaching beyond the Cold War' (Sorensen, 1965, p. 730). Kennedy called for a fresh start at Geneva, publicly announced the forthcoming Moscow talks and declared a unilateral US ban on atmospheric tests. A positive Soviet response to Kennedy's initiative ensured that the speech was a major turning point in the negotiations. Khrushchev immediately told Harold Wilson, then visiting Moscow, what he was later to tell Averell Harriman, that it was the greatest speech by an American president since Roosevelt. Khrushchev's reply came in a speech in East Berlin in July. In what was generally an uncompromising speech, he accepted for the first time that the Soviet Union would agree to a partial test ban without an unpoliced moratorium on underground testing (Jacobson and Stein, 1966, p. 453).

Reference to Khrushchev's positive response to Kennedy's speech is a useful reminder that it takes two sides to negotiate. However significant American and British efforts were, they would have achieved nothing without Soviet cooperation. The Soviet role in the achievement of a test ban treaty, therefore, cannot be ignored. While there is far less information about the Soviet policy process in this context, available analyses suggest that Khrushchev's domestic freedom of action was at least as constrained as Kennedy's (see, for example, Jonsson, 1979; Bloomfield et al. 1966). Within those constraints, however, there are clear indications of the positive role played by the Soviet Union and the importance of Khrushchev's personal involvement.

It is unlikely to have been a coincidence, for example, that the initial Soviet moratorium on testing was announced at the end of March 1958, only days after Khrushchev had become prime minister, thereby taking overall control in the Soviet Union. However cynical that suspension was, with the Soviet Union having completed and the United States about to start a test series, the moratorium and the accompanying letters to Eisenhower and Macmillan, urging them to follow suit, encouraged the American president to reciprocate. Eisenhower's invitation to a conference of experts was eventually accepted by Khrushchev and the pattern of events leading to substantive negotiations at Geneva had been set in train.

Thereafter, it can be assumed that Khrushchev's contributions to the negotiations reflected in part at least his standing with the more conservative elements of the political hierarchy in Moscow. Until the middle of 1960, as noted earlier, the Soviet contribution as a whole compared favourably with that of the United States. After the U-2 incident and the collapse of the Paris summit, however, the Soviet contribution became increasingly negative until the September 1961 atmospheric test series had been completed early in 1962. Only then was Khrushchev able to play a more positive role again. He was noticeably enthusiastic in his response to the Kennedy–Macmillan proposal for a new initiative in the context of the forthcoming ENDC negotiations. In a letter to Kennedy, he argued that the new talks were so important that heads of state should participate from the outset, though he eventually agreed to allow foreign ministers to open the conference. There was no immediate breakthrough, however, and the resumption of atmospheric testing by the Americans deferred any further progress.

It took the experience of the Cuban missile crisis in October 1962 to impress upon both Khrushchev and Kennedy the need to make common cause. Seaborg describes the impact:

> That brush with calamity seemed to forge a bond between them. They appeared now to understand each other better, to buttress each other's efforts, to avoid making the other look bad. They began to consult each other more frequently, to work together on problems of common interest (Seaborg, 1981, p. 300).

But if the two leaders were now committed to a test ban treaty, Harold Macmillan also appreciated the significance of the Cuban crisis as a potential turning point. He wrote to Khrushchev at the height of the crisis suggesting that the resolution of the Cuban situation would open the way for a test ban agreement. 'I therefore ask you to take the action necessary to make all this possible. This is an opportunity which we should seize' (Nunnerly, 1972, p. 91).

Khrushchev responded positively to Macmillan's invitation. He made a major speech to the December session of the Supreme Soviet, in which he called for the Western powers 'to remove the last barriers to an agreement on ending nuclear tests for all time to come' (quoted in Brown, 1968, p. 269). He then wrote a long letter to Kennedy, in which he accepted the principle of on-site inspection and appealed for a joint effort to reach agreement. Kennedy's response was encouraging. By the end of 1962, an exchange of correspondence between the leaders and an agreement to hold private talks in the new year had generated popular as well as governmental expectations that a treaty would be signed in the near future.

In less than two months, however, that optimism had evaporated. Shortly after the ENDC reconvened in February, deadlock again prevailed. What appears to have happened is that perceptions of a heightened possibility of a test ban agreement, following the successful resolution of the missile crisis, mobilized opposition forces in Washington and Moscow to step up their efforts. While it was important in the longer term that Khrushchev and Kennedy now appeared to share a common conviction of the desirability of a treaty, this was a necessary but not a sufficient condition for getting a treaty signed and, in the American context, ratified. Both leaders still had to carry their domestic oppositions.

Khrushchev's task was arguably the more difficult because he had backed down over the Cuban missiles and this must have affected his domestic standing. The issue of what the Americans had or had not told the Russians about the number of on-site inspections they would be prepared to accept offers an interesting insight into Khrushchev's position. The Soviet leader believed that the Americans would accept three inspections a year and he made what he thought was the critical concession by accepting that number in his December letter to Kennedy. But, as he told Norman Cousins in an interview in Moscow, he had had a lot of trouble persuading the Council of Ministers to accept this concession. When the Americans rejected this number as inadequate, Khrushchev felt that he had been made to 'look foolish' and could not go back to the Council to increase the number of inspections (Seaborg, 1981, pp. 180, 208). Thus it may be surmised that Khrushchev, from a position of relative weakness, had used up what political capital he had left after Cuba and could go no further to meet the Americans. He told Cousins that the next move was up to Kennedy.

The president, for his part, however, was finding it increasingly difficult to make any moves as his administration's policy on the test ban issue came under increasing fire. Leading senators and congressmen made it clear in speeches and letters that the concessions already made to the Russians were causing concern and that further concessions would be resisted. By the end of February, it was clear that the administration would face major problems in getting a comprehensive treaty ratified. Expressions of congressional opposition occasioned a major effort by the administration at the beginning of March to justify its test ban policy (Jacobson and Stein, 1966, pp. 444–6).

The extent of the domestic opposition that surfaced in Washington and Moscow in the early weeks of 1963 and the resulting impasse in Geneva have been spelt out in some detail here because they provide the immediate context for the Macmillan initiative of 16 March. It can be argued that neither Kennedy nor Khrushchev could make any further moves to break the deadlock and sustain the momentum generated by the successful resolution of the missile crisis. Hence the British initiative, which triggered the talks in Moscow four months later, was crucially important and perfectly timed. The use of personal emissaries maximized the ability of the Western leaders to influence the outcome of the talks and the Moscow location enabled Khrushchev personally to oversee the proceedings (see Harriman, 1971, p. 91). An appreciation of the context of the March 1963 initiative strengthens the argument that this was indeed the most significant of the initiatives taken by the Macmillan government during the course of the negotiations.

Having said that, there were other developments between March and July 1963 that made an important contribution to the eventual outcome. However important the setting up of the Moscow talks, the achievement of even a partial treaty was not a foregone conclusion. Reference has already been made to the Dodd–Humphrey resolution, Kennedy's American University speech and Khrushchev's response in East Berlin. The agreement to set up a direct communications link, a so-called 'hot-line' between Moscow and Washington should also be mentioned in order to establish the situational context in which the treaty was eventually signed. The Cuban crisis had demonstrated the necessity of the closest possible contact between leaders during a crisis if disaster was to be averted. It served to convince a sceptical US government that a hot-line was desirable and Arthur Dean made a formal proposal to that effect in December 1962. It should be noted that the Soviet government did not accept the proposal until April 1963, a further indication perhaps of the domestic constraints operating in Moscow in the early weeks of that year.

Turning finally to the Moscow talks themselves, the British role in retrospect appears to have been less crucial than Lord Hailsham's testimony would suggest. The successful outcome owed more to the context in which the talks were held and the evident determination of the two major parties to secure an agreement. On the Soviet side, this determination was indicated from the outset by the designation of Foreign Minister Gromyko as the chief negotiator (there had been speculation that the Soviet team would be led by a deputy foreign minister) and by Khrushchev's personal involvement in the first day's discussions. The Soviet leader managed to establish a relaxed atmosphere and at the same time to convince Averell Harriman that he genuinely wanted an agreement. The importance of Harriman's presence in Moscow for the success of the mission cannot be overstated. Given his standing in Moscow, sending Harriman to negotiate a test ban agreement was a clear signal to the Soviet leadership of the president's commitment to a treaty. As someone from the Moscow embassy remarked to Arthur Schlesinger, 'when I heard that Harriman was going, I knew you were serious' (Harriman, 1971, p. ix). Harriman was ably assisted by an excellent negotiating team in Moscow. According to Duncan Wilson, who was a member of Hailsham's team, the entire

American delegation was 'formidably effective' (Seaborg, 1981, pp. 252–3).

By implication at least, the role of the small British delegation in Moscow was secondary to the efforts of the major parties. Lord Hailsham has claimed that the British presence in Moscow acted as a 'catalyst', but, with the possible exception of helping to clear away the non-aggression pact issue, there is little to substantiate this (Hailsham, 1975, p. 219). There were differences concerning a couple of the clauses in the treaty, but they were resolved without apparent British help. Perhaps Hailsham's directness was his most important contribution to the outcome. His attitude was clear at an early stage of the negotiations. As he himself later described it, 'I was satisfied that both sides were fully determined to go on testing underground and, having reached this conclusion fairly early on, I went all out for a partial ban' (Hailsham, 1975, p. 218).

But if the important British contribution to the achievement of a test ban had already been made before the Moscow talks began, this does not detract from the overall significance of that contribution. The claims made at the beginning of this chapter have in general terms been substantiated here, though the importance of a British input at the beginning and at the end of a long negotiating process has been disputed. Of the public initiatives, the intervention in March 1963 was ultimately the most important in terms of crucially affecting the outcome. That intervention apart, what was most important and certainly most remarkable was the ability of the Macmillan government over an extended period to influence the domestic political processes of its negotiating partners. Much of the credit for this must go to the single-minded determination of the prime minister. Macmillan's central role in the negotiation of the treaty was later recognized by President Kennedy. In a letter to Macmillan, he offered this generous tribute:

> This morning, as I signed the instrument of ratification of the Nuclear Test Ban Treaty, I could not but reflect on the extent to which your steadfastness of commitment and determined perseverance made this treaty possible . . . History will eventually record your indispensible role in bringing about the limitation of nuclear testing; but I cannot let this moment pass without expressing to you my own keen appreciation of your signal contribution to world peace (quoted in Fisher, 1982, p. 333).

However 'indispensible' the contribution of Macmillan and his government, though, and perhaps no third party could have done more, the argument that there would have been no test ban treaty without British participation in the negotiations is difficult to sustain. The treaty would not have been signed if the situational context had not been favourable or, more important, if it had not served the interests of the United States and the Soviet Union as perceived by their respective leaders.

THE PARTIAL TEST BAN TREATY AND DÉTENTE

Having evaluated the British contribution to the test ban treaty, this chapter concludes with a brief assessment of the treaty as a turning point in the détente process. Some indication of British perceptions of the significance of the treaty can be gleaned from the reflections of Lord Hailsham and his prime minister. While Hailsham regretted that the treaty was not, as he had hoped, 'immediately followed by a détente between East and West', he believed nevertheless that it was 'the biggest step forward in international relations since the beginning of the cold war' (Hailsham, 1975, p. 219). Macmillan himself had no doubts about the importance of the treaty. He made his views clear in a newspaper interview given shortly before the Moscow talks took place. He maintained that there had been an East–West détente since 1959 'not in treaties or documents, but in tone'. If a test ban treaty could be secured, he was convinced that 'one actual agreement would symbolize the détente which everyone knows has taken place but which it is difficult for any of us to grasp' (Sampson, 1967, pp. 232–3).

After the treaty had been signed, the prime minister expressed his satisfaction to an emotional House of Commons. 'The House will, I know, understand my own feelings at seeing at last the results of efforts made over many years, and of hopes long deferred' (Nunnerly, 1972, p. 108). His private thoughts were, as ever, confided to his diary: 'So was realised at least one of the great purposes which I had set myself.' He was confident that 'once the rivalry of tests between the great nuclear powers was brought to an end some progress could be made in the limitation of the ever-increasing number and complexity of nuclear weapons'. The treaty was regarded as the key turning point in the nuclear age because it represented the necessary 'solid achievement' in East–West negotiations that would secure and advance the détente process (Macmillan, 1973, p. 484). The prime minister wanted the test ban treaty to be followed by a non-proliferation treaty and an agreement to hold a series of summit meetings. Significantly, Macmillan was not alone in explicitly linking the achievement of a test ban treaty to an East–West détente. Kennedy and increasingly Khrushchev, particularly after the Cuban crisis, shared the prime minister's sense of urgency about the need to establish a political climate in which the arms race could be controlled and other states prevented from acquiring nuclear weapons.

It can be argued with hindsight, of course, that the hopes and expectations associated with the treaty were scarcely realized. The failure to achieve a comprehensive ban was clearly important and naturally limited the impact of the treaty on the arms race. As Robert Divine succinctly put it, 'nuclear tests did not end in 1963; they simply went underground' (Divine, 1978, p. 317). For the nuclear signatories, including Britain, underground testing has been adequate to develop the warheads of numerous delivery systems since the treaty was signed. Indeed, it is difficult to dissent from Seaborg's conclusion that 'while the absence of atmospheric testing may have impeded the acquisition of some weapons knowledge, it cannot be claimed that, overall, the Limited Test Ban Treaty has had the effect of slowing down the arms race between the superpowers' (Seaborg, 1981, p. 288).

As for the nuclear proliferation problem, it was recognized that a comprehensive test ban would be far more effective in preventing proliferation. Nevertheless, it was hoped that states signing the treaty would be constrained by the technical difficulties and the costs of underground testing. The predictable refusal of France and China to sign the partial treaty, however, quickly dispelled such optimism, and it was soon realized that the proliferation problem had to be approached more directly. After several years of negotiation, a non-proliferation treaty was eventually signed in July 1968, although, to date, several of the states most likely to 'go nuclear' have either not signed or not ratified the treaty.

But if the contribution of the test ban treaty per se to arms control was less than impressive, its broader impact was far more significant. From a détente perspective, the test ban treaty was the first example in the nuclear age of a detailed and complex arms control negotiation resulting in a positive outcome. As such, it provided a breakthrough, demonstrating that successful arms control negotiations between East and West were possible. Moreover, it provided a learning experience, the confidence to make further progress in other areas and it generated the necessary impetus for a series of arms control agreements in the late 1960s and early 1970s. As Peter Calvocoressi comments, the treaty 'raised the question of what to try next. It gave a fillip to the partial approach and therefore to the search for parts ripe for tackling' (Calvocoressi, 1982, p. 33). To the extent that the treaty stimulated further arms control negotiations, it made an important contribution to détente.

The structural link with the process of East–West détente derives from the extent to which the treaty, to borrow Jacobson and Stein's phrase, 'hastened the dilution of bipolarity' (Jacobson and Stein, 1966, pp. 500–1). Both superpowers were clearly alarmed at the threat to their control of international relations posed by the proliferation of nuclear weapons to allied states, and this provided a powerful incentive on both sides to negotiate a test ban treaty. But, paradoxically, the signing of the treaty only served to hasten the diffusion of power in the international system, demonstrating as it did that neither bloc was monolithic. The treaty helped to seal the rift between Moscow and Peking and it further alienated France from the other Western allies. Despite obvious limitations and the rather inflated expectations associated with it, however, the conclusion must be that the test ban treaty was a powerful symbol of détente. Thus, given the British role in the achievement of that treaty, the Macmillan government had made a significant contribution to the détente process.

Chapter 6

The decline of British influence on East–West relations

From a historical perspective, the signing of the Partial Test Ban Treaty in August 1963 emerges as the last peak of British influence on the direction of East–West relations. Thereafter, the ability of British governments to play a major East–West role began to decline. If a single 'turning point' can be identified, it was not the test ban treaty or even the Paris summit débâcle of May 1960, so often pinpointed in this context, but the Eisenhower–Khrushchev summit at Camp David in September 1959. This meeting was crucial because, as argued in the last chapter, it effectively legitimized direct negotiations between the superpowers at heads of government level. In the longer term, personal contacts between Soviet and American leaders were bound to limit the ability of third parties to influence East–West relations: personal contacts of an exclusive nature were particularly ominous in this respect, as Macmillan realized (Macmillan, 1972, pp. 78–80). Paradoxically, to the extent that unremitting British pressure on Washington was responsible for the Camp David summit, the Macmillan government had been almost too successful. The more the leaders of the two superpowers got into the habit of consulting directly, the less they needed Britain's services as an intermediary.

This does not mean, of course, that British governments did not try to influence the direction of East–West relations after 1963. Indeed, there is some substance in the provocative Northedge comment that the 'test ban agreement . . . had the effect of fostering in Britain hallucinations of world power no longer justified by the realities' (Northedge, 1974, p. 292). The problem was that not only were the superpowers beginning to negotiate bilaterally, thus narrowing the opportunities for Britain to play the 'honest broker' role, but other sources of British influence on East–West relations also began to weaken. In particular, the 'special relationship' with Washington looked distinctly less 'special' in the decade or so after the signing of the test ban treaty, and British nuclear weapons became much less significant as an instrument of political influence. Moreover, Britain's distinctive role in the alliance was challenged by the new assertive role in East–West relations played by the Federal Republic of Germany (FRG) and Britain's relations with Western Europe as a whole became complicated by the perceived requirements of joining the European Economic Community (EEC).

In the context of these changing patterns of relations, this chapter reviews the attempts by British governments to promote East–West détente between 1963 and 1975. It focuses on three issues: the attempts to mediate in the Vietnam war in the mid-1960s; the contribution to the negotiations that produced the Nuclear Non-Proliferation Treaty (NPT) in 1968; and finally the British role in the series of interrelated developments in European security affairs, which began with the FRG's *Ostpolitik* in 1969 and culminated with the Helsinki Accords of 1975. With each issue, the concern is to evaluate the impact of British policy and, more generally, to identify the mainsprings of British détente policy in this period, using the explanatory framework developed earlier.

BRITAIN AND THE VIETNAM WAR

Before looking at the substance of the attempts by the Wilson government to act as an intermediary between the Americans and the North Vietnamese, it might be useful to note two important contextual factors. First, British governments had a history of mediation in South East Asia as one of the co-chairmen (the other being the Soviet Union) of the 1954 Geneva Conference. Moreover, the Macmillan government had had some success in this role with respect to Laos, certainly up to 1962 (see Chapter 4). This experience helped to generate the expectation that Britain could play a similar role in relation to Vietnam. In the context of Vietnam, however, the Wilson government found this position of little use, mainly because the Russians were unwilling to give the Chinese an international platform by reconvening the conference. The other factor that is germane to the outcome of this issue is the fact that Anglo-American relations had sharply deteriorated after 1964, mainly because of the refusal of the Wilson government to provide either material assistance or, more important to Washington, overt diplomatic support for the Americans as they escalated the conflict in Vietnam. The state of Anglo-American relations meant that Wilson did not have the necessary influence in Washington for the mediation effort to have any chance of success.

Wilson's attempts to mediate began inauspiciously in February 1965 with an offer to fly to Washington to 'advise' the president on policy in Vietnam. Johnson's angry response to what was seen as Wilson's 'interference' ensured that relations between the two leaders thereafter were strained at best. The prime minister, however, returned from a meeting with Johnson in April convinced that the president would back any British initiative that had a chance of getting peace talks started (H. Wilson, 1974, p. 136). There followed two abortive attempts by Wilson to send personal emissaries to initiate talks with Ho Chi Minh, which followed, in turn, a proposed Commonwealth 'peace mission' to South East Asia that never took place. At the end of 1965, Foreign Secretary Michael Stewart was sent to Moscow to try to enlist Soviet help in mediating on Vietnam, but the Soviet leadership completed a frustrating year for the Wilson government by their unwillingness to get involved.

This pattern was repeated the following year. Indeed, British hopes of playing a mediating role appeared to weaken even further when, in June 1966, Wilson publicly disassociated the British government from the American bombing of Hanoi and Haiphong. Nevertheless, Wilson's visit to Moscow the following month opened up a more promising period of British involvement. According to his own account, the prime minister impressed on the Soviet Premier Kosygin the danger of further escalation of the war if, as they were threatening, the North Vietnamese put captured American pilots on trial. The Soviet leader apparently passed on this advice to Hanoi and the show trials did not take place. Thus, Wilson suggests, with some backing from American sources, his intervention had been significant even if he had again failed to get the Russians to agree to reconvene the Geneva Conference (H. Wilson, 1974, pp. 329–30). It was the latter objective which took Foreign Secretary George Brown to Moscow in November, but he also put to the Russians a peace plan 'authorized' by Washington. This plan, dubbed the 'Phase-A-Phase-B scheme', involved an American agreement to stop the bombing of North Vietnam (Phase-A) in return for a secret agreement with the North Vietnamese to stop the infiltration of troops south through the demilitarized zone (Phase-B). Brown made no progress in Moscow, largely because the Americans had already tried to pursue variants of this plan through other intermediaries without success.

Undaunted, the Wilson cabinet decided to pursue the phased peace plan with Kosygin during his visit to London in February 1967. In close consultation with Washington – or so Wilson thought – a text setting out the peace plan was given to Kosygin for transmission to Hanoi. The Soviet leader, for his part, seemed genuinely concerned for the first time to become actively involved in a joint effort to mediate between Washington and Hanoi. Before the text could be passed on, however, the American president was persuaded by his advisers to toughen his stance. The bombing would only be stopped once the Americans had been assured that infiltration had stopped. This stood the phased plan on its head and effectively ended any chance of movement towards peace talks at that time.

It also ended serious British attempts to mediate on Vietnam. The Wilson government played no part in getting the Paris peace talks started the following year. If British efforts overall must be deemed a failure, was an important opportunity missed at the beginning of 1967 to bring the Vietnam war to an earlier negotiated conclusion? Probably not. The complexities of negotiating the details of an agreement, as evidenced later at the Paris talks, and the all too apparent divisions within the Johnson administration suggest that progress was not possible at that stage (see Gore-Booth, 1974, p. 362). British efforts not only failed materially to effect the eventual settlement, but the divisions in Washington made the Wilson government look particularly inept. Moreover, the outcome of the February 1967 episode in particular had a very negative impact on Anglo-American relations, producing irritation and friction on both sides of the Atlantic and further souring the personal relationship between Wilson and Johnson.

With hindsight, Wilson was clearly ill-advised to invest so much international credibility in the Vietnam issue. He certainly fell foul of some clumsy, poorly coordinated American diplomacy. The use of different channels at different times to test out North Vietnamese reactions reflected an administration that was deeply split. Indeed, it was not until the Tet offensive twelve months after the Kosygin visit to London that Johnson and his closest advisers finally concluded that a negotiated settlement was necessary. The Soviet government too was an uncertain ally on this issue. Soviet leaders remained unwilling to reconvene the Geneva Conference throughout this period and it was never clear how much influence they had on Hanoi. George Brown certainly took the view that Kosygin on his London visit overestimated the limits of Soviet manoeuvrability. 'I think the Russians were leading everybody up the garden path, including us' (Brown, 1972, p. 139). But even if the Soviet government could have 'delivered' Hanoi to the negotiating table, the way the British government was treated by the Americans was unlikely to inspire the necessary confidence in Moscow that London was close to Washington.

Given the evident difficulties that mediation on this issue presented, it is difficult to resist Brown's conclusion that the British 'were too anxious to be intermediaries' (Brown, 1972, p. 135). This judgement can certainly be applied to the prime minister, who, according to his cabinet colleagues, was 'obsessed' by the idea that he could bring the Vietnam conflict to a negotiated conclusion. As Denis Healey put it, 'Harold had an obsession that he could settle the war in Vietnam, and that Britain could play the role of a major power at the conference table. He was convinced that he could prove to be the great peacemaker – the honest broker' (Williams and Read, 1971, p. 215). The respected journalist Henry Brandon talks about Wilson using the Kosygin visit as an opportunity 'to step onto the world stage as a mediator between the Americans and the North Vietnamese' (Brandon, 1970, p. 82). Not only did Wilson as prime minister appear to see himself acting in the tradition of his recent predecessors on East–West relations, but, according to Crossman, he believed that he had special negotiating talents that could be deployed on this issue, having successfully completed trade deals with Kosygin and Gromyko many years before (Howard, 1979, p. 137).

But, Wilson's obsessions and possibly 'hallucinations of world power' apart, an explanation of British policy has to focus on domestic considerations in order to understand the prime minister's plight. The evidence suggests that it was domestic imperatives, perhaps more than any other set of factors in this context, that spurred Wilson into rather desperate attempts to mediate on Vietnam in a vain attempt to square a circle of conflicting pressures and demands. On the one hand, the Labour

Party was pushing him into an outright denunciation of American policy in Vietnam and, on the other, the Foreign Office was consistently arguing for a more committed pro-American line.

As early as March 1965, Crossman notes in his diary the growing concern of many Labour MPs about Vietnam and his own concern that the issue might become as divisive for Wilson as Korea had been for Attlee. 'Certainly there is a growing suspicion in the PLP that we ought to be playing a much more active mediating role along with the Russians instead of siding so closely with the Americans' (Howard, 1979, p. 86). In Crossman's view, Wilson's peace mission proposal at the 1965 Commonwealth Conference, his 'Vietnam stunt' as Crossman dismissively refers to it, was designed in part to deflect criticism from Rhodesia, but, more important, 'to calm the left-wing of the Party' (Howard, 1979, pp. 115–16). By the end of 1966, despite the public disassociation from American bombing of Hanoi, the government was, in George Brown's words, 'under tremendous pressure' from the Party as a whole to go further in outright condemnation of American policy. 'We had been defeated at the Party Conference on Vietnam and he [Wilson] wanted desperately to find a new initiative to take' (Brown, 1972, p. 136).

On the other hand, the prime minister himself notes on several occasions the other 'horn' of his dilemma, the persistent attempts by the Foreign Office to get him to take a more committed pro-American line on Vietnam (H. Wilson, 1974, pp. 120, 122, 266, 320). The state of the British economy and its dependence on American financial support during this period made it prudent to give some measure of diplomatic support to American policy in Vietnam. This, Bartlett suggests, was clearly recognized by the cabinet (Bartlett, 1977, p. 232). George Brown stresses in his memoirs the other more overtly political concern of the Foreign Office that the Americans should not be hounded out of Vietnam by international criticism until they could honourably withdraw, leaving a reasonably stable situation behind. The fear was that, if the United States was forced to leave Vietnam 'dishonourably', this might stimulate isolationist sentiments in the USA and a possible withdrawal from Europe might be precipitated (Brown, 1972, pp. 133–4). In the face of these conflicting demands on the prime minister, the search for a negotiated settlement in Vietnam, albeit in vain, clearly offered an attractive way of getting him off the hook.

BRITAIN AND THE NUCLEAR NON-PROLIFERATION TREATY

British governments of both political persuasions in the 1960s displayed a clear commitment to the non-proliferation of nuclear weapons. Despite powerful constraints on their freedom of manoeuvre on this issue, a consistent and determined stand enabled Britain to play a significant if not central role in the achievement of a Non-Proliferation Treaty (NPT) in 1968. If Wilson was obsessed with Vietnam, Macmillan in the earlier part of the decade was obsessed with the dangers of proliferation in relation both to Britain's nuclear status and, less self-interestedly, because it represented a potent threat to the stability of what was then called the 'central nuclear balance'. It was these fears that fuelled his final push for a test ban treaty in March 1963. Macmillan, the Chatham House Survey suggests, 'regarded the possibility of achieving a treaty banning further nuclear tests, with what he saw as its essential concomitant, a treaty banning the dissemination of nuclear weapons, as the crown of his political career' (Watt, 1977, p. 5). At British urging, the idea of a non-proliferation treaty was even put to the Russians by Averell Harriman at the tripartite Moscow meeting in July 1963, although it was not pursued. After the signing of the test ban, the British, and Foreign Secretary Lord Home in particular, continued to press his opposite numbers in Washington and Moscow on the subject of an NPT, but they, for different reasons, were less than responsive (Watt, 1977, pp. 19, 26).

The commitment to work with some urgency towards a non-proliferation agreement was taken up in 1964 by the Wilson government, which demonstrated its general commitment to arms control by the appointment of a Minister for Disarmament, Lord Chalfont, and by the setting up of the Arms Control and Disarmament Unit at the Foreign Office. While it was recognized that the government would have to work closely with the Americans on arms control, it was also felt that Britain could make a distinctive contribution. As Chalfont put it to the Commons, 'We in this country have an important and specific role to play: we have our own ideas for initiatives designed to break the stalemate that has . . . frozen serious disarmament negotiations for the past year or so' (*Hansard*, vol. 704, col. 575, 16 December 1964). A non-proliferation treaty had particular attractions for a Labour government, because it promised both to restrain any nuclear ambitions harboured by the Federal Republic of Germany (FRG) and to calm evident Soviet fears of a revanchist Germany.

A non-proliferation agreement was also attractive to the Wilson government to the extent that it would distract attention from its volte-face on the British deterrent. An electoral promise to 'renegotiate' the Nassau Agreement had resulted only in the decision to construct four Polaris submarines instead of the planned five. The effective continuation of the Polaris programme left Wilson exposed to the powerful anti-nuclear lobby in the Labour Party. Thus, as with Vietnam, domestic political imperatives underpinned the urgency of the British push for an NPT in 1964–65. Wilson was anxious to make progress, and to be seen to be making progress, to establish his arms control credentials.

The British contribution to the eventual NPT between 1964 and 1968 can best be considered in two broadly chronological stages: first, by looking at the British contribution in a NATO context to the abandonment of the proposed multilateral nuclear force (MLF) idea and its variants between 1964 and 1966, and then by reviewing British efforts in 1966–67 to persuade the non-nuclear representatives at the Eighteen-Nation Disarmament Conference (ENDC) in Geneva to support a draft treaty, the FRG and the developing countries in particular.

Without giving a detailed history of the complex MLF issue, it is sufficient to note that, in this context, the British and the Americans were on opposite sides of what became known as the 'nuclear-sharing' debate in NATO. While the Americans and especially the 'Europeanists' in the State Department were convinced that a multilateral nuclear force was a necessary structural innovation in the alliance to give the FRG and the other non-nuclear allies a greater say in nuclear decision-making, the British became increasingly concerned about the proposal. The problem as the Wilson government saw it was, as Freeman succinctly notes, 'how to prevent Germans getting close to the nuclear trigger. The MLF might have helped the Germans politically, but Britain was deeply suspicious of a device that appeared to encourage nuclear proliferation, albeit within the alliance' (Freeman, 1986, p. 169.

What follows in this section draws extensively on Freeman's study).

In inter-alliance terms, the problem was that the American pre-occupation with satisfying the assumed nuclear demands of its allies both diverted attention from and, more important, conflicted with its attempts to interest the Soviet Union in an NPT. The Russians had made it very clear as early as 1963 that they would not entertain a non-proliferation agreement unless the MLF proposal was dropped. Given an overriding commitment to an NPT, the objective of British diplomacy was clear – to stall the MLF negotiations and work towards their eventual abandonment – but getting there in concert with the Americans was extremely difficult. The Wilson government even devised an alternative 'nuclear-sharing' scheme at the end of 1964, the so-called Atlantic Nuclear Force, largely though not exclusively to give British representatives an alternative position from which to stall the MLF negotiations without coming into open conflict with Washington.

The British worked hard to focus American minds on the paramount importance of a non-proliferation agreement and specifically to secure American agreement to a British draft treaty, which would have ruled out a future European nuclear option. By the Summer of 1965, however, differences were so marked that the Americans were pressing the British, albeit in vain, not to table their draft treaty at the ENDC. In Geneva, where Anglo-American differences remained largely hidden, the British eventually accepted an American working draft, but insisted on a clause that retained a veto by an existing nuclear state over the control of nuclear weapons by any future European association of states. This helped to make the American draft marginally more acceptable to the Russians, but, during the early months of 1966, it became increasingly clear that serious negotiations would not be possible until NATO nuclear-sharing schemes in any form had been abandoned (Freeman, 1986, pp. 209–23).

It was not until the Summer of 1966, however, following a policy review in Washington in which the powerful MLF lobby was successfully challenged by the arms control community, that the Americans finally came round to the British view. The notion of nuclear sharing was quietly dropped in favour of alternative intra-alliance consultative arrangements, and there followed a number of important bilateral meetings between the superpowers in the

Autumn of 1966 at which an understanding was thrashed out with respect to the broad outlines of a treaty.

If the dropping of the MLF effectively resolved what might be called the East–West dimension of the NPT problem, there remained at the beginning of 1967 crucially important problems to be resolved of a West–West and a North–South variety. The superpowers and the British may have reached an agreement on a draft NPT, but it was not at all clear that the FRG would go along with it. The new Grand Coalition in Bonn had virtually given up hope of a multilateral nuclear force in NATO, but was raising a number of serious objections to the treaty. If the United States and Britain could not 'deliver' the Federal Republic, the Russians would not sign. It was as simple as that.

Thus, the British, with the Americans, played an important part through much of that year in coaxing and reassuring the Germans that the NPT would not be discriminatory in any way and that it would not damage either their security or their technological interests in civil nuclear technology. A particular problem of a more overtly political nature raised by the Germans related to the safeguards regime to be established by the treaty. It was proposed in the draft treaty that the International Atomic Energy Agency (IAEA) should be the body responsible, but the Germans were insisting that the European Atomic Energy Community (EURATOM) should also play a role. The British eventually proposed a safeguard arrangement that involved both bodies, and this paved the way to a compromise on this issue that was satisfactory to all parties (Freeman, 1986, pp. 247–50).

The developing countries, for their part, made clear their objections to what they regarded as a 'naked' NPT, in a joint memorandum to the ENDC in August 1966. They were as much concerned with what they called 'vertical' proliferation as the nuclear powers were with 'horizontal' proliferation, and were determined not only to extract security guarantees from the nuclear powers in return for their participation in a non-proliferation regime, but also to secure a commitment from the nuclear powers to take positive steps in the form of 'related measures' to curb the nuclear arms race.

There is some evidence that the British used their extensive links with the developing countries represented at ENDC to play a useful role in assuaging their concerns about the proposed NPT. Freeman, for example, concludes from his interview material that:

> Britain's Commonwealth connection and influence among many of the new nations gave her, to some degree, a special position from which to interpret their demands to the other nuclear countries. Many participants in the NPT process . . . emphasise the important role Britain played as an interlocutor between the two groups during the framing of the treaty (Freeman, 1986, p. 224; see also p. 295, fn. 78).

Other commentators such as Elizabeth Young, however, argue that British spokesmen were rather insensitive to the anxieties of the developing countries, insisting that their genuine fears were unfounded (Young, 1972, pp. 96, 98). What appears to have happened is that the British were taking up public and private positions, putting up a united front publicly with the superpowers in order to push the treaty through, but working rather hard behind the scenes to find solutions to the problems identified by India and the other developing countries at ENDC (see Freeman, 1986, p. 244).

It is important not to overstate the importance of the British role in the non-proliferation negotiations. Clearly, there would have been no treaty without the bilateral understanding worked out by the superpowers in the second half of 1966 and the more flexible line towards the NPT adopted by the Grand Coalition in Bonn with the supportive Willy Brandt as Foreign Minister. But, nevertheless and not for the first time, the singlemindedness and the persistence of the British from 1963 onwards was important. As noted above, the Americans were diverted from the issue until 1966 because of their efforts to appease FRG nuclear anxieties, and the Soviet leaders were not interested in an NPT until nuclear-sharing schemes in NATO had been abandoned. Even then, continuing Soviet suspicions of the FRG made their agreement to a treaty rather tentative. The British had a role to play here, because they, unlike the Americans, had some sympathy with or could at least understand Soviet fears. In a series of meetings with Soviet leaders between 1965 and 1967, British ministers endeavoured to allay those fears. Perhaps the most important of these meetings was Kosygin's 1967 visit to London, so ill-fated a trip with respect to Vietnam. The government attempted during this visit to persuade the Russians to agree to a treaty by the Summer and, as Freeman suggests:

> lobbying at this particular time was especially propitious because of the Soviet Union's tacit acceptance of German participation in the MacNamara Committee [later called the Nuclear Planning Group] in return for American agreement not to allow German participation in a Western nuclear strike force (Freeman, 1986, p. 236).

If the British contribution to the achievement of an NPT was more modest than it might have been given the domestic political demands, this is hardly surprising given also the constraints on independent action, which, if anything, were even more complex and onerous than those operating in the context of the Vietnam issue. Many of the things that appealed to the British about being at the heart of the non-proliferation negotiations and ultimately securing a treaty – demonstrating great power status, protecting nuclear status, being seen to be close to Washington, having influence with the Russians, simply being different from the other West Europeans – created problems for a power now evidently in decline and one, moreover, preparing a rather ignominious second application to join the EEC.

In the earlier NATO phase, the Wilson government would doubtless like to have lined up with the Russians more overtly and to have pressed the Americans more strongly to drop the MLF, but lukewarm relations at best combined with a growing dependence upon Washington ruled this out. (The 1962 Nassau Agreement, after all, can be interpreted as committing Britain to some form of nuclear-sharing scheme in return for Polaris.) Times were evidently changing fast and the contrast with the British role in the test ban negotiations provides a measure of these changes. In the non-proliferation talks, there was no scope for dramatic initiatives to push the negotiations along. There was no David Ormsby-Gore in Washington with the president's ear. The close relationship between Macmillan and Kennedy was scarcely replicated by Wilson and Johnson. Britain was now much more evidently the junior partner forced to line up with the Americans, in public at least, and to work patiently and rather self-effacingly towards a treaty.

Room for manoeuvre was further constrained by the requirement not to alienate the Europeans, if Britain's second application to the

EEC was to have any chance of success (Young, 1972, pp. 98–9). The NPT issue was a minefield in this context. Pushing too hard on the MLF, of course, would have alienated both the Americans and the Germans. Later efforts to persuade Bonn to accept the draft treaty were equally hazardous. The British could not appear to be too close to the Americans or too distant from European concerns. The role of EURATOM in the NPT was a particularly difficult issue to handle, to the extent that it was regarded in Europe as a test case of British 'Europeanness'. The Wilson government did its best to mollify its potential EEC partners by extensive and almost continuous inter-governmental exchanges during the latter stages of the NPT negotiations (for details, see Freeman, 1986, pp. 244–5).

Given this complex pattern of demands and constraints on British policy, it is difficult not to conclude that the British used their limited influence on this issue as effectively as possible. If a non-proliferation agreement was an even more blatantly self-interested objective than a test ban treaty, at least the pursuit of an NPT, albeit 'naked', was consistent with the British view of détente as a process in which each arms control agreement builds upon the achievement of the last and paves the way for the next. From this perspective, the British contribution to the NPT, unlike the abortive efforts to mediate in the Vietnam war, was a solid indication of a continuing contribution to East–West détente.

BRITAIN AND EUROPEAN SECURITY

Compared with the Vietnam and the non-proliferation issues, the British role in European security affairs in the late 1960s and early 1970s is less clearly focused as an issue for analytical purposes, certainly until attention became directed towards the serious prospect of a multilateral conference, the Conference on Security and Cooperation in Europe (CSCE) and the parallel Mutual and Balanced Force Reduction (MBFR) negotiations. Nevertheless, an attempt will be made to identify and evaluate the British contribution to the interrelated series of developments that effectively linked a process of détente in Europe to the wider East–West dimension.

Clearly, the major development in Europe in the late 1960s, with crucial implications for East–West détente, was the FRG's *Ostpolitik* associated with the Chancellorship of Willy Brandt. This long-awaited flexibility in FRG policy was welcomed by the Wilson government, both as a significant boost to the détente process and as a policy orientation that was very much in line with the thrust of British policy over a number of years. On his visit to Washington at the beginning of 1970, according to Henry Kissinger's account, Harold Wilson 'urged on Nixon the benefits of Brandt's policy as if no other approach was conceivable' (Kissinger, 1979, p. 416). At the end of that year, Denis Healey, now in opposition, told the House of Commons that the influence of *Ostpolitik* on the whole shape of European politics had been 'stupendous'. The European situation had been transformed in the previous twelve months by Brandt's courage and vision with treaties signed by the FRG with both the Soviet Union and Poland (the Moscow and Warsaw treaties). Brandt personally inspired confidence and trust, particularly with fellow social democrats such as Healey. The Conservatives, like the French, were more cautious if not suspicious of the direction of FRG policy, but they were no less forthcoming in their public support for *Ostpolitik* after they came to power in 1970.

If the British contribution to *Ostpolitik*, like that of the other European allies, could only be supportive and indirect, it was important that the West Germans had what Elisabeth Barker calls 'a secure and stable base' within NATO from which to pursue their Eastern initiatives. Here, the British could make a contribution by helping to create and sustain such an environment. Indeed, as will be discussed later, by helping NATO to recover from the shock of the French withdrawal from the integrated military command structure of the alliance in 1966, it can be argued that the British played an important role in creating the conditions necessary for *Ostpolitik* to succeed (see Barker, 1971, p. 261).

Also crucial to the success of *Ostpolitik*, however, given the concerns of the Americans and the other allies both about German intentions and Soviet good faith, was an East-West agreement on Berlin. As Stephen Kirby notes, 'Berlin [had] become the crucial test of the Soviet Union's sincerity in seeking political accommodation with the West' (Kirby, 1972, p. 78). Mindful of the need to maintain allied support for *Ostpolitik* and under some pressure from Kissinger, Brandt had agreed to defer the ratification of the Moscow and Warsaw treaties pending a successful outcome to the quadripartite Berlin talks, which had begun through ambassadorial channels in March 1970. As one of the occupying powers, Britain did have some opportunity here to play a more direct role in the détente process, though opinions vary on the significance of the British contribution. The Heath government, not surprisingly perhaps, later took the view that the 'British representative played a particularly distinguished part' in negotiating the final treaty in September 1971 (see Watt and Mayall, 1974, p. 897). Other commentators, however, suggest that the British, like the French, played a supporting role only. Garthoff, for example, following Kissinger's account, claims that the negotiations were 'finally concluded primarily through confidential American (White House)–Soviet negotiations, then funneled through the four-power ambassadorial forum' (Garthoff, 1985, p. 120). Bowker and Williams comment that the Kissinger account 'downplays the contribution that was also made by the British and French negotiators', but they give no indication of the substance of that contribution (Bowker and Williams, 1988, p. 89).

The Quadripartite Agreement, in turn, stimulated further progress both in terms of European and superpower détente. Ray Garthoff neatly conveys in an extended footnote the interrelatedness of all these developments:

> By design, the final protocol of the Berlin agreement, and the West German treaties with Poland and the USSR, went into effect on the same day, June 3rd 1972. This was just a few days after the first Nixon–Brezhnev summit meeting, at which it had been agreed to proceed in parallel with the CSCE and MBFR (Garthoff, 1985, p. 121, fn. 32).

One immediate effect of the Berlin agreement was to clear the way to a general acceptance of the German Democratic Republic (GDR) by the West. The British had made a point of eschewing any links with the GDR in deference to the *Ostpolitik* initiative, but they now led the way in pressing for recognition and the normalization of relations. Having been dismissive of the British role in the Berlin negotiations, even Donald Watt grudgingly admits that 'Britain did perhaps play a larger role in urging the recognition of East Germany.' Although, he insists, 'the main drive . . . came from Dr Kissinger' (Watt, 1984, pp. 153–4).

If the British contribution to the quadripartite agreement was essentially supportive, direct negotiations between the superpowers in 1972–73 promised even less for Britain. Surprisingly, though, Britain was given what might be called a 'cameo' role to play in the negotiation of the Prevention of Nuclear War Agreement (PNW), the centrepiece of the June 1973 US–Soviet summit meeting in

Washington. This agreement had a potentially explosive European security dimension, to the extent that the Soviet Union had been pressing the Americans prior to the Washington summit to sign an agreement banning the first use of nuclear weapons. If the United States had signed such an agreement, of course, this would have crucially undermined its nuclear guarantees to the European allies. Nevertheless, Kissinger was keen to build on the success of the Moscow summit and to maintain the momentum of superpower détente. In a move that demonstrated unusual sensitivity to growing allied concerns, Kissinger consulted the British as early as August 1972 and secured the services of a small FCO team, headed by Sir Thomas Brimelow, to assist his staff in redrafting the original Soviet PNW draft. According to Garthoff, this collaboration, with Brimelow apparently doing most of the redrafting in Washington, was very successful.

> The crux of the Kissinger–Brimelow counterdraft was to remove from the Soviet draft anything that smacked of a priority to American–Soviet relations over American–allied relations and that singled out nonuse of nuclear weapons, as contrasted with nonuse of force or threat of force with any weapon (Garthoff, 1985, p. 337; see also Kissinger, 1982, pp. 278–86).

With respect to a proposed European security conference, the British shared the concerns of their allies that persistent Soviet pressure for such a conference reflected an attempt to persuade the West to underwrite the political and territorial status quo in Europe or, more sinister, was a device to divide Western Europe from the United States. But, if certain preconditions could be met and these included an acceptable Berlin agreement, the British were prepared to give the idea serious consideration. At the NATO anniversary meeting in April 1969, Foreign Secretary Michael Stewart 'urged that the allies should not respond with a flat negative, though they must insist on the full representation of the United States and Canada at any conference' (quoted in Barker, 1971, p. 283). At the NATO Council meeting at the end of 1969, ministers were still sceptical, but, at least, they were now publicly discussing the possibility of a conference. For his part, Stewart suggested a study to see whether the issue could best be dealt with in a conference or by some other method. By the time of the next NATO Council in May 1970, British ideas had firmed up into a proposal for a 'standing commission', perhaps in a neutral city, charged with the task of 'identifying' a broad agenda of subjects for future negotiation, such as force reductions, freedom of human relations, and so on. In Stewart's view, this was a significant contribution to pushing along the idea of a European security conference and making it acceptable to as many parties in Europe as possible (see Watt and Mayall, 1971, pp. 343–4).

At an early stage in the actual proceedings of the CSCE, the Foreign Secretary Sir Alec Douglas-Home made it clear that the main British objective as far as the conference was concerned was to see that it achieved practical results (see F.C.O., 1977, p. 19). The British delegation made some important contributions to this end. With respect to so-called Basket One issues, for example, which dealt with rather general statements on military security and human rights, the British tabled the original paper on confidence-building measures and played an important role in resolving some of the final differences. Another specific contribution at a late stage in the negotiations related to helping resolve problems with the texts on human contacts and information in Basket Three (for details, see F.C.O., 1977, pp. 21–2, 166–8). Other British contributions, if less specific, were no less important. In close consultation with NATO and increasingly with European Community allies, the British government worked particularly hard on the Basket Two provisions relating to East–West economic cooperation, and pressed for binding commitments from the Eastern bloc on human rights.

BRITISH ATTITUDES TOWARDS DÉTENTE

What emerges from this analysis of British policy is the conclusion that, with the possible exception of the non-proliferation issue, Britain played a supporting role at best with respect to the important developments in East–West détente in the decade or so after the test ban treaty. It is now necessary for explanatory purposes to put a discussion of specific issues into a broader framework, starting with a review of British attitudes that underpinned policy. Did British attitudes towards détente undergo identifiable changes in this period? Do these attitudinal changes help to explain the more peripheral role played by Britain? If, as in the 1950s, détente can be defined from a British perspective as the normalization of diplomacy and the seeking of more open contacts between East and West, then there are clear indications in this period of continuing pro-détente attitudes. Shorn of the dramatic initiatives perhaps, there is much in the British approach to the issues discussed above that is reminiscent of earlier attitudes: the need to defuse potential East–West crises by attempting to mediate; the idea of détente as a continuing process; the need to make piecemeal progress by patient diplomacy; the importance of the broad agenda; the focus on practical issues, and so on.

In addition to the indications of British attitudes that emerge from the specific issues discussed above, great efforts were made through the 1960s to expand trade and other contacts with the Soviet Union and Eastern Europe. However, there appears to have been a greater emphasis in this period on establishing links with Eastern Europe than on developing contacts with the Soviet Union, with whom relations could best be described as 'patchy' (see Barker, 1971, pp. 263–70). The development of these commercial and cultural contacts with the Soviet bloc was interrupted by the Soviet invasion of Czechoslovakia in 1968, but the British reaction to this event is interesting in terms of continuing attitudes. Although there was great shock and outrage, the prime minister certainly was adamant that the invasion should not block the progress of détente. As Wilson commented to the House in November 1968, 'while we must increase vigilance, there must be no return to the cold war . . . we must keep before us the continuing objective of a détente' (F.C.O., 1977, p. 58). East–West accommodation was still regarded as desirable and necessary, not least because of the continuing dangers of a nuclear confrontation between the superpowers. When Nixon visited London in February 1969, he found Wilson vigorously pressing for détente. Kissinger recalls the prime minister arguing that the main purpose of NATO was no longer defence: its 'principal justification' was becoming the relaxation of tension. 'The Alliance had to move from security to such positive ends as "cooperation and peace".' Michael Stewart's related theme was that US–Soviet negotiations, particularly on strategic arms limitation, were 'essential' for the unity of the West (Kissinger, 1979, pp. 89, 94).

Expressions of support for the détente process continued after the Heath government came to power. As Michael Clarke notes, although relations with the Soviet Union were strained after 'the unprecedented expulsion of 105 Soviet personnel from Britain in 1971 . . . the visits of Andrei Gromyko to London in October 1971 and Alec Douglas-Home to Moscow in 1973 were marked by polite communiqués which were filled with expressions of hope that détente would be deepened in all areas' (Clarke, 1988, pp. 58–9). Despite this fulsome 'pro-détente' rhetoric, what is significant about the development of British attitudes by the early 1970s is signs of a growing ambivalence towards and even a certain scepticism about the détente process. This stemmed from a greater awareness of the risks and dangers associated with an accommodation between the superpowers than had been apparent in the 1950s. An interesting indication of this scepticism comes from Rab Butler's reflections upon his period as Foreign Secretary in the Home administration. Writing in 1971, he recalled what he referred to as 'the illusion of the bear hug [that] hung like a sort of mirage before various prime ministers' eyes'. In his view, both Churchill and Macmillan had been overly susceptible to the belief that East–West summitry was the key to international peace and security. Sir Alec Douglas-Home, on the other hand, did not suffer from the 'bear hug complex'. He took a more realistic view about the ideological bases of Soviet policy and was therefore more cautious in his dealings with Moscow and had more limited expectations of the benefits of détente (Butler, 1971, pp. 257–8).

It is difficult to date the beginnings of this more cautious, ambivalent attitude, but the opening of the Strategic Arms Limitation Talks (SALT) in 1969 seemed to focus British attention as well as that of the other European allies on the desirability, but also the potential dangers, of a superpower accord. With fears heightened by exclusion from these negotiations and with what was generally regarded by the NATO allies as inadequate consultation about their contents, the concern grew that the Americans might sign agreements that were detrimental to West European interests. The superpowers might, for example, reach an understanding to preserve each other's homelands in the event of a nuclear war, or a SALT agreement might also limit allied nuclear arsenals and options as well as those of the superpowers. Equally if not more disturbing was the possibility that a series of superpower agreements might dilute the American pledge to defend Western Europe. Understandably, the Americans found this ambivalence very frustrating. As Kissinger notes wryly, 'in times of rising tension, they [the Europeans] feared American rigidity; in times of relaxing tension, they dreaded a US–Soviet condominium' (Kissinger, 1979, p. 94).

By 1970–71, nevertheless, the tone of British ministers' speeches on East–West relations was markedly different. While not exactly wanting to hold back the process of détente, they were much more aware of possible problems in terms of the potential destabilization of the structure of European security. An illustrative example is a speech the Defence Secretary Lord Carrington made to the Lords in November 1971. Although he welcomed the progress that had been made on East–West relations (the Berlin agreement had recently been signed), he was still loath to press too hard for a European security conference:

> I beg that we should be careful not to neglect the NATO Alliance . . . It has become a truism to say that NATO stands for the twin concepts of defence and détente [but] we must not fall into the trap of striving for détente and forgetting about defence. For logically these two things are complementary' (Watt and Mayall, 1973, p. 959).

There was a sense in which the Heath government was beginning to feel that détente was getting rather out of hand. Carrington himself later referred to this period as one of 'competitive détente' with the West engaged in an 'undignified scramble for Eastern markets' (Carrington, 1983, p. 152). The Soviet Union and the Eastern bloc as a whole were being asked to make little if any concessions as far as their domestic arrangements were concerned, in order to reap the benefits of détente.

By 1972, this growing British scepticism towards the process of East–West détente had become focused on the CSCE. Though they had limited expectations about these negotiations, the British were determined that the Soviet bloc should be forced to make concessions with regard to human rights and other basic liberal freedoms. This goal was related to a new dimension to the British approach to détente – implicit in the attempts to expand contacts with East European countries in the 1960s – which emphasized what might be called 'quality of life' objectives (Dougherty, 1975, p. 89). A number of speeches by British leaders in a CSCE context stressed that détente must have a practical output in terms of producing beneficial changes in the lives of ordinary people in the Soviet bloc. In this sense, détente was being evaluated less in terms of intergovernmental agreements and more in terms of the quality of interpersonal contacts both within and between the blocs.

At the opening of the first stage of the CSCE in Helsinki in July 1973, Foreign Secretary Sir Alec Douglas-Home argued that it was time 'to move from general declarations of principle to their application to the lives of ordinary people'. 'Politics', he continued, 'is essentially about people [who] will not thank us or congratulate us for adding more solemn declarations to the world's archives . . . they will want to know whether their lives will be affected for the better by our efforts.' Two years later, at the opening of the final stage of the conference, Prime Minister Harold Wilson reiterated the point that 'détente means little if it is not reflected in the daily lives of our peoples . . . there is no reason why, in 1975, Europeans should not be allowed to marry whom they want, hear and read what they want, travel abroad when and where they want, meet whom they want' (F.C.O., 1977, pp. 158, 219). By 1975–76, a sceptical approach had been reinforced by the apparent paucity of tangible benefits that had resulted from the Helsinki process and the 'era of negotiation' as a whole.

If an ambivalent British approach to détente in the 1970s is not inconsistent with the 'balanced' approach to defence and détente noted in the 1950s, this growing scepticism, reinforced by a sharpened awareness of the associated risks and dangers, produced an underlying set of attitudes during this period that weighted the defence rather than the détente side of the balance. Even before the détente negotiations of the 1970s began in earnest, the active British diplomacy to limit the damage done to NATO by the French withdrawal from the military organization and the British role in the establishment and development of the Eurogroup, were clear indications that a concern to maintain NATO cohesion and solidarity was beginning to have a higher priority in British foreign and defence policy than pressing for an East–West accommodation.

Allied reaction to De Gaulle's announcement about the French withdrawal at the end of February 1966 was rather tentative. The Americans in particular were divided about how to respond. While the Pentagon took a fairly relaxed view about the military significance of the prospective loss of French territory, the State Department, steeled by Under Secretary of State George Ball's blunt views, favoured a tough line with De Gaulle. There was an evident lack of leadership within the alliance at this crucial time until the British stepped into the breach. Foreign Secretary Michael Stewart struck the right note in a speech he gave to the Western European Union on 15 March. Although he stressed the seriousness of the French action, he avoided engaging in a diatribe. He made it clear that a 'calm and dignified' approach to the problem was accompanied by a firm British commitment to continue with NATO and the integrated military system (see Harrison, 1981, pp. 145–7).

Meanwhile, the fourteen NATO Permanent Representatives were endeavouring to work out a common response. That they were able to publish an important declaration on 18 March, to the effect that all the other allies would continue to operate under the terms of the 1949 Treaty, owed much to the work of Minister of State George Thompson, who visited many of the NATO capitals during this period, and to Evelyn Shuckburgh, the British Permanent Representative, who handled the day-to-day negotiations (Gore-Booth, 1974, pp. 340–3). This declaration was confirmed at the NATO Council meeting in June and the crisis in the alliance was well on the way to being managed successfully, thanks largely to quiet but decisive British diplomacy at a critical time. As Harrison comments, 'British policy was characterized by a practical concern for keeping NATO together' and, moreover, it was Foreign Secretary Michael Stewart who 'formulated the first proposals for transferring the entire Alliance machinery out of France and streamlining it in the process' (Harrison, 1981, p. 147).

A continuing concern with NATO cohesion was also reflected in the leading role played by Britain in the establishment from 1968 onwards of a distinct European defence identity within NATO, based upon the so-called Eurogroup. Initiated by Defence Secretary Denis Healey as a forum for ministerial discussion, the Eurogroup spawned a number of subgroups in the early 1970s, largely under the auspices of Healey's successor, Lord Carrington, and Helmut Schmidt, his opposite number in Bonn, which dealt with particular areas of practical cooperation. Britain also played a leading role in the creation of the Independent European Programme Group (IEPG) in 1976. This forum, which, significantly, included the French, was designed to generate greater European defence cooperation and to facilitate a genuine 'two-way street' in defence technology with the United States (see Heyhoe, 1976/77).

While these institutional developments were intended to improve the military effectiveness of the alliance, they were also a political response to the concerns noted earlier about the relative weakness of the 'European pillar' of NATO at a time when the United States was engaged in bilateral strategic arms talks with the Soviet Union. It was important to ensure that the European members of the alliance could maximize their influence on these negotiations by consulting together on a regular basis and speaking with a common voice. Thus, as John Baylis comments, Britain 'found herself increasingly in common accord with other Eurogroup states in a collective effort to ensure that the United States did not sacrifice Europe's strategic interests in its search for accommodation with the Soviet Union' (Baylis, 1984, p. 167).

There are clear indications, therefore, that British attitudes towards détente did undergo significant changes towards the end of the 1960s. While there was a continuing desire to support the détente process in a variety of ways, there was a growing concern about the less desirable consequences of an East–West accommodation. This produced a policy orientation that emphasized the importance of reinforcing the bases of British security in a NATO context rather than promoting East–West détente. To some extent, therefore, a more sceptical view of détente does help to explain the more peripheral British role in the détente process during this period. This caution was further underscored in more general terms by an apparent erosion of confidence in Britain's ability to influence international events. Britain was the exception to the general regeneration of West European states in political and economic terms during this period and the resultant mood meant, as Michael Smith notes, that 'the self-confidence of the early postwar period had given way to the stagnation and uncertainty of the 1960s' (Smith, 1984, p. 57). This apparent lack of confidence came as a surprise to Henry Kissinger at the end of the 1960s:

> Britain still possessed the experience and intellectual resources of a great power . . . But with every passing year [British leaders] acted less as if their decisions mattered. They offered advice, usually sage; they rarely sought to embody it in a policy of their own. British statesmen were content to act as honored consultants to our deliberations (Kissinger, 1979, p. 421).

This mood can also be explained, however, in terms of structural changes to which we now turn to throw additional light upon British détente policy during this period.

BRITISH POLICY AND STRUCTURAL CHANGES

As implied in earlier sections, it was apparent by the early 1970s that Britain had been 'marginalized' as far as the détente process and, indeed, as far as East–West relations as a whole were concerned (Williams, 1986, p. 225). If the abortive attempts to mediate in the Vietnam war illustrated the limits of British influence in rather stark terms and raised fundamental questions about the 'special' nature of Anglo-American relations, at least Britain's status as a nuclear weapons power provided a 'seat at the top table' as far as the non-proliferation negotiations were concerned. But the signing of the NPT in 1968 became another marker in the decline of British influence. As Watt explains:

> its signature transferred the search for balance . . . from the nuclear explosives to the long range delivery systems. With the opening of the Strategic Arms Limitation Talks, Britain, having abandoned its own missile programme in 1958–9 . . . ceased to have any *locus standi* (Watt, 1984, p. 153).

As if to make that point, the superpowers chose the very day that the NPT was signed to announce that they were embarking on bilateral negotiations to limit strategic forces.

If the superpowers no longer needed an intermediary, there was little contribution that Britain could make to détente in Europe. In effect, Britain's distinctive role within the alliance had been usurped by the Federal Republic who, consciously or not, followed the British and the more recent French example, by exploiting the potential of a high-profile East–West role. The success of this policy made it only too evident that the British, like the French, no longer had the capabilities or the resources to carry off the ambitious role of mediator between East and West. As Harrison comments, 'détente depended much more on the US and West Germany, the two powers who could offer concrete and valuable concessions to the Soviet Union' (Harrison, 1981, p. 70).

While the British were very supportive of *Ostpolitik*, they could not be unaware that this policy had less desirable structural implications for British influence. In particular, a successful *Ostpolitik* threatened significantly to reduce British influence in Moscow. A normalization of FRG–Soviet relations inevitably reduced Soviet fears of a revanchist Germany. To the extent that Moscow had hitherto looked to the British and the French to restrain the Germans, their value was consequently reduced. Not surprisingly, given growing FRG influence in both European and East–West politics, the British and the French were keen to assert their rights to be involved in the Berlin negotiations. If they were able to play a limited role only in these negotiations, there were also limits to how far the British and, indeed, the West Europeans collectively could push their demands in the multilateral CSCE negotiations, as Dougherty illustrates:

> At Helsinki and Geneva, British diplomats and their West European colleagues pressed harder than the US Department of State for political change in the East, especially on human rights, as a sign of good faith. But in the final analysis, the British realised that there were definite limits to how far the West Europeans could go in demanding conditions for a Helsinki Accord once the superpowers decided that the time had come to terminate the conference (Dougherty, 1975, p. 88).

Clearly there was now little to be gained in terms of Britain's international status or, indeed, in terms of the reputations of Britain's leaders from even attempting to play a high-profile East–West role, and this reinforced a preoccupation during this period with Europe and specifically with entry to the EEC. Whatever the other powerful arguments that propelled Britain towards Europe, the idea of the Community as a vehicle through which to wield political influence became an increasingly attractive one the more marginalized Britain became as an actor in East–West relations. The concern to be seen to be a 'good European', however, also provided an additional set of constraints on independent action in the East–West arena, as noted above in the context of the NPT issue. There was some attempt to argue that membership of the Community would actually strengthen Britain's ability to influence East–West détente, but this was to turn a perceived necessity into a virtue.

Having objected to the first Macmillan application to join the EEC in 1961 on the grounds that membership would restrict Britain's freedom of action to promote East–West détente, Wilson proceeded to argue in 1966–67 that British entry would positively benefit the détente process. In April 1967, for example, he told the Parliamentary Labour Party that:

> our purpose is to make a reality of the unity of Western Europe. But we know this will be an empty achievement unless it leads first to an easing of tension and then to an honourable and lasting settlement of the outstanding problems that still divide Europe . . . I am convinced that if Britain is a member of a

united European community our chances of achieving this will be immeasurably greater (see Barker, 1971, p. 264).

The following month, George Brown too was telling the House that 'the success of this growing détente would be immeasurably greater if Britain were a member of a united European Economic Community' (see Barker, 1971, p. 265).

The fact was that the priority of securing membership of the EEC, together with the concerns about the direction of American policy discussed earlier, meant that West–West relations were beginning to overshadow East–West relations for British policy-makers. The need to adapt to changing structural factors was reinforced by the second French veto of Britain's application in November 1967. The Europeanization of British foreign and defence policy was apparent thereafter in the promotion of an effective 'European pillar' in NATO and was a particular feature of Britain's role in the CSCE negotiations, where the harmonization of British policy with that of its European partners through the political cooperation mechanism was a major innovation in the policy process (see Clarke, 1985). In a Commons debate on European security in December 1972, Foreign Office Minister Anthony Royle made a point of noting that all the positions that British representatives would take up at CSCE had been discussed exhaustively both within NATO and the EEC:

It would be impossible to exaggerate the value of the work undertaken in [NATO], but it may not be generally realised what a high degree of harmonization of positions has been achieved in recent months within the EC, through the medium of the D'Avignon Committee (Watt and Mayall, 1974, p. 890 ff).

Britain had to become used to being a 'team' player with respect to East–West relations in order to achieve other objectives and, inevitably, this further limited the opportunities to play a significant independent role.

THE DOMESTIC POLITICAL CONTEXT

The argument that British détente policy was essentially a function of policy-makers attempting to adapt – relatively successfully in this period – to structural changes in the international political and economic environment is a powerful one, particularly in the period from 1969 onwards as Britain became evidently marginalized in the détente process. However, there is also some substance to the domestic imperatives hypothesis, particularly in the earlier part of this period. As noted in relation to Vietnam and the NPT issue, there were powerful lobbies active on the left wing of the Labour Party, hostile both to American policy in Vietnam and to nuclear weapons, who were pressing for particular policy responses. On both issues, Wilson faced a troublesome but influential section of the Labour Party that he ignored at his peril. Thus, domestic political imperatives constituted a powerful stimulus for a Labour government to work towards East–West conciliation.

If domestic imperatives become a less convincing explanation later on in this period, this was partly because of changing public perceptions. As the public began to see East–West détente as a concrete reality in the form of more and more agreements both bilateral and multilateral across the East–West divide, there appears to have been less pressure on British governments to push for détente. But this does not mean that domestic demands were insignificant after 1969. With reference to a European security conference, for example, the Heath government came under persistent pressure from the Labour opposition in 1971–72 to press more strongly for a security conference. In January 1972, for example, Lord Brockway asked whether the House could 'now have an assurance of the wholehearted support of HMG for this project as distinct from the lukewarmness, and sometimes even the obstruction of our government in association with the American Government during the last four years'. In May, Russell Kerr asked whether the minister was

> aware that, as a result of the stalling of the last twelve to eighteen months, HMG have a most regrettable reputation throughout Europe for dragging the chains on this issue. Will he try to inject some imagination into his colleagues to see that we do not have to carry this reputation around Europe for much longer?

By the end of 1972, the complaints finally produced the major speech on East–West relations by Foreign Office Minister Anthony Royle, referred to above, in which he felt compelled to justify government policy at some length and to some effect (see Watt and Mayall, 1974, pp. 22–3, 340, 890–6).

In terms of the broader domestic context, it is worth noting that the development of more sceptical British attitudes towards détente was also a function, in part at least, of the domestic political salience of the issue. The more Britain was marginalized as a key actor in East–West relations, the less direct interest political leaders appeared to take in the détente process. East–West policy, such as it was, appears to have been framed more and more by the naturally cautious views of the bureaucrats in the Foreign Office and elsewhere, who were responsible for the day-to-day handling of negotiations in the various forums concerned. And, as Williams notes, there was still a 'somewhat sceptical attitude towards the Soviet Union in the higher levels of the Foreign Office where détente was seen as a Soviet tactic rather than as a fundamental change in Soviet objectives or ambitions' (Williams, 1986, p. 226). Moreover, although we would not want to push this point too far because, as we have seen, there was a high degree of bipartisan consensus on the essence of the British approach to détente, bureaucratic caution chimed in well with Conservative views also. The Conservatives were ideologically sceptical of doing deals with the Soviet Union, whereas, for the Labour Party, with its 'Left can talk to Left' tradition, the pursuit of détente with the East fitted in more comfortably with its basic ideological orientation.

Chapter 7

Britain, the new cold war and détente

After the return of the Labour Party to power in 1974, the essential outlines of British policy towards the Soviet bloc remained unchanged. Both the Wilson and the Callaghan governments sought to play a constructive role in East–West relations – Wilson made his much publicized trip to Moscow in 1975, for example, where he agreed a £1 billion trade and credits package – but it was becoming increasingly clear even then that the détente process was in serious trouble. As criticism of that process mounted in the West and the rhetoric about a 'new' or 'second' cold war began to be voiced by a rising New Right on both sides of the Atlantic, there was even less opportunity for Britain to play a significant détente role in the second half of the 1970s than there had been in the first. Indeed, the profound ambivalence towards the whole process of East–West détente, which had been a feature of the British approach since the beginning of that decade, was if anything more marked after 1974. The potential costs rather than the benefits of East–West détente appeared to exercise the British the more and they dictated a very cautious approach.

When, for example, President Carter sought to make human rights the centrepiece of his foreign policy in 1977–78, the British became concerned that such high-profile pressure on the Soviet system could provoke confrontation rather than promote cooperation. Thus, there was a clear preference for a low-key, soft approach on human rights at the Conference on Security and Cooperation in Europe (CSCE) Review Conference in Belgrade. As Williams comments, the British fear was that 'too much emphasis on change in Eastern Europe might not only be counterproductive in terms of its purposes, but could spill over and obstruct or undermine the moves towards accommodation that were being made at the state level'. The Callaghan government was prepared to press the Soviet Union to uphold the Final Act commitments, but was 'sensitive to the dangers of pressing too hard and too publicly. The CSCE process had turned into a weapon that could be used by the West; but it was . . . one which had to be used with care and discrimination' (Williams, 1986, pp. 227–8, 235).

During the same period, the British role in the Comprehensive Test Ban (CTB) talks, which began in June 1977, provides an interesting illustration of both the extent to which Britain had been marginalized in the détente process and also the tough line that the British were now taking on détente. By 1979, according to Ray Garthoff's account, the British were taking an even harder line than the Americans on the issue of verification. Having attempted unsuccessfully to persuade the British to increase the number of on-site seismic stations they would be prepared to accept, Carter apparently proposed to Brezhnev at the Vienna summit in June that they should proceed with a CTB without Britain if necessary (Garthoff, 1985, pp. 757–8, fn. 14). It should be noted, however, that both superpowers had already decided that a strategic arms agreement should take priority over securing a comprehensive test ban treaty.

The tone of speeches by Labour ministers in the mid-1970s shows very clearly the continuing British commitment to détente but also, with Western eyes focusing anxiously on Soviet involvement in Southern Africa, the determination to balance contributions to that process by ensuring that the West's ability to deter the Soviet Union was undiminished. A speech in January 1976 by the then Foreign Secretary James Callaghan, for example, expressed his concern that:

> in the last few years the Soviet Union has added to its existing numerical advantage over NATO in manpower and conventional weapons in Central Europe, an approximate strategic nuclear parity with the United States in addition to rapidly expanding its navy and improving its airforce and missile system (F.C.O., 1977, p. 291).

His conclusion was that 'as long as the Soviet Union and her allies devote so much of their resources to armaments, détente must also be matched by an adequate defence capability that is sufficient to deter'. The contribution of Roy Hattersley to a Commons debate on East–West relations the following month was even more hawkish.

Though he was concerned in his speech to defend détente in general and the Helsinki Accords in particular, he warned the House that 'the policy of détente has to be pursued with the greatest possible caution. It can proceed only on the secure foundation of a strong and effective Western Alliance' (F.C.O., 1977, p. 305).

It is of interest that Hattersley went on to note the absence of any 'disagreement between the two Front Benches' on this balanced approach to détente. Labour spokesmen at this time were not only reacting to a worsening climate of East–West relations after Helsinki, but they were also responding to attempts by the Conservatives, and their new leader Margaret Thatcher in particular, to suggest that the Wilson government was rather too keen on promoting close links with the Soviet Union and was bent on pursuing East–West détente with something less than 'the greatest possible caution'. Although Mrs Thatcher made few statements on East–West relations in opposition, two speeches she did make not only set out her position on détente very clearly but also established the beginnings of an international reputation on this issue, which would be very significant after she became prime minister in 1979.

She was not against détente, she told Chelsea Conservatives in July 1975, just before the signing of the Helsinki Accords. Indeed,

> détente sounds a fine word. And to the extent that there has really been a relaxation in international tension, it is a fine thing. But the fact remains that throughout this decade of détente, the armed forces of the Soviet Union have increased, are increasing and show no signs of diminishing (quoted in Young, 1990, p. 170).

Tutored by the historian Robert Conquest, a trenchant critic of détente during this period, Mrs Thatcher was already firmly of the New Right view that détente was not merely an illusion but a dangerous Soviet ploy to enable Moscow to extend its influence over the West. The assumption that this tactic was working implied that it was no longer appropriate to pursue a balanced policy of détente and defence. It was necessary to pour all the resources of government into increasing defence expenditure to match the growing Soviet threat. Even expanding trade credits to Moscow, as Wilson had done in 1975, was dangerous, because it would enable the Soviet government to divert even more resources to its military machine. A second speech, delivered in January 1976, was a more explicit anti-Soviet diatribe which contained, in Hugo Young's words, 'unfashionably strong language about Soviet iniquities'. So strong was the language, indeed, that it provoked an official protest from the Soviet ambassador and, more important, earned Mrs Thatcher the famous sobriquet of the 'Iron Lady' from Tass (Young, 1990, p. 170).

If the scene was set for a radical break from the traditional British approach to détente after Mrs Thatcher came to power, it is useful for contextual purposes to conclude this section by reviewing a major speech by Foreign Secretary David Owen delivered in March 1977 to the Diplomatic and Commonwealth Writers' Association in London. This speech is important because it contained a strong defence of the British approach at a time when there was growing scepticism about the benefits of détente both at home and abroad. In a deliberate attempt to scale down expectations of what détente could achieve, Owen talked about what he called the 'Jekyll and Hyde nature of détente – competition on the one hand, cooperation on the other'. Détente cannot remove the areas of competition, he stressed; they are endemic to the continuing bipolar struggle between East and West and the global nature of Soviet power. But what détente can and must do is to expand the areas of cooperation and gradually contract the areas of competition.

Again, détente is seen as a historical process that began in the early 1950s (interestingly, from a British perspective, the Foreign Secretary specifically cites 1953 as the starting date) but, Owen argued, we are still 'witnessing the early stages of this process, not its culmination. Détente has solved some of the most urgent and obvious problems in East/West relations and it has established a basic framework for the solution of those which remain. But there is still a long way to go.' The first and 'easier' stage of détente – managing the security politics relationship between the superpowers and stabilizing East–West relations – was over. But, the Foreign Secretary warned his audience, don't expect the momentum of the early 1970s to be maintained, because the next stage of détente involves issues 'which are more complex, more contentious and far more intractable . . . [because they] . . . encroach on fundamental attitudes, on human behaviour, and the issues go to the heart of each side's perception of itself and its interest'. Thus, while the Helsinki Final Act is deliberately located by Owen within a long-term framework as far as the détente process is concerned, it is regarded, nevertheless, as crucially important because it provided 'a charter and code of behaviour for what we hope will in time become a more normal and open relationship between both governments and peoples in East and West. It reflects détente's highest aspirations.'

Significantly, 'normal and open' continued to include the widest possible agenda for détente – Owen refers to détente as 'an immensely complex process, comprising innumerable strands and relationships on different levels: political dialogue, commercial and technological exchange, cultural contacts, ideological debate and military vigilance'. Progress towards détente is to be measured in practical terms rather than in terms of political posturing. In language that had now become familiar from British leaders in the 1970s, Owen asserts that progress towards détente 'cannot simply be a matter of inter-state relations, but has to be reflected in people's daily lives'. The key to the British approach, however – and this underpins Owen's speech – is caution, limited expectations and, centrally, maintaining a 'balance . . . between the elements of confrontation and cooperation'. This explains the guarded approach to human rights noted at the beginning of this chapter. The Callaghan government, Owen suggests, was more concerned to 'help provide and sustain the framework of peace and security within which human rights can be discussed, championed and enlarged' than to promote high profile 'campaigns of denunciation' that would provide little practical assistance to people in the Soviet bloc and which might well provoke a confrontational response (F.C.O., 1977, pp. 331–40).

THE FIRST THATCHER GOVERNMENT AND THE NEW COLD WAR

Little changed in terms of the substance or the intensity of British East–West policy during the period of the first Thatcher government from 1979 to 1983, but, in the context of an ever worsening climate of East–West relations, a great deal changed as far as the tone was concerned. Taking some pride in her 'Iron Lady' label, the new prime minister was openly critical of a détente with the Soviet Union. Her instincts told her that the appropriate response to the expansion of Soviet power was to increase vigilance, spend more on defence and move closer to the Americans, who ultimately guaranteed British security. Thus, during her first year in office, decisions to purchase the Trident missile system from the United States, to support the NATO decision to increase defence spending by 3 per cent per annum and to endorse the 'dual track' approach to the deployment of Cruise and Pershing 2 missiles, all contributed to an 'image of strength' as far as foreign and defence policy was concerned (Clarke, 1988, p. 62).

When the Soviet Union invaded Afghanistan at the end of 1979, an act which can only have served to confirm the prime minister's anti-Soviet convictions, Mrs Thatcher, as Smith notes, was 'among the first and the most enthusiastic supporters of President Carter's firm stand against the Soviet invasion' (M. Smith, 1988, p. 15). In March 1980, the government condemned the invasion in a House of Commons motion and called on British competitors to boycott the forthcoming Olympic Games in Moscow. When the Chairman of the British Olympic Committee refused to support this call, Mrs Thatcher made her displeasure very clear. Similarly, after the imposition of martial law in Poland at the end of 1981, American demands for sanctions against both the Soviet and Polish governments again evoked a strong, supportive response from the prime minister.

The impression that the Thatcher era would indeed mark a radical break from the balanced approach to détente favoured by previous British governments was further strengthened by the prime minister's preoccupation with human rights violations in the Soviet bloc and also, in broader terms, by her apparent impatience with the whole process of diplomacy during her first period in office. As noted earlier, there had been a reluctance in the late 1970s to push too hard on human rights for fear that this would provoke a hostile and counterproductive reaction from the East. At the second CSCE review conference in Madrid, however, the British delegation was instructed 'from a very high level' to press as hard as possible on human rights issues (see Young and Sloman, 1986, p. 117). For Mrs Thatcher, armed with her readings of Solzhenitsyn if little else, violations of human rights were clearly a powerful symbol of the wickedness of communist regimes.

A hostile approach to détente with the Soviet Union was not only consistent with Mrs Thatcher's ideological convictions, but also with her approach to foreign policy in general and diplomacy in particular. It was evident from her first year or two in office that she saw foreign policy almost wholly in terms of a handful of basic principles, chief among which was anti-communism, and that she was impatient at best with the 'give and take' nature of diplomacy and indeed with diplomats who, in her view, were far too predisposed towards compromise on issues she regarded as matters of principle. 'Détente', moreover, would have been precisely one of those 'frenchified' words that would have raised all her hackles about the pretentious intellectual language of the Foreign and Commonwealth Office (FCO) (see Young, 1990, in particular, pp. 175, 248, 381, 408; Clarke, 1988, p. 61). What détente meant in plain English, she must have thought, was perilously close to 'doing deals with the Devil'. After all, in her 1983 reformulation of Reagan's 'evil empire' thesis, Mrs Thatcher did describe the Soviet Union as 'a modern version of the early tyrannies of history – its creed barren of conscience, immune to promptings of good and evil' (quoted in Jenkins, 1987, p. 288).

It would not be accurate, however, to equate the uncompromising principles and the steely rhetoric of the 'Iron Lady' with the substance of British policy on East–West relations during the first Thatcher period. There was a marked gap between the declaratory posturing, which was consistently tough and unyielding, and the substantive action, which was remarkably restrained. On Afghanistan, for example, the specific demands posed by American policy in relation to economic and diplomatic sanctions against the Soviet Union 'met with a distinctly muted British response' (see M. Smith, 1988, p. 15). Similarly, the substance of the reaction to the imposition of martial law in Poland, in terms of the rather mild package of sanctions announced by the government in February 1982, 'belied the strength of the political declarations which surrounded it' (Clarke, 1988, p. 66).

There was more than a hint of pragmatism too in the British response to the deliberate American inclusion of a major European contract to build a gas pipeline from Siberia to the Federal German border in their list of sanctions against the Soviet Union. Gesture politics was one thing but, as Mrs Thatcher made quite clear to the American Secretary of State Alexander Haig at the beginning of 1982, she was not prepared to see British and other European firms sustain losses on the massive scale that would have resulted from a retrospective embargo on the pipeline project (Young, 1990, pp. 255–7). Finally, on the Cruise missile issue, which in many respects dominated the foreign and defence policy agenda in Mrs Thatcher's first term, the gap between rhetoric and action is particularly instructive with respect to British policy. While the prime minister was concerned to demonstrate the strength of the British commitment to NATO policy on Cruise deployment, there was continuous pressure on Washington to implement the other half of the dual track policy. Indeed, as Smith again notes, there were 'open expressions of British concern' in 1982 about the repeated refusal of the Americans to respond positively to Soviet offers to negotiate on intermediate-range nuclear systems (M. Smith, 1988, p. 15).

If the substance of British policy in this period was marked by an essential continuity despite the dramatic change of tone, how significant was the British contribution to East–West relations during the first Thatcher period? The prime minister's strident anti-communism certainly made a contribution to the worsening atmosphere in East–West relations in the late 1970s and early 1980s, but the British contribution was essentially a reaction to the parlous state of East–West relations. The Thatcher government – and the prime minister in particular – was ideologically in tune with a second cold war, but Britain was in no sense an initiator, still less an architect, of Western policy in the way that the Attlee government had been with respect to the first cold war in the late 1940s.

THE SECOND THATCHER GOVERNMENT AND DÉTENTE

What is interesting about the second Thatcher period in this context is the more intensive and the more significant role played by Britain in East–West relations. How radical the change actually was in policy terms, given the analysis offered in the last section, however, needs some discussion here. Certainly, the policy of the Thatcher government towards the Soviet bloc after the Conservative victory in June 1983 appeared to represent a dramatic volte-face, given the uncompromising principles that had underpinned policy in the 1979–83 period. Following a major review of East–West policy in the Summer, the new Thatcher government launched its version of *Ostpolitik*. This began with a visit by Foreign Secretary Sir Geoffrey Howe to Hungary in September, and a successful meeting in the new year with his Soviet opposite number Gromyko in Stockholm, followed by Mrs Thatcher's visit to Hungary in February 1984, her first to a Soviet-bloc state. A sustained and remarkably successful attempt to improve the climate of East–West relations lasted throughout the second Thatcher period.

What appeared to be a new direction in British policy certainly represented a change of approach for the prime minister herself, something which, unusually, Mrs Thatcher admitted in an interview for the *New York Times* in January 1984. For a prime minister who had shown herself to be less than sympathetic to the virtues of patient negotiation, she now sounded positively Churchillian in a 1950s' rather than a 1940s' sense. 'In a dangerous world', she told the *New York Times*,

> the thing is not whether you agree with the other very powerful bloc's political views. The important thing is that you simply must make an effort the more to understand one another . . . We've got to do more talking' (*New York Times*, 22 January 1984; Young, 1990, pp. 389–90).

On her visit to Hungary the following month, Mrs Thatcher began to assert that countries with different social systems must find a way of living together and to stress the need for the superpowers to return to the negotiating table as soon as possible. What had happened to persuade the Iron Lady to modify her views or at least to curb the hostile rhetoric? The most obvious line here is to suggest that the prime minister, like her Conservative predecessors Churchill and Macmillan, spotted an opportunity in 1983 to gain some personal kudos and national prestige from attempting to initiate a more conciliatory period in East–West relations. The situational context in both domestic and international terms was certainly propitious for such a move.

Not only had Mrs Thatcher won a convincing second victory at the polls, but that election had, of course, been preceded the previous year by her even more famous victory in the Falklands. These successes produced a buoyant, confident prime minister, who appeared keen to establish in her second term a claim to be regarded as an international stateswoman of the first rank. An influential East–West role – not for the first time – fitted the bill perfectly. Pressing for a renewed dialogue with the East, moreover, had the added bonus in domestic political terms of helping to neutralize the potent anti-nuclear movement that had re-emerged in the wake of the Cruise/Pershing debate (the domestic context is considered in more detail in a later section). The evident determination in Washington to continue a policy of confrontation with the Soviet Union and the growing concern in Western Europe about the negative consequences of an impasse in East–West relations were the important international components of a situation that presented the opportunity for a more flexible approach.

What might be called 'pragmatic opportunism' provides an attractive explanation of this new direction in British policy, but it understates the continuing impact of the traditional British concern to balance the diplomatic and the military elements of Western policy towards the East. Not for the first time, the 'guardian' of this tradition was the Foreign Office (FCO) and its ministerial representatives, past as well as present. Two months before the 1983 election, for example, former Foreign Secretary Lord Carrington used the platform provided by the Annual Alastair Buchan Memorial Lecture in London to remind his audience of the advantages of the British approach.

In his speech Carrington not only criticized what he called 'megaphone diplomacy' but also a 'crude, one-dimensional moralism' in dealings with the East. Carrington, it should be remembered, was commenting on NATO policy as a whole, but, as a barely coded critique of the Iron Lady posture of the prime minister, the point was not lost on a domestic audience. What was being neglected, Carrington argued, was the 'broader political dimension of East–West relations'. What was needed was a return to a more balanced policy – a 'sweet and sour' approach as he called it – with the emphasis now on the 'sweet', stressing the importance of 'our own tradition . . . the peaceful resolution of potential conflict through energetic and forceful dialogue' (Carrington, 1983, pp. 151–2). Carrington's speech is significant as another powerful restatement of the traditional British approach to East–West relations, but it was even more important politically at this time because he continued to have influence on the prime minister after his resignation over the Falklands, if only because, as Peter Jenkins notes wryly, 'he lived near Chequers and was easily available for Sunday morning drinks' (Jenkins, 1987, p. 288).

After the election, the pressure on the prime minister for a more flexible approach was stepped up. In his first speech from the back benches, Francis Pym, Carrington's shortlived successor at the FCO, made a point of calling for more top-level contacts to be established between London and Moscow. The FCO, meanwhile, while still under Pym's leadership, had been 'tactfully tutoring [the prime minister] in occasional little seminars with their Soviet experts' (Jenkins, 1987, p. 288). By the end of the Summer, under the ministerial guidance of the new Foreign Secretary Sir Geoffrey Howe, a policy review that included confidential meetings with Soviet experts outside government had been concluded. The general conclusions were that the Soviet Union had begun a process of change and that a new diplomatic initiative towards the East had some prospect of success. The view emerged from these discussions that a policy of 'differentiation' with respect to the Soviet bloc was most likely to produce results. More accessible East European countries, such as Hungary, should be approached first and contacts then broadened and built up slowly and patiently (see House of Commons, 1986).

Whether the new focus on East–West relations that resulted from this review was a product of political opportunism, sustained bureaucratic pressure or traditional imperatives – or a combination of all three factors – the second Thatcher government did make a significant contribution to the development of a less confrontational and more constructive relationship between the superpowers and, moreover, helped to open up contacts with Eastern Europe. There were two important phases here: from the beginning to the end of 1984, and from the middle of 1986 to the end of 1987.

Until the re-election of President Reagan in November 1984, there were scarcely any high-level contacts between the United States and the Soviet Union. As an influential third party who at that time enjoyed excellent relations with Washington and rapidly improving relations with the Soviet Union and various members of the Soviet bloc, Britain was in a good position to play an important and timely role in helping to initiate a new period of East–West relations. Moreover, after the thorny issue of Britain's contribution to the European Community was resolved at the Fontainebleau summit in May 1984, the prime minister was able to lay some claim to a European leadership role when pressing the United States to adopt a more conciliatory approach to the East. Mrs Thatcher made an important speech to the European Atlantic Group in July, for example, which was characteristically critical of the Soviet Union, but made it clear that in her view business could be done with Moscow on a realistic basis. If the prime minister appeared to face an uphill struggle through 1984 in persuading the Americans to renew an effective East–West dialogue, there were indications that the Reagan administration was beginning to adopt a more conciliatory tone during that Summer as the presidential election entered its final stages. An important meeting between Reagan and Gromyko at the White House in October was followed in the new year by tangible improvements in the superpower relationship. As if to point up the significance of the British role during the previous twelve months, the then heir-apparent Mikhail Gorbachev led a delegation of the Supreme Soviet on a visit to Britain in December 1984, just a few weeks as it turned out before he took over the leadership.

After Mr Gorbachev became General Secretary, it soon became apparent that cultivating good relations with the Thatcher government would be useful if he were to achieve his general objective of improving relations with the West. The fact that the British were prepared to initiate a dialogue with him before the United States and the other major West European states underlined their importance. Mrs Thatcher qua 'Iron Lady' was particularly useful to Gorbachev in much the same way that Churchill had been to the post-Stalin leadership in the 1950s. As Pravda and Duncan put it, the prime minister had 'unimpeachable hardline credentials which made any endorsement of *perestroika* and Soviet new thinking all the more valuable'. Gorbachev made it clear on his later visits to Britain how much he appreciated Mrs Thatcher's early and enthusiastic support for him personally and her role in breaking the deadlock between the superpowers (see Pravda and Duncan, 1990, pp. 131, 240–1).

The Thatcher–Gorbachev relationship was clearly significant (special?), not least for the way in which each helped to give the other credibility on the international stage. But, more important in terms of British influence, it was the development of this relationship after December 1984, allied to the existing relationship between Mrs Thatcher and President Reagan, that gave the prime minister the opportunity to play if not a mediatory role at least an important communications role between the superpowers and their respective leaders. In Hugo Young's words, 'Mrs Thatcher, politically on Reagan's wavelength, and intellectually on Gorbachev's, had some of the qualities required to interpret the one to the other.' The importance of this interlocutory role can be seen with respect to the Strategic Defence Initiative (SDI) issue. The Camp David Accord, signed during Mrs Thatcher's visit to Washington at the end of 1984, went some way to meeting the objections to SDI voiced by Mr Gorbachev and, indeed, the concerns of Britain and other West European states, and laid the groundwork for a compromise on this issue, which was a necessary prerequisite for the later signing of the Intermediate Range Nuclear Force (INF) Treaty (Young, 1990, pp. 394–400; Bluth, 1990, pp. 113–14).

The Thatcher government continued through 1985 and into 1986 its policy of developing high-level contacts with the East – indeed, the ubiquitous Geoffrey Howe became the first British

Foreign Secretary to visit all the Warsaw Pact countries – but that policy began to have less impact for a variety of reasons. Once the superpowers had resumed direct contacts, restarted arms control negotiations and even by the end of 1985 held their first summit meeting at heads of government level for more than six years, the scope for mediation was inherently limited. Also, not for the first or the last time, improving Anglo-Soviet relations suffered a setback when diplomats were expelled from both capitals for alleged spying activities. Even the smooth path of Anglo-American relations registered a blip when Geoffrey Howe's overtly critical speech on SDI received favourable publicity in the East. It was significant in terms of declining British influence that Gorbachev chose Paris to launch his European policy initiatives on his first official visit to the West as Soviet leader in October 1985.

The visit of his Foreign Secretary Shevardnadze to London in July 1986, however, not only indicated that both countries wished to put the diplomatic expulsions episode behind them, but also signalled the start of a second period in which Britain again became, in Howe's phrase, 'a serious player in the peace process' (*Guardian*, 30 January 1987). Given the indications that the Soviet leadership was engaged in a wholesale review of foreign policy in the early part of that year, and that Soviet–American relations continued through 1986–87 to be delicate at best, Britain again served as an apparently valuable 'back-channel' of liaison between Washington and Moscow (Clarke, 1988, pp. 71–2). In particular, British reservations about SDI must have given the Russians some hope that they (the British) might persuade Reagan to compromise. After all, though this key issue had been deferred at the first Reagan–Gorbachev summit, the American President's continuing unwillingness to compromise led to the collapse of their second meeting at Reykjavik at the end of 1986. The British line at this time was to seek to dissuade the Soviet government from pursuing apocalyptic nuclear-free solutions and to persuade them to adopt a step-by-step approach to arms control. To opt for an INF agreement shorn of a space agreement, it was argued, would enable Reagan to prevail against his anti-arms control lobby and go for further agreements.

It was during this 1986–87 period that Mrs Thatcher could fully exploit her position as the senior Western leader in her dealings with the East. This was most evident perhaps during her visit to Moscow at the end of March 1987 when, having made a point of consulting with both Chancellor Kohl and President Mitterand in advance, she let it be known that she was representing European interests. As the superpowers moved inexorably towards an INF agreement, those interests included growing European resistance to any further 'denuclearization' of Europe. Significantly, the Western European Union (WEU) at British and French insistence signed a 'European Security Charter' in October 1987, which included support for a large continuing nuclear element in West European defence. Again, as if to symbolize Britain's leading role in East–West deliberations, President Gorbachev had a brief meeting with Mrs Thatcher on his stopover at Brize Norton en route to the Washington summit at the end of that year.

THE THIRD THATCHER GOVERNMENT AND STRUCTURAL CHANGES IN EAST–WEST RELATIONS

If the impact of British policy during the second Thatcher period indicated the continuing scope for some autonomous British influence on the direction of East–West relations, the limits of that influence soon became evident during the prime minister's third term. The signing of the INF Treaty at the third Reagan–Gorbachev summit in December 1987 heralded a period in which the underlying weakness of the British position became more apparent, perhaps, than ever before. The distinctly cool reception that Sir Geoffrey Howe received in Moscow in February 1988 was an early indicator that the sources of British influence on East–West relations were being further eroded. While direct superpower relations were becoming more and more institutionalized, Britain's bilateral relations with each of them became more difficult and certainly less 'special'. As a result of highly publicized differences about the future of the European Community, Britain's relations with her West European partners also entered a particularly difficult stage. Finally, less tangibly perhaps but no less significantly, Mrs Thatcher began to appear more and more as an unreconstructed cold warrior, preoccupied with security politics and either unwilling or unable to adapt to the changing mood of East–West relations. This was partly a matter of attitudes, but it was also a response to the impact of structural changes on what Pravda and Duncan called Britain's 'Euro-Atlantic standing and role' (Pravda and Duncan, 1990, p. 10).

As noted earlier, the response of the Thatcher government to the downturn in East–West relations at the beginning of the 1980s had been to increase defence spending and move closer to the Americans, who were seen as providing the ultimate security guarantee. Underpinned by the close personal and ideological relationship between the prime minister and President Reagan and apparently evidenced by the extensive assistance afforded to Britain during the 1982 Falklands conflict, the 'special' nature of the Anglo-American relationship received greater emphasis in London than it had for twenty years. Thereafter, however, the continuing assumption of special links with Washington appeared increasingly anachronistic. If, as David Reynolds and others have argued, the relationship never has been special except in the particular areas of defence and intelligence collaboration, even in these areas Britain appeared to become increasingly dependent upon the United States (Reynolds, 1985/86). The notion that the relationship as a whole is characterized by dependence rather than 'specialness' was highlighted by what appeared to be an excessive willingness to underwrite American policy in 1985–86. A series of decisions, including following the United States out of UNESCO, being the first NATO ally to agree to participate in SDI research programmes, sanctioning the takeover of Westland Helicopters by an American-led consortium and allowing the United States to stage the April 1986 attack on Libya from bases in Britain, produced unflattering references in the British press to the prime minister as 'Little Lady Echo' or 'Reagan's Poodle'.

An even more important problem for the Anglo-American relationship in the context of East–West relations was the extent to which it rested on the personal relationship between President Reagan and Mrs Thatcher. This began to concern the British as President Reagan approached the end of his second term. President Bush's first visit to Europe in June 1989 confirmed the worst British fears. The new president offered reassurances in London that 'from our side of the Atlantic, this relationship is strong and will continue to be so', but the fact that he felt compelled to offer such reassurances both privately and to the press only served to draw attention to the concern on the other side of the Atlantic that British influence in Washington was indeed on the wane (*Guardian*, 2 June 1989). This seemed to be underlined when the British government received only the most cursory advance notification of the first Bush–Gorbachev summit in Malta.

By the end of 1989, it was clear that the revolutionary events in Eastern Europe were confirming, dramatically in the case of the opening of East Germany's borders, that the West Germans had become the 'special' partner of the United States in Europe. From Washington's perspective, the fact of West German economic strength, not least the strength of the mark against the dollar, was at the heart of this deepening relationship. But, in political terms, it was also clear that the Americans were increasingly impressed by German assertiveness through 1989, initially in deferring the nuclear modernization issue until after the 1990 German elections and later in terms of the more active leadership role played by Chancellor Kohl in the wake of the dramatic changes in the East.

If the Anglo-American relationship was becoming increasingly problematic as a source of British influence on East–West issues, the pendulum nature of the relationship with the Soviet Union was also helping to marginalize British influence. Despite the considerable efforts to revive Anglo-Soviet relations after 1984, critics might argue with some justification that Britain managed to squander opportunities to regularize those relations. At their first meeting in London, Mrs Thatcher had immediately taken to a man she recognized as a fellow 'conviction' politician and declared that Gorbachev was a communist leader she could do business with. But, in contrast to the West Germans, for example, whose relationship with the Soviet Union also improved dramatically after 1987, surprisingly little business was done in the form of securing an increased share of Soviet trade with Western Europe. Although there were commercial reasons for this, the general climate of political relations appears to have had a significant impact (Pravda and Duncan, 1990). Perversely, it appeared, the alleged spying activities of Soviet diplomats were allowed to interfere with efforts to normalize relations. In 1985, the expulsion of thirty-one Soviet diplomats, which was reciprocated in Moscow, had precipitated the worst expulsion crisis since 1971. It led to the immediate shelving of a planned visit to London by Foreign Minister Gromyko and, more important, as noted above, it helped to bring to an end a period in which Britain had played an important role in improving East–West relations.

After a substantial repair of Anglo-Soviet relations, which culminated in a third visit to London by Mr Gorbachev in April 1989, relations were immediately soured yet again by the expulsion from London of eleven alleged KGB operatives. The Soviet response on this occasion was not only to reciprocate by expelling the same number of diplomats and journalists from Moscow, but also to threaten to cut the number of British citizens allowed to work in Moscow. Once again, the effect was to make it that much more difficult for Britain to have a distinctive impact on East–West relations. It is ironic that, while governmental contacts between London and Moscow positively mushroomed after 1987, Britain's influence on wider East–West developments was clearly waning.

If Britain's relations with both superpowers had become problematic at the same time, relations with her partners in the European Community also became more strained during the prime minister's third term. During Mrs Thatcher's first period in office, the continuing need to be a 'good European' had imposed some constraints upon independent action in the East–West arena. The fact noted earlier, that the substance of British policy on East–West issues did not match the Thatcherite rhetoric, owed something to the perceived need to stay in line with Britain's partners in the Community, who were less predisposed to cast aside the benefits of détente. The actual British policy responses to the Soviet invasion of Afghanistan and to the imposition of martial law in Poland – to the gas pipeline issue, in particular – were not inconsistent with the line taken by Britain's partners. There are also indications that the 'new' policy adopted towards the East in 1983–84 was in part a response to some pressure from Europe – from the West Germans, in particular – for a more flexible approach (see Wallace, 1986, p. 222).

Until 1984, however, the long-running saga of Britain's budgetary contributions to the Community had not only soured relations with her partners but made it difficult to wear a 'European hat' on East–West issues. An important spin-off from the resolution of that issue was to enable Mrs Thatcher to do just that, which in turn had increased her ability to influence East–West developments during her second term. After 1987, however, the prime minister's if not the British government's ambivalence about the future direction of the European Community clearly had a detrimental impact on Britain's East–West policy. Having ratified the Single European Act in 1987, the British government, like its partners, was committed to working towards political and economic union. The prime minister's well-publicized speech in Bruges in September 1988, however, served to confirm existing doubts on the Continent about the reliability of the British commitment to that objective. This speech and its repercussions not only soured relations once again with Britain's partners but made it more difficult to work collectively with those states to influence East–West relations.

In a BBC interview in October 1988, the Foreign Secretary felt it necessary to deny that Britain was being isolated and left behind as West Germany, France and Italy intensified their contacts with Eastern Europe. Britain's relations with Eastern Europe, Howe stressed, 'are absolutely in the mainstream, and have indeed been setting the pace in many respects' (*Guardian*, 25 October 1988). There was some substance to this claim, as we have seen, but differences over fundamental Community issues served to highlight differences with Britain's partners over East–West issues. At the end of 1988, for example, there were highly publicized disagreements about the extent of Western aid needed to help Gorbachev's economic reforms, and Mrs Thatcher was taking a notably tougher line than her partners on human rights in the context of the Soviet proposal to stage the 1991 meeting of the Conference on the Human Dimension (CDH) in Moscow.

Indeed, the suspicion grew through 1988–89 that the Thatcher government or at least the prime minister – a distinction it was becoming increasingly difficult to make – was fundamentally out of sympathy with the dramatic changes that were occuring in East–West relations. This was not surprising, perhaps, to the extent that these changes undermined British influence rather more than that of other key players. A cautious response, moreover, was arguably only prudent in the wake of the revolutionary changes in Central and Eastern Europe that ended the 1980s. But the responses of the prime minister to change and the prospect of further change over a longer period almost suggested a desire to turn back the clock. As the mood of East–West relations was transformed from a preoccupation with threats, confrontation and high defence spending towards the contemplation at least of radically new political, economic and security structures in Europe, Mrs Thatcher appeared unwilling or unable to shake off an Iron Lady image that looked increasingly anachronistic.

The prime minister's response to the INF Treaty, for example, was to call a special NATO summit in March 1988, to reaffirm NATO's traditional policy of nuclear deterrence and to secure an unambiguous commitment to the modernization of short-range nuclear systems. Although she failed to secure that commitment, Mrs Thatcher continued through 1988–89 to be preoccupied with the issue of nuclear modernization. Only after the East German elections in March 1990 produced a massive vote in favour of German unification did the prime minister finally give up her modernization crusade. Although she now had little choice but to accept that land-based, short-range nuclear missiles – whose principal targets are in East Germany – had to be phased out, her grudging willingness to tolerate any changes in NATO strategy was a clear indicator of her ambivalent attitude to radical changes in Central Europe.

With respect to changes in the Soviet Union, having offered Mr Gorbachev effusive support for his *perestroika* reforms during her Moscow visit in 1987, Mrs Thatcher and her government made clear attempts towards the end of 1988 to discourage the evident enthusiasm of Britain's Community partners for Soviet reforms. A feeling that the prime minister was ambivalent at best about the whole reform process in the Soviet Union was further heightened by suspicions about the timing of the revelations concerning Soviet spies in London. Coming as they did just before President Bush's first NATO summit – with nuclear modernization again on the agenda – led some to suspect that the British were trying to create the impression that nothing had really changed in Moscow.

BRITISH ATTITUDES TOWARDS DÉTENTE

Despite the declaratory posturing of the first Thatcher government and, perhaps, the excessive commitment to cold war certainties in the third Thatcher government, it is difficult not to be struck once again by the elements of consistency in the British approach to East–West relations from the mid-1970s to the end of the 1980s. This is suggested both by the policy statements of Labour ministers in the 1970s, which were quoted at some length in the first section of this chapter, and by the policy orientation if not always the rhetoric of the Thatcher governments in the 1980s. Not surprisingly, given the dramatic downturn in East–West relations from the mid-1970s to the mid-1980s, there was a growing scepticism about the benefits of détente during this period, and a corresponding emphasis on the necessity of maintaining effective structures of deterrence and defence. But the desirability of maintaining an essential balance between détente and defence continued to find expression both in policy terms and in the statements of government spokesmen.

In conceptual terms, historical observers could be forgiven for having a sense of *déja vu* at the start of Mrs Thatcher's second term. The prime minister's call for an 'easement of relations' with the Soviet Union borrowed Churchill's phrase from the 1950s, and there were many other evocations of that period. Speaking at the end of 1984, for example, Defence Secretary Michael Heseltine did his impression of Churchill *circa* 1953 in a speech that called for greater mutual understanding between East and West. Both sides, he maintained, should seek better political and economic relations, which would enable arms reductions to be achieved. As a contribution to that understanding he, like Churchill, was prepared to concede that the build-up of Soviet military strength in recent years had not been solely designed to threaten the security of the West in accordance with some grand ideological design. Developing the theme of 'Russia in Historical Perspective', the Defence Secretary argued that Russian governments had been preoccupied for centuries with their security and the West should understand that the Soviet Union also has legitimate security interests to defend. His thesis was not that Western vigilance is inappropriate but that the West, in his words, should 'couple this essential policy of deterrence with a manifest willingness to talk and listen'. The prime minister was an evident convert to the 'talk and listen' philosophy, particularly after her first meeting with Gorbachev, when, to her surprise, she realized that here was a Soviet leader with whom she could have a real dialogue rather than some scripted diplomatic exchange.

The need to increase high-level, personal contacts between leaders of East and West was one of the familiar themes that Foreign Secretary Geoffrey Howe took with him on his forays into Eastern Europe. These contacts, Howe and his prime minister hoped, would gradually increase trust and contribute to an improved political atmosphere, which might in turn facilitate progress in East–West negotiations. The negotiations, however, should not be restricted to arms control. The aim, Howe asserted, should be to develop and sustain an East–West dialogue covering the broadest possible agenda including trade and human rights issues. Thus, Howe was concerned to try to boost trade with Eastern Europe and the Soviet Union. He also raised whenever possible, and sometimes to the embarrassment of his hosts, particular human rights cases and the general human rights situation in the country he was visiting.

Significantly, however, the approach to human rights after 1983 was now more consistent with the traditional approach. It was no longer a case of singling out and condemning violations of human rights as symbols of the evils of communism and the manifest need for change. Representations on human rights cases were now located within broader discussions on a range of issues, and the emphasis once again was on securing practical improvements at a human level rather than on changing political systems. As one minister commented to Hugo Young, Mrs Thatcher 'wasn't interested any more in changing the Russians, or recovering Eastern Europe for the Western way of life. She might detest their system, but she didn't even want to talk about anything except the strictly practical' (Young, 1990, p. 391). A cautious, piecemeal approach to East–West relations with the object of opening contacts and normalizing those relationships was again dominant.

It became clear in the 1980s, however, that the government was as concerned with relationships with the individual countries of Eastern Europe as it was with the Soviet Union. Again, this was not a wholly new dimension of British East–West policy to the extent that it continued a trend that had been evident since the 1960s. But the focus on Eastern Europe after 1983 was new in terms of the intensity with which those relationships were fostered. The development of these relationships is significant in terms of British attitudes, because it gave the Thatcher governments a number of opportunities to demonstrate their commitment to practical, 'quality of life' objectives. In terms of influence, these links highlighted the new British activism on East–West détente after 1983 and became particularly important in bilateral terms after the break up of the Soviet bloc at the end of the 1980s.

The British reaction to these revolutionary changes in Europe at the end of the decade can also, to some extent at least, be explained in terms of traditional attitudes. The persistent cautioning against premature changes in the structure of Western security in the wake of these changes reflected the traditional concern with any developments that might destabilize that structure. In the second half of the 1980s, as in the early 1970s, there was a growing feeling that détente was getting rather out of hand. Thus, as early as 1984 in the context of the SDI issue, and in some earnest following the Reykjavik summit in 1986, Mrs Thatcher threw her not inconsiderable political weight behind the status quo as far as the East–West security environment was concerned. This position was not inconsistent with the traditional British concern to maintain a balance between détente and defence.

For a prime minister who had built her international reputation on her 'iron' opposition to communism, however, the apparent demise of the communist system in Eastern Europe in 1989–90 did pose a fundamental problem. In particular, it made her defence of the status quo appear to be a rather desperate swimming against the tide of precisely the sort of changes she should have welcomed. As Hugo Young comments:

> events in Eastern Europe saw the destruction of the most potent demon in her international rhetoric, the onward march of communism. The Iron Lady noted these developments, congratulated herself on her part in, as she believed, inspiring them, but showed no sign of revising her strategic analysis (Young, 1990, p. 547).

The argument here is that the ambivalence towards these dramatic changes cannot be understood solely in terms of traditional attitudes or even Thatcherite orthodoxy. It reflected more fundamentally, perhaps, the impact of structural changes on Britain's ability to influence East–West relations. After all, the ending of the cold war era fundamentally transformed the established Euro-Atlantic frameworks through which British influence had been exercised throughout the postwar period. Given that the future had suddenly become very uncertain, it is not wholly surprising that familiar reference points were tenaciously clung to. However, there were also domestic political reasons why Mrs Thatcher could not without difficulty revise her 'strategic analysis', and this provides an appropriate point to turn finally to the domestic political environment for clues that might help us to explain British East–West policy in the period from the mid-1970s to the end of the 1980s.

THE DOMESTIC POLITICAL CONTEXT

Until the election of the first Thatcher government, it has to be said, little significance can be attached to domestic politics as an explanation of British policy. The Conservatives in opposition, as suggested earlier, were more sceptical of the fruits of the 'Helsinki Process' than the Labour Party, and this may have encouraged the Wilson and Callaghan governments to adopt a more cautious approach to détente than they might have preferred. But a continuation of the traditional, balanced approach to détente and defence – even if weighted towards the defence side of the balance – received broad bipartisan support during these years and, in so far as it can be determined, seemed to attract broad support in the country generally. With both Soviet capabilities and intentions still viewed with some popular concern at this time, there was little apparent opposition to the growing emphasis towards the end of the Callaghan period on providing an effective defence to counter the Soviet threat.

After 1979, however, the domestic political context began to change rather dramatically. With a focus provided by the debate on the siting of American Cruise missiles in Britain, the nuclear issue with all its ramifications began to acquire a salience in British politics it had not had for twenty years. Quantitative indicators of this included a massive rise in the membership of the Campaign for Nuclear Disarmament (CND) from something like 2,000 in 1979 to a figure approaching 100,000 in 1983. This was accompanied by regular, large-scale demonstrations during this period, with Greenham Common, designated as the first Cruise missile base, a popular target. With the growth of a significant minority of anti-nuclear opinion in the country, represented politically by the Labour Party and with the Liberal Party and new Social Democratic Party also refusing to support important elements of Conservative nuclear policy, the broad consensus on defence that had lasted since the 1960s was destroyed.

In what had now become a genuine party political debate on defence in Britain, new propositions were introduced into the debate that fundamentally questioned conventional assumptions about the defence environment. These included the idea that the Soviet Union, the invasion of Afghanistan notwithstanding, did not pose the military threat that had been assumed for many years. Some began to argue that Soviet capabilities had been overestimated and Soviet intentions misunderstood. The United States also began to be perceived by some as less the ultimate guarantor of Western defence interests and more, under Reagan's leadership, as a danger-ously militaristic power seriously contemplating the possible use of nuclear weapons in a 'limited' nuclear war in Europe. The deterrent function of those weapons began to be questioned or, at least, the deterrent rationale for the deployment of new nuclear weapons such as Cruise and Pershing 2 in the European theatre.

With hindsight, it would be easy to ignore these ideas and regard them as of little political significance. After all, they clearly failed to impress the British electorate either in 1983 or 1987. Indeed, the anti-nuclear policy of the Labour Party helped that party to a succession of crushing electoral defeats and, conversely, the military orthodoxy of the Thatcher governments helped the Conservative Party to their sweeping victories (see Butler and Kavanagh, 1984, 1988). Certainly with respect to the 1983 election, the image of strength comprising high defence spending, a robust anti-Soviet rhetoric and a reassertion of the efficacy of the British deterrent, appeared to make a significant contribution to Mrs Thatcher's re-election. Nevertheless, *before* that result was achieved – and in the context of the aforementioned defence debate – the stridency, the closeness of the links with Washington and the unqualified nature of the commitment to nuclear orthodoxy exposed the Thatcher government to potentially adverse electoral consequences. There are clear historical parallels here with the domestic political situation faced by Harold Macmillan in the run up to the 1959 election. Significantly, there are indications that Mrs Thatcher, like her predecessor, was sensitive to this threat and began to realize that the pursuit of a 'naked' deterrence policy might have undesirable political consequences in the 1983 election and thereafter.

Initially, though, the first Thatcher government appeared to think that it could ignore or, if necessary, subvert the anti-nuclear movement. Until 1983, as Freedman notes, the government did not engage the anti-nuclear or 'peace' movement very effectively. They underestimated 'its sophistication and popular appeal . . . and the debate was often left to junior ministers' (Freedman, 1989, p. 146). In January 1983, however, with Cruise missiles due in Britain within months, growing governmental concern about the peace movement was reflected in the appointment of Michael Heseltine as Secretary of Defence. Given Heseltine's acknowledged public relations skills, part of his remit was to stem the tide as far as the arguments of the anti-nuclear lobby was concerned. We also know from the revelations of the MI5 operative Cathy Massiter that the government was prepared to use the resources of the security organizations to discredit the leaders of the peace movement.

If the result of the 1983 election was the most effective way of rebutting the arguments of the anti-nuclear lobby, the Thatcher government's apparent change of direction on East–West issues immediately thereafter indicates a more subtle response to domestic concerns and provides an explanation for British attempts to improve the climate of East–West relations in the second Thatcher period, which cannot be ignored. The continuing domestic salience of the nuclear issue, particularly after the arrival of Cruise missiles in November 1983, positively required, in Freedman's phrase, 'a hawkish military orthodoxy to be balanced by a doveish diplomatic orthodoxy' (Freedman, 1989, p. 145). Domestic political support for a détente policy continued through the second Thatcher period and beyond, moreover, in the shape of changing popular perceptions of the superpowers as reflected in opinion polls. Between 1984 and 1986, as Clarke notes, 'the Reagan presidency slipped even further in the esteem of the British public, while the Soviet Union enjoyed an improving image'. In April 1986, for the first time ever, the United States earned a higher 'disapproval' rating in the Gallup Poll than the Soviet Union, and this trend continued thereafter. If the polls suggested that the British public was taking an increasingly cynical view of both superpowers, they clearly had little confidence in Reagan and were increasingly impressed by Gorbachev (Clarke, 1988, p. 70; Clarke, 1990, pp. 82–3, 87).

These indications of changing public perceptions provide an important context for evaluating the contribution of Mrs Thatcher's East–West policy to the winning of the 1987 election. A focus here is provided by the prime minister's timely and very successful visit to the Soviet Union at the end of March, only six weeks before the election was called. The historical parallel that inevitably comes to mind here is, of course, Macmillan's Moscow trip in February 1959. Like Macmillan, Mrs Thatcher could not have been unaware of the media impact of this trip and her advisers were careful to maximize the opportunities to present media images of the prime minister as an international leader of the first rank. Mrs Thatcher was helped by the evident willingness of Mr Gorbachev to play his supporting role on the Soviet stage and by the apparently spontaneous welcome accorded to Mrs Thatcher by the Soviet people. The reaction at home to this spectacular also seems to have been very positive. While summit meetings generally were regarded with some scepticism at this time, an exception was made for the Thatcher–Gorbachev meeting, which, Clarke again suggests, was regarded as a 'worthwhile and sincere attempt at improving relations with a superpower that wanted to be friendly' (Clarke, 1990, p. 83). In terms of imagery, the contrast with the disastrous trip which the Labour leader Neil Kinnock made to the United States the previous week could not have been greater. In electoral terms, the Thatcher visit may even have been more important than the Macmillan trip, because it diverted attention at home away from what Hugo Young calls the 'barrenness and misfortune which largely dominated both 1985 and 1986'. The Moscow trip, Young argues, was as important as the 'give away budget' earlier that month in securing Mrs Thatcher's third term in office (Young, 1990, p. 514).

Chapter 8

A British conception of détente

An important assumption made throughout this study is that there has been a consistent set of attitudes towards détente, which has underpinned British East–West policy since the 1950s. This chapter begins by drawing together the elements of the British approach, where necessary identifying changes of emphasis over time. This is followed by a more detailed attempt to locate British attitudes within a longer-term historical context to test the proposition that an explanation of British policy requires some understanding of the sources of these attitudes. Finally, we deal here with an important issue that was identified in the introductory chapter: namely, whether these attitudes can be said to constitute a British conception of détente and the extent to which they challenge the pervasive notion that the making of British foreign policy is dominated by a pragmatic ethos.

It will be recalled that an attempt to discover a distinctive British approach to détente began by contrasting British and American approaches to the cold war in the late 1940s. While the formal acceptance of the NSC-68 principles by the Truman administration in 1950 indicated that the Americans were beginning to see the cold war as an end in itself, it soon became apparent that British policy-makers were committed to containing East–West conflict not by confrontation or 'political warfare' but by a policy of military strength combined with diplomatic accommodation. From a British perspective, containment of the Soviet Union was essentially a means to an end, the object being the normalization of East–West relations. To that end, having helped to establish the North Atlantic alliance to contain the Soviet threat, it was necessary to initiate a process of negotiations with Moscow as soon as possible.

Thus, on the basis of a brief analysis of British attitudes to détente prior to 1953, it was argued that, while the Americans at that time regarded 'cold war' and 'détente' as antithetical approaches to East–West relations, the British regarded them as complementary, with détente apparently regarded as 'normal diplomacy'. This view of détente, it was suggested, was grounded upon a traditional approach to diplomacy and international relations. Implicit within this formulation, of course, is the idea that British policy-makers have had a consistent view of 'normal' international relations. This study of British détente policy since the early 1950s has provided an opportunity to identify more precisely what policy-makers have understood by détente, which might now be used to see whether their view of détente can be related to traditional attitudes that might, in turn, define a British conception of 'normal' international relations.

At first sight, British policy towards détente in the mid-1950s seemed to reflect a simple preoccupation with summitry: normal diplomacy appeared to be synonymous with summit diplomacy. In November 1955, for example, we noted that Harold Macmillan explicitly related the 'Spirit of Geneva' to what he called 'a return to normal human relations', by which he meant that it represented flexibility, 'give and take', a readiness to discuss and negotiate. By implication, more 'Genevas' would bring about a normalization of relations between East and West.

Summit meetings were indeed thought to offer the best chance of resolving major conflicts of interest and achieving a modus vivendi with the East, but there were also indications during this period that there was more to a British view of détente than summitry or even a wider process of East–West negotiations. Significantly, Churchill's idea of a new approach to East–West relations after Stalin's death consisted not only of restoring and expanding politico-diplomatic contacts but also of developing as many commercial, social and cultural contacts as possible across the Iron Curtain. This suggested that the notion of 'open contacts' might be as useful as 'normal diplomacy' in terms of capturing the essence of a British view of détente.

This was confirmed by the analysis of the approach adopted by the Macmillan government: normal diplomacy, moreover, had now acquired more specification. Although Macmillan pressed hard to institutionalize summit meetings, it was clear that normal diplomacy meant more than 'mere' summitry. This was partly a result of a learning experience following the Geneva experience, but partly a clearer articulation of the place of sum-mit meetings within a regularized cycle of negotiations. The Macmillan government assumed rightly or wrongly, on the basis of Geneva, that summit meetings would be more effective in terms of producing practical results if preparatory work was undertaken at lower-level meetings. Hence, détente as normal diplomacy connoted permanent East–West diplomatic contacts interspersed with meetings of ministers and regular if less frequent meetings of heads of state/government. It was also clear from the statements of British policy-makers in the late 1950s that they did not envisage that normalized diplomacy would of itself 'normal-ize' East–West relations. The Macmillan government shared the Churchill view that it was necessary to buttress political contacts by developing contacts across the spectrum of non-governmental relations.

By the end of the 1950s, it can be argued, the essential elements of a British approach to détente were in place. Its hallmarks were caution and limited expectations but, nevertheless, a belief that progress was both possible and necessary. Thus, détente was seen as a desirable process. It was important that the British make practical contributions to nudge that process forward both 'vertically', at every level from the highest political level down-wards, and 'horizontally', across the broadest range of issues. The key notion of balancing that contribution with due con-cern for maintaining the basic structure of security, however, placed intrinsic limits upon British enthusiasm for the détente process.

If these elements have been consistent features of the British approach since the 1950s, there have, nevertheless, been significant changes of emphasis. Most important, perhaps, we have observed the development of a more sceptical and a more ambivalent approach to détente, which can be dated from the late 1960s. Note that this scepticism was maintained both at the 'high points' of détente in the early 1970s and the second half of the 1980s and at the 'low points' of détente from the late 1970s to the early 1980s. While growing fears that détente might fundamentally destabilize the structures of European and East–West security are not inconsistent with the perceived need for a balanced approach, these fears have tended to locate British policy as often as not on the defence side of the balance during the last twenty years or so. Certainly, they served to reinforce a sense of caution and, if anything, to downgrade even further expectations of the détente process.

Not unrelated to this growing scepticism was an increasing emphasis on pursuing what was referred to in an earlier chapter as 'quality of life' objectives in relation to détente. These objectives, however, first articulated clearly in the context of the CSCE negotiations in the early 1970s, are also related to other elements of the British approach. They can be linked firstly to another 'new' dimension of that approach, the increasing concern with the individual countries of Eastern Europe rather than with the Soviet bloc as a whole, a trend which began in the 1960s and became an important focus of British policy in the 1980s. In this context, 'quality of life' objectives referred to the desirability of opening up the Soviet bloc by introducing liberal values – a concern with human rights in particular – into bilateral and multilateral negotiations. Seeking to improve the daily lives of individuals and families in Eastern Europe and the Soviet Union was also consistent with working towards practical improvements in East–West relations. Finally, the symbolic value of human rights as a focal issue was also important. It provided either a convenient expression of concern without the need actually to engage in East–West negotiations or, if pursued as a low-key issue in negotiations, it avoided the dangers of stimulating an unhelpful and possibly a confrontational response from the East.

Making due allowance for differences of emphasis over time, this confirmation of an essentially consistent British view of détente from the 1950s through to the 1980s, in terms of normal diplomacy and open contacts, provides a basis for locating attitudes towards détente within traditional British attitudes towards international relations. The next part of this chapter explores the historical antecedents of attitudes towards détente in an interrelated set of traditional attitudes towards diplomacy, defence and what might be called 'globalism'.

DÉTENTE AND TRADITIONAL DIPLOMACY

British attitudes towards détente, it can be argued, have their origins within traditional attitudes to diplomacy. Persistent efforts to mediate between the superpowers in the postwar period, whether successful or not, like the policy of appeasement in the 1930s, illustrate what Lord Strang called the 'conciliatory quality' in British diplomacy. In his formulation, 'it is a policy that usually prefers compromise to victory; that seeks by mutual concession to reach durable understandings' (Strang, 1961, pp. 359–60; for the links between the appeasement policy and a British diplomatic tradition, see Kennedy, 1976, pp. 195–215). Historically, this distinctive quality was a product of two major factors: long experience of playing a leading role in the European diplomatic system and assumptions dating from the nineteenth century about how to maintain Britain's global position in world affairs in the face of growing challenges to that position.

The idea of détente as normal diplomacy suggests a link with a historically familiar European system where conciliation was the important norm of diplomacy. Macmillan's description of a return to 'normal human relations' positively evokes that system, which, in contrast to the inflexible bipolar system of the postwar period, was characterized by shifting alliances, shared interests in maintaining the system and the absence of ideologically oriented confrontation politics. In the context of that system, normal diplomacy meant a willingness to bargain, to make concessions and to compromise in order to maintain a modus vivendi with the other members of the system. There was no shortage of conflicts of interest between those states, but they could normally (though not always, of course) be resolved by an institutionalized process of communication, dialogue and negotiation.

The 1983 lecture by Lord Carrington referred to in the last chapter also alludes implicitly at least to that system and helps to establish the origins of a British approach to détente in traditional European diplomacy. Speaking about the new cold war, Carrington chided those in the West who would reduce East–West diplomacy to 'nothing but nuclear accountancy'. Our own tradition, he stressed and we noted, 'must be for the peaceful resolution of potential conflict through energetic and forceful dialogue'. By implication, simply to 'face the Russians down in a silent war of nerves, broken only by bursts of megaphone diplomacy' was abnormal diplomacy, the very antithesis of a British and European diplomatic tradition (Carrington, 1983, p. 151; see also Owen, 1984, pp. 3–8).

From this perspective, differences between British and American approaches to détente during the postwar period can be explained either by the United States' lack of experience in, or rejection of, the techniques and the objectives of European diplomacy. Northedge suggests the former and exemplifies a fundamental difference of approach by reference to the idea of peaceful coexistence 'which for the European Powers is the normal rule and *raison d'être* of diplomacy' but which for the Americans has generally had 'the overtones of cohabitation with the devil' (Northedge and Wells, 1982, p. 237; an alternative ideological explanation is outlined in Calvocoressi, 1984, pp. 89–101).

If British attitudes learnt during more than two centuries of experience in the more pragmatic European school of diplomacy reappeared in attitudes towards détente, those attitudes also reflected traditional assumptions related more specifically to the maintenance of Britain's global interests. In particular, it had long been assumed, certainly since the middle of the nineteenth century, that the preservation of peace was central to the protection of global politico-economic interests. This was the premise that Harold Nicolson had in mind when he argued in his classic work on British diplomacy that British policy-makers have traditionally had a 'civilian' or a 'commercial' as opposed to what he called a 'warrior' conception of diplomacy (Nicolson, 1939, pp. 52–4).

Unlike the other European powers, Britain had an empire of genuinely global dimensions, and this provided special reasons for pursuing a conciliatory foreign policy. As the so-called 'workshop of the world' in the nineteenth century, Britain was at the centre of a global system of trade and finance. The new liberal orthodoxy held that this position of pre-eminence could best be maintained and, indeed, exploited by pursuing a policy of free trade. This policy had important commercial advantages, but it also made the British imperial economy highly vulnerable to any disruption of trade and to war in particular. Hence, to the extent that global economic interests required a policy of free trade, that policy in turn required the preservation of peace by conciliatory diplomacy.

As Britain's economic position in relation to other states began, nevertheless, to decline in the second half of the nineteenth century, the preservation of peace became even more vital. Similarly, other challenges to Britain's global position, which revealed an increasing gap between material power and worldwide commitments, served to reinforce a predisposition to seek compromise solutions to and peaceful settlements of disputes with other states. As Paul Kennedy explains:

> This did not mean that British governments would choose peace at any price but – unlike the militaristic elites of certain other countries – they did know that war was bad for business and that the essence of diplomacy was to secure British interests without recourse to a large-scale conflict (Kennedy, 1981, p. 27. The arguments outlined in this section are developed in the first chapter of this book).

It is important to note, however, in terms of trying to identify the historical origins of British attitudes towards détente, that it was never assumed, even by the most radical liberals, that peace could be maintained solely by conciliatory diplomacy. In rather crude political terms, which oversimplify party political positions, liberal and conservative approaches to problems of war and peace can be identified in nineteenth-century Britain. The liberal approach stressed the need for a foreign policy that was pragmatic, conciliatory and reasonable but, given that liberals were suspicious of government-to-government diplomacy, they tended towards the view that peace could best be maintained by expanding non-governmental contacts across nations. The classic liberal belief in a natural harmony of interests that underpinned this view was rejected, however, by conservatives who, though not opposed in principle to conciliatory diplomacy, tended towards the older realpolitik position, which held that conflict rather than harmony is the natural state of affairs. They believed that the necessary defence of national interests required firmness and resolution as well as conciliation and reasonableness. From this perspective, indeed, war could *only* be avoided by combining diplomacy and defence, conciliation and strength.

Significantly, this study strongly suggests that elements of both traditions of thought reappear within British attitudes to East–West détente. The notion of détente as open contacts can certainly be traced back to nineteenth-century liberal ideas associated in particular with Richard Cobden. There was, as Geoffrey Goodwin has commented, a 'deep streak of Cobdenism in much of British thinking' in the postwar period (Goodwin, 1972, p. 43). Cobden argued that a free interchange of goods and services would not only benefit the British economy but that free trade and 'as much connection as possible between the nations of the world' would give all peoples a commercial stake in maintaining peace. Popular pressure, in turn, would force governments to desist from pursuing policies that resulted in war (see Read, 1968; Cain, 1979).

British governments in the period since 1945 scarcely accepted Cobden's radical philosophy in its entirety, but Churchill's belief in trade as the 'great Mediator', for example, echoed Cobden's view that 'commerce is the great panacea'. The common assumption was that an expansion of trade could act as a solvent of political differences and serve as an alternative to war. The 'can we do business' approach to new Soviet leaders in the postwar period provides a related illustration of the continuing impact of a commercial ethos in British diplomacy. Sir William Hayter, for example, the former ambassador in Moscow, recalls in his memoirs the initial concerns about Malenkov, 'but as we got to know him in 1953 and 1954 we all concluded that though tough and secretive he was a man with whom business could be done' (Hayter, 1966, p. 107). It is interesting that Mrs Thatcher found Malenkov's most recent successor surprisingly open, but still drew the same conclusion, using the same sort of commercial language.

DÉTENTE, DETERRENCE AND DEFENCE

If elements of classical liberal thinking about the relationship between commerce and peace reappear in British attitudes towards détente, these attitudes also reveal, more obviously perhaps, evidence of the conservative realpolitik tradition in British political thought, particularly with respect to the assumed linkage between the avoidance of war and a balanced relationship between diplomacy and defence. Collective security in a North Atlantic context may have replaced a 'balance of power' role in Europe, but the assumption persisted that conciliatory diplomacy, however desirable for all the reasons touched on here, would only be effective if wedded to a credible structure of defence or, in a nuclear context, deterrence. The unfortunate experience with an 'unbalanced' policy of appeasement in the 1930s, it can be argued, only served to reinforce this perspective.

As noted several times in this study, notions of balance and complementarity pervade descriptions of a 'proper' relationship between the political and military components of British East–West policy in the postwar period. Churchill's 'double dealing' and Macmillan's 'two-fold' policy or, alternatively, 'arm and parley' can be compared with similar aphorisms both before and since the 1950s by political leaders and commentators alike. Northedge, for example, reminds us that there was nothing inconsistent about advocating collective defence within NATO and détente with the Soviet Union. It was, he suggests, 'the continuation of a long standing British principle of foreign policy, which Lord Templewood, the Sir Samuel Hoare of the 1930s, called the "double line" – a strong defence posture combined with the energetic search for accommodation' (Northedge, 1980, p. 21). Moreover, Northedge argues elsewhere, with the exception of the first Thatcher government (an exception we might dispute):

> British policy towards the Soviet Union since 1945 has followed a consistent course of armed vigilance against aggression, coupled with a search for détente and all manner of agreements to ease international tension, as and when opportunities for making these presented themselves (Northedge and Wells, 1982, p. 133).

Addressing an American audience at the end of the 1950s, Michael Donelan also commented on the British belief that 'both strength and diplomacy [are] continuously necessary in a world of endless disharmony, in a world in which the best possible solution is the best possible bargain' (Donelan, 1959, p. 54; see also Dougherty, 1975, p. 51). More recently, as we noted in the last chapter, Lord Carrington sought to disassociate himself from the 'Iron Lady' approach to East–West relations and to place himself squarely in the 'double dealing' tradition. In his 1983 speech, he commented that:

> when he [Churchill] declared himself in favour of an East–West summit one week, and Western rearmament the next, he was wrongly accused of inconsistency . . . Churchill was ahead of his time: the *sweet and sour approach* to Moscow was not yet recognised as the tactical necessity it is today (Carrington, 1983, pp. 152–3; emphasis added).

Significantly, the problem that Carrington faced in the early 1980s was an ideological one, though he did not discuss it in these terms. There was a conflict between the traditional British approach to East–West relations, which, following the argument here, might be labelled 'liberal realist' and the ideological orientation of the Thatcher government, which might be labelled 'conservative liberal' (see Wallace and Wallace, 1990). While Mrs Thatcher claimed to be a Victorian liberal, the New Right's version of liberalism was distinctively different from its nineteenth-century predecessor. The main difference, as Porter notes, was:

> the divorce between economic and political liberalism which had been taking place slowly over the past one hundred years and was now almost complete . . . the champions of the free market [now] were also, by and large, the defenders of strong laws, a powerful police, centralised government . . . and – in foreign affairs – military might and *realpolitik*; which in Victorian times, they generally were not (Porter, 1987, p. 131).

It would appear that Lord Carrington was concerned to remind the 'Iron Lady' that military strength must be balanced by dialogue and that politico-diplomatic contacts, particularly with potential enemies, are just as important as commercial and financial links – and no less moral.

DÉTENTE AND GLOBALISM

The origins of British attitudes to détente can be located finally in the traditional assumption that Britain has a global role to play in international relations. This assumption again can be traced back at least as far as the nineteenth century, when British imperial power reached its apogee. The most recent historical experience prior to the period dealt with here, in the Second World War, confirmed the belief that Britain still had a central role to play in the international system, as one of the 'Big Three'. In Frankel's words, 'Britain's wartime record ensured for her a position perpetuating her traditional claim to be represented at the exclusive top-level councils dealing with global politics' (Frankel, 1975, p. 151). Continuing global aspirations after the war were most clearly articulated in the 'Three Circles' doctrine, which placed Britain unashamedly at the hub of world politics. Enunciated by Churchill in opposition at the 1948 Conservative Party Conference, this conception became arguably the most pervasive and influential image of what constituted an appropriate role for Britain in the postwar world.

Historically, Britain's claim to play a global role had rested principally on a combination of global interests and capabilities. But, as implied earlier, Britain's material resources alone had never been sufficient to sustain an empire of global dimensions. As Michael Howard argues, the underlying weaknesses of the British imperial structure in economic and military terms were finally exposed by the Boer War (see Howard, 1974, pp. 11–13). Even prior to this war, however, it had long been necessary to augment military strength by forging alliances, and to supplement material power with less tangible elements of power, such as skilful, flexible diplomacy and claims to moral authority. As Britain's global capabilities declined in comparison with other states and, in the postwar period, global interests contracted sharply, it became necessary to rely more and more upon collective defence and the symbols of power to sustain the image of global status.

British attitudes towards détente and, indeed, to East–West relations as a whole since the 1950s can be explained in terms of the continuing assumption that Britain could and should play an effective global role, material circumstances notwithstanding. Whether Britain was seen as a mediator, a 'bridge', an 'honest broker' or, in the more traditional language of realpolitik, a 'balancer' of power, what Northedge called 'first-rank status' was taken for granted (Northedge, 1970, p. 43). Of the range of metaphors used to explain and justify continuing British efforts to influence the direction of East–West relations during the postwar period, perhaps Macmillan's notion that Britain could play 'Greece' to the United States' 'Rome' captures the essence of this sort of imagery. While 'Rome' had the material power to act decisively in world politics, she lacked subtlety and was hampered by her naivety and lack of experience. 'Greece's' role was to complement this raw power by providing the experience, the wisdom and the practical diplomatic skills that would guide this brash, rather vulgar newcomer through the intricacies of international relations (see Sampson, 1967, p. 61; Watt, 1984, p. 135).

This basic conception, shorn over time of its more arrogant and pretentious elements, that Britain has a distinctive if not unique role to play in East–West relations, has persisted to the present day. The conclusions of Lord Carrington can again be used to exemplify this point. His argument in 1983 was that:

Britain has an important role to play in developing a more sane and secure East–West relationship [though] not as a bridge, or an intermediary, not to spot the chance to split the difference – but to contribute our knowledge, experience and mixture of firmness and flexibility to the efforts of our partners in Europe and America (Carrington, 1983, p. 152).

DÉTENTE AND PRAGMATISM

The previous sections have attempted to locate attitudes towards détente within a traditional British approach to international relations, identifying particular historical antecedents in attitudes towards diplomacy, the relationship between diplomacy and defence, and the global orientation of British policy. The object of this exercise, it will be recalled, was to consider the proposition that an explanation of British détente policy is incomplete without an understanding of relevant traditional attitudes. In this context, the contention must be that this proposition has been sustained. The continuity of British attitudes towards détente since the 1950s cannot be explained without some reference to the persistence of certain traditional attitudes to international relations.

Another justification for this historical detour is to be better placed to consider an important issue posed in the introduction. The issue can be focused by posing a question. Can British attitudes and policy towards détente also be explained in terms of a tradition of pragmatism in foreign policy-making, or has a British conception of détente been established here that challenges the pragmatic ethos that is said to infuse British foreign policy? To answer this question, rather more needs to be said about the meaning of pragmatism than the brief comments offered in the introduction.

A dictionary definition of pragmatism would suggest that it means dealing with affairs in terms of their practical significance. In the context of British foreign policy, however, the word has various connotations that seem to go beyond simply a practical approach to affairs. Unfortunately, pragmatism is rarely discussed and, when it is, more often by commentators than by policy-makers themselves, it tends to be explained in negative terms. The problem is further compounded by the fact that the absence of discussion about pragmatism is itself taken to be part of its meaning. This led Andrew Shonfield to relate pragmatism to what he called the 'cult of the implicit' (Shonfield, 1967, p. 11).

Nevertheless, a pragmatic tradition in British foreign policy is generally taken to mean a non-analytical and a non-ideological approach to international relations. Foreign policy issues are dealt with piecemeal, case by case, with little or no reference to general principles or broad objectives. Frankel, for example, suggests that 'owing to the pragmatic, non-ideological nature of British foreign policy in the past, we are unable to trace such clear patterns of tradition and principle as we can for other countries whose politicians are more articulate'. For Frankel and other commentators, pragmatism also denotes, *inter alia*, flexibility, a resistance to 'grand designs', an unwillingness to engage in policy planning, a preoccupation with immediate 'interests' rather than desired future outcomes and, finally, reacting to international events rather than taking the initiative (Frankel, 1975, pp. 3, 96, 112–17; see also Vital, 1968, pp. 98–103, 109–11; Hanrieder and Auton, 1980, pp. 181–2; Palliser, 1976; Shlaim, 1975, p. 838).

If this is taken as a broad characterization of pragmatism, British détente policy does provide clear evidence of a pragmatic approach to policy-making. A piecemeal, flexible approach to resolving a range of East–West problems is evident in the approach adopted by successive British governments since the 1950s. The British contribution to the test ban negotiations, for example, offers a case study illustration of a pragmatic approach based, in Korbel's words quoted in the introduction, on the 'ways of quiet diplomacy and practical steps of rapprochement'. The British approach to détente in the 1950s, certainly in contrast to the American approach in this period, was non-ideological and, as suggested earlier, consistent with a tradition of pragmatic European diplomacy. And, finally, there was an important element of pragmatic opportunism about the persistent efforts of British leaders to take a lead in the détente process whenever the opportunity presented itself. The initiatives taken by Churchill in 1953–54, Macmillan in the late 1950s and Thatcher after the 1983 election provide the most significant illustrations.

But it can also be argued on the basis of this study that the continuity of British détente policy, with its roots in traditional attitudes to international relations, is more difficult to explain in pragmatic terms. The article on Anglo-Soviet relations by Sir Duncan Wilson, which was cited in earlier chapters, conveniently focuses our attention on the problem of trying to explain the substance of British détente policy in purely pragmatic terms.

Commenting in 1974 on relations with Moscow in the second half of the 1950s and the early 1960s, Wilson, a former ambassador in Moscow, begins by reiterating the standard line on pragmatism. 'The conduct of foreign affairs is largely a question of reacting to various day-to-day stimuli . . . As is well known, the British diplomat's motto is ad hoc.' Consistent with this premise, he goes on to reject the argument that British contacts with the Soviet government after 1956 were 'based on any broad philosophy of "bridge-building"' (D. Wilson, 1974).

Wilson then encounters problems, however, in trying to explain what he calls the 'intensification of contacts, commercial and cultural' between London and Moscow in the period 1957–64. He tries to explain these contacts, first by suggesting that they were minor and therefore of little significance. He then argues that they can be explained in terms of the domestic political necessity of producing for a sceptical British public some positive results from the visits of Khrushchev and Bulganin to London in 1956, and Macmillan to Moscow in 1959. He also suggests that there was an element of *faute de mieux* about these contacts, before admitting finally that the intensification of Anglo-Soviet contacts was based in part at least on what he calls an 'implicit philosophy of contact':

official policy began to be determined not only by the pressure of events, but also to some small extent by the development of its own philosophy. A constant element in this philosophy was that the utmost caution is needed in dealing with the Soviet government. A less explicit but growing element, however, was the idea that changes were taking place in the internal structure of the Soviet Union, and that further changes might result from increasing contacts with the outside world (D. Wilson, 1974, pp. 380, 385–7).

The conclusion drawn here is that while pragmatic, opportunistic elements can certainly be identified within British détente policy, they are indicative of what Frankel calls a distinctive 'national style' of policy-making (Frankel, 1975, p. 23). But this characteristic style should not be allowed to obscure an approach that, as even the sceptical Duncan Wilson admits, has analytical and philosophical components that cannot be explained in terms of pragmatism. Attitudes toward détente can be related to traditional British attitudes to international relations, which constitute, if not a coherent ideology, at least a normative set of principles, which in turn define a preferred international order.

The British 'view of the world' that is revealed by this study is less concise than the conception of a global role – although this conception itself must be regarded as part of that world view – because the 'liberal realist' approach contains not wholly compatible elements of both liberal and conservative traditions of thought about international relations. But, if no ideological 'grand design' is evident, the 'normal' or preferred international order that emerges highlights a continuing preference for peace rather than war; for conciliatory diplomacy rather than the use of force, particularly in situations where the consequences of using force are unpredictable; and for a flexible international system, with contacts as open and diverse as possible, to facilitate the advancement and/or the protection of politico-economic interests.

British détente policy may reflect different traditions, but the indications here are that commentators exaggerate the difficulty of tracing 'patterns of tradition and principle'. British policy-makers may be less prepared than their counterparts in Europe and the United States to articulate the analytical assumptions upon which their behaviour is based, but the statements of policy-makers cited in this study, which convey an essentially consistent and, moreover, a bipartisan view of détente during the postwar period, suggest that this criticism is overstated (Frankel, 1975, p. 23). It would be difficult, for example, to find a more clearly articulated conception of détente than that offered by Macmillan in his September 1960 speech to the United Nations General Assembly, which certainly stands comparison with the more famous speech by President Kennedy at the American University in June 1963. The British approach to foreign policy may, as Palliser argues, be typified as reactive rather than initiatory, but the proactive, catalytic role of British diplomacy at certain key stages in the détente process is scarcely compatible with a pragmatic approach, if pragmatism is defined in these terms (Palliser, 1976, pp. 2, 6). If it is accepted that pragmatism characterizes a style of policy-making rather than providing a wholly satisfactory explanation of the substance of policy, it can be argued that a coherent British conception of détente has been established here that can legitimately be used for explanatory purposes.

Chapter 9

Conclusion

This book began with the assertion that the promotion of East–West détente has been an important but neglected theme in postwar British foreign policy. The objective of this study was not only to identify this theme historically, but also to make some assessment of the impact of British policy and to offer an explanation of that policy. Furthermore, it was suggested in the introduction that such a study might throw some additional light on the nature of détente and, it is hoped, make a contribution to an understanding of British foreign policy since the Second World War.

The extensive narrative sections of this study confirm that East–West détente has indeed been a recurring though not a dominant theme in British foreign policy. Little needs to be added here, except to say that this suggests an interpretation of British policy since the 1950s that differs from those, such as Korbel, who would deny that Britain has taken a sustained interest in détente and conclude that British policy in this context is not worthy of detailed analysis. Having established this theme, however, we do need to offer some concluding comments with respect both to the evaluation and the explanation of British policy. Given the dramatic changes in the East–West environment during the last two years or so, it is also appropriate to reflect on what lessons might be derived from this study with respect to how effectively British policy will adapt to that new environment through the 1990s.

THE SIGNIFICANCE OF BRITISH DÉTENTE POLICY

An evaluation of the British contribution to détente since the 1950s has to begin, as we did here, with the concept of détente itself. To the extent that this study has demonstrated the utility of the concept, it has provided a response to those who would question whether détente can be used as an analytical term. From a British perspective, détente is not 'wishful thinking', as George Ball would have it, nor is it an artificial construct divorced from the real world of international relations. Détente is not simply an 'attitude' or a 'mood' if these terms connote an atmosphere, an approach to or a style of policy-making, rather than a substantive phenomenon. Although closely related to traditional diplomacy, détente is not merely a synonym for it.

In essence, a British perspective has reinforced the argument that détente can be effectively analysed as both a policy and as a process of systemic change over a longer time-frame than many of the conventional uses of the term would suggest. For British policy-makers, a détente between East and West in terms of keeping the 'door' open to Moscow was, arguably, a policy aspiration in the late 1940s, and has certainly been a recurring policy instrument and policy objective since the 1950s. British governments of both political persuasions, it can be concluded, have pursued a consistent policy towards détente, based on a coherent and consistent conception of détente throughout the postwar period.

Given that successive British governments since the 1950s have regarded East–West détente as an important process of change in international relations, however, this poses a challenge to those who would locate détente within a specific and delimited historical period, such as the 1970s. From a British perspective, to regard détente as a temporary period or phase in postwar international relations seems arbitrary; to regard détente as a prelude to entente appears both mechanistic and deterministic; and regarding détente as synonymous with appeasement in a pejorative sense is revealed as an overtly ideological use of the term. From this perspective, indeed, the continuing search for détente appears as an essential part of international relations rather than an 'optional extra'. Even more fundamentally perhaps, 'détente', like 'cold war', might reflect the special conditions of the nuclear age, but both terms can be located and explained within a pattern of international relations conceived as a mix of conflict and cooperation.

It is from this important notion of 'normal' international relations that the contribution but also the limits of British policy with respect to détente emerges. When East–West relations were judged to have become 'abnormal' or 'unbalanced' in the postwar period,

British governments sought with some success to throw their weight behind an attempt to normalize or balance those relationships. In periods of intense cold war or 'new' cold war conflict, British policy was oriented towards the promotion of détente and British influence was used as a catalyst in a détente process. For reasons that have been developed here, this role was played most effectively in the 1950s and early 1960s. Over this period as a whole, it can be argued that British diplomacy made a more significant contribution to the initial development of an East–West détente than any other state on either side of the ideological divide. Thus, this earlier period has received disproportionate attention in this study. The later British contribution to détente in the mid-1980s is important, but less significant. Britain was less and less able to exercise an autonomous influence on East–West relations after the 1960s and, arguably, the high-profile British role in the 'new détente' of the 1980s was more a function of the personal standing of Mrs Thatcher in East–West relations and of the triangular relationship she managed to establish with Presidents Reagan and Gorbachev than a reflection of continuing British influence per se.

The important corollary of the British position, however, was that the 'balance principle' prescribed a different role for Britain when, in the judgement of British leaders, the process of East–West conciliation developed to a point where it threatened to destabilize or even to undermine the structure of Western security. Thus, in the 1970s and the late 1980s, in particular, we see British governments continuing to support détente in principle, but acting less as an active participant and more as a 'brake' in seeking to slow down the process of accommodation. Nevertheless, it can be argued that both dimensions of the British approach made an important contribution to East–West relations at different times. In the 1950s, the early 1960s and the mid-1980s, British attempts to promote détente served to highlight the dangers of the West relying excessively on the essentially negative strategy of deterrence in its dealings with the Soviet bloc. In the 1970s, on the other hand, the more cautious British approach highlighted the dangers of overselling détente in the West, and helped to deflate some of the more exaggerated expectations of what détente could achieve. In the final analysis, the decline in British influence in the postwar period notwithstanding, it is perhaps the very consistency of the British approach to East–West relations that has been the major contribution to international peace and stability.

AN EXPLANATION OF BRITISH DÉTENTE POLICY

If East–West détente has been an important theme in postwar British foreign policy and the impact of British détente policy has been more significant than many scholars would suggest, how can British policy be explained? The approach adopted here, it will be recalled, was to set up an analytical framework operating at three different levels of analysis in an attempt to develop an explanation. From an international system or 'systemic' perspective, the aim was to explain British policy in terms of a persistent attempt over time to adapt to the new postwar structure of East–West relations. From this perspective, a détente policy that exploited Britain's continuing 'strengths' was seen as a useful vehicle for maintaining British influence at the global level in the face of challenges to that position, most evidently from material decline.

On the basis of this study, however, we can conclude that British governments adapted most successfully and used détente most effectively in the 1950s, when a tight bipolar structure and the absence of direct superpower diplomacy, in particular, provided an opportunity for British governments to play an important mediating role – an opportunity that was not to reappear again during the postwar period in quite such a stark form. What were called here the 'symbols of power' were effectively deployed until the early 1960s to maximize British influence and to maintain a position in world affairs which, even then, was scarcely justified by British power defined in narrow material terms.

This analytical perspective has been particularly useful in explanatory terms. By providing a focus on the way in which the postwar structures or patterns of East–West relations have changed since the 1950s, it has identified the consequent erosion of the sources of British influence on the direction of those relationships. In particular, it has identified the transformation of the Euro-Atlantic or transatlantic frameworks, which British governments helped to construct and through which British influence has been exercised since the 1950s, and has highlighted the growing tension between the 'European' and the 'Atlantic' dimensions of British policy. By the end of the 1980s, the limits of Britain's ability to adapt to the now radically changing structure of East–West relations were apparent. Despite the attempts by the Thatcher governments after 1983 to play what might be called a residual mediation role with, admittedly, some success, it is clear from a structural analysis that

Britain was being increasingly marginalized as far as East–West relations were concerned.

The attempt to explain the continuity of British détente policy from a domestic politics perspective has been less successful, although this outcome was not unexpected for reasons identified in the introductory chapter. But if the pursuit of détente over the postwar period as a whole cannot be explained satisfactorily in terms of domestic politics, an explanation of British policy in two important periods – the late 1950s and the mid-1980s – does clearly benefit from the application of an analysis pitched at this level. It can be argued that domestic political factors did constitute an imperative in both periods, because détente was significant in electoral terms and the related nuclear issue was also particularly salient. This stemmed largely from the fact that a nuclear deterrence strategy was highly 'visible' in domestic political terms, and the political leadership appeared to be sensitive to the domestic ramifications of this strategy. The indications are that both the Macmillan and the Thatcher governments in these periods were aware of the potential electoral advantage to be derived from a successful détente policy. Or, to put it another way, they appeared to be aware of the electoral damage that might be done by not pursuing or at least by not appearing to pursue a détente policy.

The interesting dimension of the domestic political environment not developed here in analytical terms – though there are some pertinent comments in this study – is the extent to which government officials and Foreign (and Commonwealth) Office officials in particular have served during the postwar period as a repository of traditional values with respect to détente. The fact that the 'balanced' approach to détente has been pursued so consistently over a long period of time by a number of different governments of both political persuasions, and with a remarkable degree of bipartisan support, suggests that an explanation of British détente policy might derive considerable benefit from an analysis that focuses on bureaucratic attitudes and the operation of administrative politics in this context.

Whatever the source and the nature of the transmission of traditional values into the policy process, the final level of analysis, pitched at the level of the policy-makers themselves and focused on an attempt to identify their attitudes towards détente, has been particularly instructive in explanatory terms. Appropriate conclusions in this context were drawn in the last chapter, but it is worth adding here that this study adds weight to the argument advanced elsewhere, with reference to the development of nuclear weapons policy, for example, that the substance of postwar British foreign and defence policy owes much to the continuing impact of traditional attitudes to international relations, shaped by historical experience. British policy towards détente provides useful insights into a British 'view of the world' and what has been conceived by policy-makers as an appropriate role for Britain in that world. However, in the context of studies that emphasize the impact of a realpolitik tradition on British thinking and seek to explain policy largely in terms of power politics, a study of policy in relation to East–West détente serves as an important reminder not only of the continuing influence of a liberal tradition but also of the broader mix of traditions of political thought that have influenced policy-makers in the postwar period.

The conclusions with respect to an explanation of British détente policy can, therefore, be summarized simply. While the demands of domestic politics provide some illuminating insights into British policy, alternative analytical perspectives, which focus on changes in East–West relations over time, allied to an understanding of the continuities of British attitudes, offer the most satisfactory explanation of British policy. An analysis of changing patterns of East–West relations is necessary to appreciate the declining ability of British governments to influence East–West relations. What constituted effective adaptation in the 1950s – using particular 'symbols of power' to substitute influence for power – had become less and less effective by the 1980s. A structural analysis explains why Britain became increasingly marginalized in East–West relations. On the other hand, an understanding of decision-makers' attitudes towards détente over time is crucial not only to explain the continuity of British policy, but an appreciation of the historical sources of those attitudes also helps to explain the growing problem of adaptation to change at the systemic level. To this extent, the results achieved by applying analytical perspectives that are distinctively different can be usefully combined to provide an explanation.

BRITAIN AND EAST–WEST RELATIONS IN THE 1990s

An explanation of British détente policy since the 1950s, which draws so heavily on changing patterns of East–West relations

and consequent problems of adaptation, together with the continuing impact of traditional attitudes on policy-makers, inevitably
raises important questions about how effectively Britain will adapt
through the 1990s to the very different and still emerging environment of East–West relations. It is appropriate, therefore, to
conclude with some brief comments about the implications that
might be drawn from this study, comments that necessarily have
a prescriptive flavour. Given the revolutionary changes that began
this decade, the past, it might be argued, is a very poor guide
to the future. After all, the fixed points of that past–the cold war,
two competing superpowers, two military alliances confronting
each other, the ideological rift between Marxism–Leninism
and capitalism, the continuing elements of a bipolar structure of
international relations – appear finally to have disappeared from
the international scene in a quite dramatic way. But a number
of questions flow from this. What will constitute 'East–West'
relations in the 1990s? How will Britain influence the new structures and processes that emerge? Will 'détente' be an appropriate
policy objective? More fundamentally perhaps, how relevant is an
approach grounded essentially in the past for facing a very different
future?

Some elements of the British approach to détente, it can be
argued, have an essentially timeless relevance: the notion that
normal international relations is a mix of conflict and cooperation even in a 'post-cold war' world; that a cautious approach
to change is prudent; that policy should always be concerned
with maintaining security, although not necessarily defined in
military-strategic terms; that the military elements of policy should
always be balanced by the politico-diplomatic, and so on. The
traditional British conception of détente as normal diplomacy
and open contacts should be sufficiently flexible to be useful
in the new environment of the 1990s. The problem is that the
specific policy implications of these premises in a highly dynamic
environment are not necessarily apparent. The clear danger that
emerges from the analysis here is that British governments may
remain excessively attached both to institutions and relationships
that have served as sources of influence in the past, but which,
we have concluded, were being eroded well before more recent
changes took place. In the context of East–West relations – and
beyond – this not only raises questions about how to respond to
a radically changing Soviet Union, but it also raises fundamental

questions about Britain's attitude to NATO and the appropriate pattern of relationships to develop with the United States and with Britain's partners in the European Community – in short, questions about the established transatlantic context of British policy and the international identity of Britain in the foreseeable future.

If transatlantic unity or 'Atlanticism' has been a guiding leitmotif of the British approach to East–West relations in the past, it is not at all clear that this will be appropriate in the future. In the absence of a unifying threat from the East, growing divergences between the United States and Western Europe across a range of issues may mean that Britain has to choose between Atlantic and European unity. Détente or, more appropriately perhaps, East–West cooperation will undoubtedly take different forms in the 1990s and will be enacted through transformed if not entirely different institutional structures. It is already evident, for example, that the European Community will be a major player in that process and Britain's relations with the Community will be crucial. Clearly, if British governments are not able to think creatively to meet new challenges, they risk being further marginalized and left out of the mainstream as far as future developments are concerned.

This sort of new thinking, however, may not be aided by the pragmatic elements in the British tradition. Pragmatism should facilitate unavoidable changes of direction. As Frankel puts it, 'the natural reaction of pragmatic policy-makers is to retain as much flexibility as possible, to keep the options open' (Frankel, 1975, p. 114). But in Britain's case, as Hill notes, pragmatism has often meant avoiding making 'major choices and sticking with known assets at all costs' (Hill, 1988, p. 40). Britain may have a long and relatively successful history of adapting to change in international relations, but one of the central challenges facing the post-Thatcher leadership in Britain will be how effectively it adapts to new structures and patterns of East–West relations in the future in order to maintain an influential British voice.

Indications of a new approach to East–West relations in the first few months after the resignation of Mrs Thatcher were ambivalent at best, partly because the foreign policy agenda in Britain as elsewhere was dominated by the crisis and the eventual war in the Gulf. While this issue served as a temporary diversion from confronting the broader questions outlined above, it did illustrate in a powerful way the continuing influence of traditional thinking as far as British policy-makers were concerned. British policy under the new Major administration, not surprisingly perhaps, followed the lines established by Mrs Thatcher. The former prime minister was in the United States at the time of the Iraqi invasion in August 1990, and there was speculation at the time that she had helped to persuade President Bush to take a tough line in response. As the British role developed, however, it took on more and more the appearance of an ill-fitting perhaps but nevertheless comfortable old suit. Once the Gulf crisis turned into a military confrontation it triggered all the familiar, traditional images: Britain again playing a significant global role upholding international law by military force; Britain acting again as the closest and most loyal ally of the United States; British leaders berating the 'Europeans' again for allegedly contributing inadequately to the coalition efforts to liberate Kuwait; British leaders using the Gulf example to pour scorn once more on the possibility of European political and economic union.

With the ending of the Gulf War, however, attention turned back to the issues dramatically highlighted by Mrs Thatcher's resignation. Given the increasingly high-profile role played by Europe – and the European Community in particular – in the evolving structure of East–West relations, one central question was whether the Major government would adopt a more positive approach to the Community to avoid the isolation that had been such a feature of the last twelve months or so of the Thatcher period. Alternatively, would the Gulf experience – like the Falklands war – be used to justify a continuing adherence to Atlanticism? More broadly, given the structural changes in Europe, was the traditional British transatlantic posture any longer an option?

Early indicators did not allow any firm conclusions to be drawn. With respect to the Community, there was certainly a change of style, although this was to be expected. And there is a sense in which style and attitudes are substantive in this context. Contacts at Community meetings and elsewhere were cordial, and there were clear indications that the new government was seeking to build bridges with Community partners. There was a determined effort, for example, to develop a good working relationship with the Germans after a series of frosty exchanges during the Gulf crisis. Despite a headline speech in Bonn by John Major in March 1991, however, in which he promised to put Britain 'at the very heart of Europe' in working towards an integrated European Community, it was still not clear at the time of writing whether the substance of British European policy would undergo a significant change. Much hinges on this with respect to whether or not the Community can serve as a vehicle for British influence in the wider international arena.

What was clear though was the dilemma that faced British policy-makers. Not only was the pace of change rapid, but change in one area of policy cut across others. When issues could be compartmentalized – economic and social issues dealt with in an EC context and security issues in a NATO context, for example – institutional arrangements roughly matched Britain's self-appointed role as a manager of transatlantic relations. With the transformation of cold war structures and processes, however, the process of institutional change in Europe speeded up and forced British policy-makers to confront some uncomfortable choices – such as whether to support the Franco–German plan to integrate the Western European Union (WEU) into the European Community by the time the WEU Treaty expires in 1998. This is precisely the sort of development that would cut right across the Atlantic/European institutional distinction that the British have sought so hard to preserve.

Such institutional changes would, of course, threaten Britain's relationship with the United States, at least in the way in which it has been traditionally conceived. The problem with seeing that relationship in terms of its 'specialness' or otherwise is that it prevents a realistic reassessment of it from a European perspective. The analysis here suggests that such a reassessment is necessary. Certainly, British governments in the 1990s can no longer regard the Washington connection as an alternative to a more European orientation. This does not mean that relations with Washington would not continue to be important in the 1990s, but they would need to be evaluated from an unambiguous position within European institutional structures rather than from some position on the Atlantic periphery of European affairs. Apart from a brief visit to Washington in December 1990, in which the new prime minister used the very Euro-sounding phrase, a 'community of interest' to describe the Anglo–American relationship, there were no clear indications of any new directions in this context.

To revert finally to the crucial European context of British policy, there were no indications either that a post-Thatcher government would be prepared to do what successive British governments since the 1970s have signally failed to do – namely, to educate the British people with respect to the extent of British involvement in the interdependent network of relationships that constitutes contemporary European politics. Without government being prepared to gear the domestic polity and popular perceptions to the facts of interdependence and the extent of the Europeanization of policy, there will be no domestic consensus to underpin a new European orientation. In the absence of change with respect to a range of traditional British attitudes, we might conclude, the 1990s will see continuing tensions between 'Atlanticism' and 'Europeanism', and this false dichotomy will in turn further undermine British efforts to wield influence both in Europe and in the wider East–West arena.

Notes

1 INTRODUCTION

1 See, for example, Shlaim, 1983–4; Ovendale, 1985; Best, 1986; Smith, R. 1988; Deighton, 1987, 1990. For a more sceptical view of the British contribution, see Rothwell, 1987.
2 See, for example, Shlaim, 1975, Barker, 1971. A notable exception is Northedge, who argued consistently in several publications that Britain played a crucial role in initiating East–West détente in the 1950s and early 1960s (see Northedge, 1970, 1974, 1980; Northedge and Wells, 1982).
3 For a useful discussion of analytical methods and perspectives in the context of British foreign policy studies, see Smith and Smith, 1988.
4 The tension between 'Atlantic' and 'European' orientations in British policy is explored further in White, 1991.

3 BRITAIN, THE COLD WAR AND DÉTENTE

1 A clear statement of this position appeared in an interdepartmental steering committee paper prepared for the forthcoming Churchill visit to Washington in January 1952. 'Our fundamental objectives vis-à-vis the USSR are to contain its aggressive expansionism within the present territorial limits which it controls or dominates, to encourage and create, if possible, a situation within the Soviet satellite countries of Eastern Europe which would lead to the relaxation of Soviet control and domination over them and deter the Kremlin from acts which might result in general war. To achieve these objectives, the US Government has adopted two fundamental policies:

> 1 To create military, political, economic and psychological unity among the free nations and particularly among NATO countries.
> 2 To exploit and promote weakness, disunity and discontent behind the Iron Curtain through political warfare.'

Steering Group Negotiating Papers TCT D-1/5a, 6 January 1952, *Harry S. Truman Papers.*

2 ibid.

4 BRITAIN AS A CATALYST OF DÉTENTE

1 Memorandum to the president from C.D. Jackson, Special Assistant for Psychological Warfare, Administrative File, Jackson, C.D. 1953 (2) 3 June 1953, *D.D. Eisenhower Papers.*

2 In his diary entry on 5 February 1959, Macmillan describes his 'idea of a more or less continuous or permanent Conference – adjourning for long periods and reassembling for new work, with Ministers attending from time to time, and officials (Ambassadors, etc.) working on committees and reporting to Ministers. Such a Conference, or Congress, would in itself "relieve tensions"' (Macmillan, 1971, pp. 588–9). It is worth noting that this conception, which appears to borrow from nineteenth-century European congresses, is very different from Churchill's notion of a summit, which used Second World War conferences as a model.

3 The relevant extracts from Lloyd's speeches can be found in King, 1963, pp. 69–74 and in Gott *et al.*, 1964, pp. 2–3.

4 Department of State Memorandum dated 5 May 1954 (Library of Congress documents on microfiche series, 002370, 1983).

5 BRITAIN AND THE PARTIAL TEST BAN TREATY

1 On the important contribution of British scientists to nuclear arms control during this period, see Freeman, 1986, ch. 2.

2 The 'big-hole' obsession was a reference to a method of evading detection of underground tests that emerged from American seismic research in 1959. The argument, associated with Professor Albert Latter, was 'that it might be possible to muffle underground nuclear tests by conducting them in large subterranean cavities or holes which would make them difficult if not impossible to detect' (Wright, 1964, p. 125).

3 There is some debate about the extent of British responsibility for what turned out to be the critical final initiative. Schlesinger (1965) and Sorensen (1965) give at least equal credit to Kennedy. Other sources, however, which focus on the resistance within the Kennedy administration to a new initiative, argue convincingly that the initiative came from London. Kennedy overruled those who advised against the initiative and Macmillan ignored the advice of his ambassador in Moscow. (See, in particular, Jacobson and Stein, 1966, p. 447; Nunnerly, 1972, p. 106; Freeman, 1986, pp. 139–42.)

4 It should be noted that British sources on this issue, apparently following Wright's account, are misleading to the extent that they imply that the call for test ban negotiations, following the Experts' report, and the commitment to suspend testing, were British initiatives.

The argument is that the Americans and Dulles in particular were still unwilling to negotiate a test ban agreement separate from other disarmament measures, and had to be persuaded to negotiate and to suspend testing. (See Wright, 1964, p. 130; Nunnerly, 1972, p. 92; Sampson, 1967, p. 227; Freeman, 1986, p. 80.) American sources, on the other hand, argue convincingly from primary sources that the Eisenhower administration had effectively decoupled a test ban from other disarmament measures as early as April 1958. This was not a problem, therefore, after the Experts reported. Eisenhower and Dulles had already won the internal battle on this issue and they took the initiatives. Macmillan merely deferred to the American position, though not without protest. (See, in particular, Divine, 1978, pp. 206–12, 227–31: also Jacobson and Stein, 1966, pp. 85–94; Seaborg, 1981, p. 14; Macmillan, 1971, pp. 560–3; Eisenhower, 1965, p. 477.)

Bibliography

Alting Von Geusau, F.A.M. (ed.). 1979. *Uncertain Détente*. Alphen aan den Rijn: Sijthoff & Noordhoff.

Ball, G. 1976. *Diplomacy for a Crowded World*. London: Bodley Head.

Barker, E. 1971. *Britain in a Divided Europe 1945–70*. London: Weidenfeld & Nicolson.

Barker, E. 1983. *The British between the Superpowers 1945–50*. London: Macmillan.

Barnet, R. 1977. *The Giants*. New York: Simon & Schuster.

Barnet, R. 1983. *The Alliance*. New York: Simon & Schuster.

Barraclough, G. and Wall, R.F. 1960. *Survey of International Affairs 1955–56*. London: RIIA/Oxford University Press.

Barraclough, G. 1964. *Survey of International Affairs 1959–60*. London: RIIA/Oxford University Press.

Bartlett, C.J. 1977. *A History of Postwar Britain 1945–74*. London: Longman.

Baylis, J. 1982. Britain and the Dunkirk Treaty: the origins of NATO. *Journal of Strategic Studies* 5: 236–47.

Baylis, J. 1984. *Anglo-American Defence Relations 1939–84*, 2nd edn. London: Macmillan.

Bell, C. 1962. *Negotiation From Strength*. London: Chatto & Windus.

Bell, C. 1971. *The Conventions of Crisis*. London: Oxford University Press.

Bell, C. 1977. *The Diplomacy of Détente*. London: Martin Robertson.

Best, R.A. 1986. *'Cooperation with Like-Minded Peoples': British Influences on American Security Policy 1945–49*. New York: Greenwood Press.

Bloomfield, L.P., Clemens, W.C. and Griffiths, F. 1966. *Khrushchev and the Arms Race: Soviet Interests in Arms Control and Disarmament*. Cambridge, Mass.: MIT Press.

Bluth, C. 1990. The security dimension. In A. Pravda and P.J.S. Duncan (eds), *Soviet–British Relations since the 1970s*, pp. 92–119. Cambridge: RIIA/Cambridge University Press.

Boardman, R. 1976. *Britain and the People's Republic of China 1949–74*. London: Macmillan.

Bowker, M. and Williams, P. 1988. *Superpower Détente: A Reappraisal*. London: RIIA/Sage.

Brand, C.F. 1974. *The British Labor Party*. Stanford, Calif.: Hoover Institution Press.

Brandon, H. 1970. *Anatomy of Error*. London: André Deutsch.

Brown, G. 1972. *In My Way*. Harmondsworth: Penguin.

Brown, S. 1968. *The Faces of Power*. New York: Columbia University Press.

Bullock, A. 1985. *Ernest Bevin: Foreign Secretary 1945–51*. Oxford: Oxford University Press.

Butler, D.E. 1952. *The British General Election of 1951*. London: Macmillan.

Butler, D.E. and Kavanagh, D. 1984. *The British General Election of 1983*. London: Macmillan.

Butler, D.E. and Kavanagh, D. 1988. *The British General Election of 1987*. London: Macmillan.

Butler, D.E. and Rose, R. 1970. *The British General Election of 1959*. London: Frank Cass & Co.

Butler, R.A. 1971. *The Art of the Possible*. London: Hamish Hamilton.

Buzan, B. 1983. *People, States and Fear*. Brighton: Wheatsheaf.

Cain, P. 1979. Capitalism, internationalism and imperialism in the thoughts of Richard Cobden. *British Journal of International Studies* 5, 3: 229–47.

Calvocoressi, P. 1953. *Survey of International Affairs 1949–50*. London: RIIA/Oxford University Press.

Calvocoressi, P. 1982. *World Politics since 1945*, 4th edn. London: Longman.

Calvocoressi, P. 1984. Nuclear weapons in the service of man. *Review of International Studies* 10, 2: 89–101.

Carlton, D. 1981. *Anthony Eden*. London: Allen Lane.

Carlton, D. 1982. Potential threats to European security. In W. Gutteridge (ed.), *European Security, Nuclear Weapons and Public Confidence*, pp. 177–82. London: Macmillan.

Carlyle, M. (ed.). 1953. *Documents on International Affairs 1949–50*. London: RIIA/Oxford University Press.

Carrington, P. 1983. The 1983 Alastair Buchan memorial lecture, *Survival* 25, 4: 136–53.

Chomsky, N. 1982. *Towards a New Cold War*. London: Sinclair Brown.

Clarke, M. 1985. The implementation of Britain's CSCE policy, 1975–84. In S. Smith and M. Clarke (eds), *Foreign Policy Implementation*, pp. 142–65. London: Allen & Unwin.

Clarke, M. 1988. The Soviet Union and Eastern Europe. In P. Byrd (ed.), *Foreign Policy under Thatcher*, pp. 54–75. Oxford: Philip Allan.

Clarke, M. 1990. British perspectives on the Soviet Union. In A. Pravda and P.J.S. Duncan (eds), *Soviet–British Relations since the 1970s*, pp. 68–91. Cambridge: RIIA/Cambridge University Press.

Clemens, W.C. 1974. The impact of détente on Chinese and Soviet Communism. *Journal of International Studies* 28, 2: 133–57.

Colville, J. 1976. *Footprints in Time*. London: Collins.

Colville, J. 1981. *The Churchillians*. London: Weidenfeld & Nicolson.

Colville, J. 1985. *The Fringes of Power. Downing Street Diaries 1939–55*. London: Hodder & Stoughton.

Conquest, R. *et al.* 1974. Détente – an evaluation. *Survey* 20, 2/3: 1–27.

Cousins, N. 1972. *The Improbable Triumvirate*. New York: Norton & Co.

Craig, G.A. and George, A.L. 1983. *Force and Statecraft*. Oxford: Oxford University Press.

Cyr, A. 1979. *British Foreign Policy and the Atlantic Area*. London: Macmillan.

Deighton, A. 1987. The 'frozen front': the Labour government, the division of Germany and the origins of the cold war 1945–7. *International Affairs* 63, 3: 449–65.

Deighton, A. (ed.). 1990. *Britain and the First Cold War*. London: Macmillan.

Divine R.A. 1978. *Blowing on the Wind: the Nuclear Test Ban Debate 1954–60*. New York: Oxford University Press.

Donelan, M. 1959. Britain's foreign commitments 2. In report of a Princeton University conference (12–13 May), published as *Britain Today: Economics, Defence and Foreign Policy*. Princeton, NJ: Princeton University Press.

Dougherty, J.E. 1975. *British Perspectives on a Changing Global Balance*. London: Sage.

Draper, T. 1974. Détente. *Commentary*, June 1974: 26–40.

Draper, T. 1976. Appeasement and détente. *Commentary*, February 1976: 27–38.

Eden, A. 1960. *Full Circle*. London: Cassell.

Edmonds, R. 1975. *Soviet Foreign Policy 1962–73*. London: Oxford University Press.

Eisenhower, D.D. 1965. *The White House Years. Volume 2. Waging Peace 1956–61*. New York: Doubleday.

Epstein, L.D. 1954. *Britain – Uneasy Ally*. Chicago: Chicago University Press.

Evans, H. 1981. *Downing Street Diary: The Macmillan Years 1957–63*. London: Hodder & Stoughton.

Farrar, P.N. 1983. Britain's proposal for a buffer zone South of the Yalu in November 1950: was it a neglected opportunity to end the fighting in Korea? *Journal of Contemporary History* 18: 327–51.

Finley, D.D. 1975. Détente and Soviet–American trade: an approach to a political balance sheet. *Studies in Comparative Communism* 8, 1/2: 66–97.

Fisher, N. 1982. *Harold Macmillan*. London: Weidenfeld & Nicolson.

Folliot, D. (ed.). 1956. *Documents on International Affairs 1953*. London: RIIA/Oxford University Press.

Foreign and Commonwealth Office. 1977. *Miscellaneous No. 17: Selected Documents Relating to Problems of Security and Cooperation in Europe 1954–77*, Cmnd 6932. London: HMSO.

Frankel, J. 1975. *British Foreign Policy 1945–73*. London: Oxford University Press.

Frankland, N. (ed.). 1958. *Documents on International Affairs 1955*. London: RIIA/Oxford University Press.

Freedman, L. 1989. Thatcherism and defence. In D. Kavanagh and A. Seldon (eds), *The Thatcher Effect*, pp. 143–53. Oxford: The Clarendon Press.

Freeman, J.P.G. 1986. *Britain's Nuclear Arms Control Policy in the Context of Anglo-American Relations 1957–68.* London: Macmillan.

Gaddis, J.L. 1982. *Strategies of Containment.* New York: Oxford University Press.

Gallie, W.B. 1962. Essentially contested concepts. In M. Black (ed.), *The Importance of Language,* pp. 121–46. New York: Prentice-Hall.

Garthoff, R. 1985. *Détente and Confrontation: American–Soviet Relations from Nixon to Reagan.* Washington, DC: Brookings Institution.

George, A.L. 1980. *Presidential Decision-Making in Foreign Policy.* Boulder, Colo: Westview Press.

Gilbert, M. 1988. *'Never Despair'. Winston S. Churchill 1945–65.* London: Heinemann.

Gladwyn, Lord. 1972. *Memoirs.* London: Weidenfeld & Nicolson.

Goodwin, G. 1959. Britain's foreign commitments 1. In report of a Princeton University conference (12–13 May), published as *Britain Today: Economics, Defence and Foreign Policy.* Princeton, NJ: Princeton University Press.

Goodwin, G. 1972. British foreign policy since 1945: the long odyssey to Europe. In M. Leifer (ed.), *Constraints and Adjustments in British Foreign Policy,* pp. 35–52. London: Allen & Unwin.

Gore-Booth, P. 1974. *With Great Truth and Respect.* London: Constable.

Gott, R., Major, J. and Warner, G. (eds). 1964. *Documents on International Affairs 1960.* London: RIIA/Oxford University Press.

Hailsham, Lord. 1975. *The Door Wherein I Went.* London: Collins.

Halliday, F. 1983. *The Making of the Second Cold War.* London: Verso.

Hanrieder, W.F. and Auton, G.P. 1980. *The Foreign Policies of West Germany, France and Britain.* Englewood Cliffs, NJ: Prentice-Hall.

Harriman, A. 1971. *America and Russia in a Changing World.* London: Allen & Unwin.

Harrison, M.M. 1981. *The Reluctant Ally: France and Atlantic Security.* Baltimore, Md: Johns Hopkins University Press.

Hassner, P. 1977. Eurocommunism and détente. *Survival* 19, 6: 251–4.

Hayter, W. 1966. *The Kremlin and the Embassy.* London: Hodder & Stoughton.

Herz, J.H. 1964. The relevance and irrelevance of appeasement. *Social Research* 31, Autumn: 296–320.

Heyhoe, D.C.R. 1976/77. *The Alliance in Europe: Part 6. The European Programme Group.* Adelphi Papers no. 129. London: International Institute for Strategic Studies.

Hill, C. 1988. The historical background: past and present in British foreign policy, in S. Smith, M. Smith and B. White (eds), *British Foreign Policy: Tradition, Change and Transformation,* London, Unwin, Hyman, pp. 25–49.

Hoffman, S. 1972. Will the balance balance at home? *Foreign Policy,* Summer: 60–87.

Holsti, O.R., Siverson, R.M. and George, A.L. 1980. *Change in the International System.* Boulder, Colo: Westview Press.

Horne, A. 1989. *Macmillan 1957–86.* London: Macmillan.

House of Commons. 1986. *Observations by the Government to the Second*

Report from the Foreign Affairs Committee 1985–86, Cmnd 9842, July. London: HMSO.

Howard, A. (ed.). 1979. *The Crossman Diaries. Selections from the Diaries of a Cabinet Minister 1964–70. Richard Crossman*. London: Magnum.

Howard, M. 1958. *Disengagement in Europe*. London: Penguin.

Howard, M. 1974. *The Continental Commitment*. London: Penguin.

Howe, G. 1987. East–West relations: the British role. *International Affairs* 63, 4: 555–62.

Jacobson, H.K. and Stein, E. 1966. *Diplomats, Scientists and Politicians: The United States and the Test Ban Negotiations*. Ann Arbor, Mich.: University of Michigan Press.

Jenkins, P. 1987. *Mrs Thatcher's Revolution*. London: Cape.

Jonsson, C. 1979. *Soviet Bargaining Behaviour: The Nuclear Test Ban Case*. New York: Columbia University Press.

Kennan, G. 1982. *The Nuclear Delusion*. New York: Pantheon.

Kennedy, P. 1976. The tradition of appeasement in British foreign policy 1865–1939. *British Journal of International Studies* 2, 3: 195–215.

Kennedy, P. 1981. *The Realities Behind Diplomacy: Background Influences on British External Policy 1865–1980*. London: Fontana.

Kilmuir, Lord. 1964. *Political Adventure*. London: Weidenfeld & Nicolson.

King, G. (ed.). 1963. *Documents on International Affairs 1959*. London: RIIA/Oxford University Press.

Kirby, S. 1972. Britain's defence policy and NATO. In M. Leifer (ed.), *Constraints and Adjustments in British Foreign Policy*, pp. 70–85. London: Allen & Unwin.

Kissinger, H. 1979. *White House Years*. Boston, Mass.: Little, Brown.

Kissinger, H. 1982. *Years of Upheaval*. Boston, Mass.: Little, Brown.

Korbel, J. 1972. *Détente in Europe*. Princeton, NJ: Princeton University Press.

Luard, E. 1967. Conciliation and deterrence. *World Politics* 19: 167–89.

Macmillan, H. 1971. *Riding the Storm 1956–59*. London: Macmillan.

Macmillan, H. 1972. *Pointing the Way 1959–61*. London: Macmillan.

Macmillan, H. 1973. *At the End of the Day 1961–63*. London: Macmillan.

Marantz, P. 1975. Prelude to détente: doctrinal change under Khrushchev. *International Studies Quarterly* 19, 4: 501–27.

Nicholas, H.G. 1968. *The British General Election of 1950*. London: Frank Cass.

Nicolson, H. 1939. *Diplomacy*. London: Thornton Butterworth.

Nixon, R. 1984. *Real Peace*. London: Sidgwick & Jackson.

Northedge, F.S. 1970. Britain as a second rank power. *International Affairs* 46: 37–47.

Northedge, F.S. 1974. *Descent from Power: British Foreign Policy 1945–73*. London: Allen & Unwin.

Northedge, F.S. 1980. The coordination of interests in British foreign policy. Unpublished paper presented to the annual conference of the British International Studies Association, University of Lancaster, December 1980.

Northedge, F.S. and Wells, A. 1982. *Britain and Soviet Communism*. London: Macmillan.

Nunnerly, D. 1972. *President Kennedy and Britain*. London: Bodley Head.

Ovendale, R. 1982. Britain, the USA and the European cold war 1945–48. *History* LXVII: 217–36.

Ovendale, R. (ed.). 1984. *The Foreign Policy of the British Labour Governments 1945–51*. Leicester: Leicester University Press.

Ovendale, R. (ed.). 1985. *The English-Speaking Alliance: Britain, the United States, the Dominions and the Cold War 1945–51*. London: Allen & Unwin.

Owen, D. 1984. A new realism in East–West relations. *Journal of the Royal United Services Institute* 129: 3–8.

Palliser, M. 1976. *Britain and British Diplomacy in a World of Change*. London: David Davis Institute.

Pelling, H. 1968. *A Short History of the Labour Party*. London: Macmillan.

Pipes, R. 1981. *US–Soviet Relations in the Era of Détente*. Boulder, Colo: Westview Press.

Porter, B. 1987. *Britain, Europe and the World 1850–1986*, 2nd edn. London: Allen & Unwin.

Pravda, A. and Duncan, P.J.S. (eds). 1990. *Soviet–British Relations since the 1970s*. Cambridge: RIIA/Cambridge University Press.

Read, D. 1968. *Cobden and Bright: A Victorian Partnership*. London.

Reynolds, D. 1985/86. A 'special relationship'? America, Britain and the international order since the Second World War. *International Affairs* 62: 1–20.

Richardson, J.L. 1966. *Germany and the Atlantic Alliance*. Cambridge, Mass.: Harvard University Press.

Rosecrance, R. 1975. Détente or entente. *Foreign Affairs* April: 464–81.

Rothwell, V. 1987. Britain and the first cold war. In R. Crockatt and S. Smith (eds), *The Cold War Past and Present*, pp. 58–76. London: Allen & Unwin.

Sampson, A. 1967. *Macmillan: A Study in Ambiguity*. London: Penguin.

Schlesinger, A.M. 1965. *A Thousand Days*. Boston: Houghton Mifflin.

Seaborg, G.T. 1981. *Kennedy, Khrushchev and the Test Ban*. Berkeley, Calif.: University of California Press.

Senate Foreign Relations Committee (SFRC). 1974. *Hearings on United States Relations with Communist Countries before the Committee on Foreign Relations*. August–October 1974.

Shlaim, A. 1975. Britain's quest for a world role. *International Relations* May: 838–56.

Shlaim, A. 1983–4. Britain, the Berlin blockade and the cold war. *International Affairs* 60: 1–14.

Shonfield, A. 1967. The pragmatic illusion. *Encounter*, June 1967.

Shulman, M.D. 1966. *Beyond the Cold War*. New Haven, Conn.: Yale University Press.

Shulman, M.D. 1973. Towards a Western philosophy of coexistence. *Foreign Affairs* 51: 35–8.

Smith, M. 1984. *Western Europe and the United States: The Uncertain Alliance*. London: Allen & Unwin.

Smith, M. 1988. Britain and the United States: beyond the 'special relationship'? In P. Byrd (ed.), *British Foreign Policy under Thatcher*, pp. 8–34. Oxford: Philip Allan.

Smith, R. 1988. A climate of opinion: British officials and the development of British Soviet policy 1945–47. *International Affairs* 64, 4: 631–47.

Smith, S. and Smith, M. 1988. The analytical background: approaches to the study of British foreign policy. In S. Smith, M. Smith and B. White (eds), *British Foreign Policy: Tradition, Change and Transformation*, pp. 3–23. London: Unwin Hyman.

Sorenson, T. 1965. *Kennedy*. New York: Harper & Row.

Stevenson, R.W. 1985. *The Rise and Fall of Détente*. London: Macmillan.

Strang, Lord. 1961. *Britain in World Affairs*. Westport, Conn.: Greenwood Press.

Ulam, A. 1968. *Expansion and Coexistence*. New York: Praeger.

Ulam, A. 1976. Détente under Soviet eyes. *Foreign Policy* 24, Fall: 145–59.

Urban, G.R. (ed.). 1976. *Détente*. London: Temple Smith.

Vernon, G.D. 1979. Controlled conflict: Soviet perceptions of peaceful coexistence. *Orbis* 23, 2: 271–97.

Vital, D. 1968. *The Making of British Foreign Policy*. London: Allen & Unwin.

Wallace, W. 1986. Foreign policy: the management of distinctive interests. In R. Morgan and C. Bray (eds), *Partners and Rivals in Western Europe: Britain, France and Germany*, pp. 205–23. London: Gower.

Wallace, W. and Wallace, H. 1990. Strong state or weak state in foreign policy? The contradictions of conservative liberalism 1979–87. *Public Administration* 68: 83–101.

Watt, D.C. 1965. *Survey of International Affairs 1961*. London: RIIA/Oxford University Press.

Watt, D.C. 1977. *Survey of International Affairs 1963*. London: RIIA/Oxford University Press.

Watt, D.C. 1984. *Succeeding John Bull: America in Britain's Place 1900–1975*. Cambridge: Cambridge University Press.

Watt, D.C. and Mayall, J. (eds). 1971. *Current British Foreign Policy: Documents, Statements, Speeches 1970*. London: Temple Smith.

Watt, D.C. and Mayall, J. (eds). 1973. *Current British Foreign Policy: Documents, Statements, Speeches 1971*. London: Temple Smith.

Watt, D.C. and Mayall, J. (eds). 1974. *Current British Foreign Policy: Documents, Statements, Speeches 1972*. London: Temple Smith.

Weede, E. 1977. Threats to détente: intuitive hopes and counter-intuitive realities. *European Journal of Political Research* 5: 407–32.

West, D. 1978. Détente in trouble – or is it? *New Zealand International Review*, January–February: 29–33.

White, B.P. 1991. Britain: an Atlantic or a European relationship? In R.S. Jordan (ed.), *Europe and the Superpowers. Essays on European International Politics*, pp. 155–74. London: Pinter.

Wiesner, J.B. 1965. *Where Science and Politics Meet*. New York: McGraw-Hill.

Williams, G. and Read, B. 1971. *Denis Healey and the Politics of Power*. London: Sidgwick & Jackson.

Williams, P. 1986. Britain, détente and the Conference on Security and Cooperation in Europe. In K. Dyson (ed.), *European Détente*, pp. 221–37. London: Pinter.

Wilson, D. 1974. Anglo-Soviet relations: the effect of ideas on reality. *International Affairs* 50, 3: 380–91.

Wilson, H. 1974. *The Labour Government 1964–70*. Harmondsworth: Penguin.

Windsor, P. 1971. *Germany and the Management of Détente*. London: Chatto & Windus.

Wright, M. 1964. *Disarm and Verify*. New York: Praeger.

Young, E. 1972. *A Farewell to Arms Control?* Harmondsworth: Penguin.

Young, H. 1990. *One of Us*, rev. edn. London: Pan.

Young, H. and Sloman, A. 1986. *The Thatcher Phenomenon*. London: BBC Publications.

Young, J.W. (ed.). 1988. *The Foreign Policy of Churchill's Peacetime Administration 1951–55*. Leicester: Leicester University Press.

Zuckerman, S. 1982. *Nuclear Illusion and Reality*. London: Collins.

Index